RAISING LOKI

RAISING LOKI

ELLIOT MANARIN

Quill & Crow
NONFICTION

RAISING LOKI
WRITTEN BY ELLIOT MANARIN
PUBLISHED BY QUILL & CROW PUBLISHING HOUSE

Edited by Cassandra Thompson, Lisa Morris

Cover Design by Fay Lane

Photography by Elliot Manarin

Printed in the United States of America

ISBN (ebook): 978-1-958228-75-3

ISBN (paperback): 978-1-958228-76-0

Publisher's Website: quillandcrowpublishinghouse.com

For all those who felt like they never quite fit in...

CONTENTS

INTRODUCTION

In the first week of September 2017, I found myself, as I do every year, looking out toward the salt marshes on the Norfolk coast. It was peacefully slow. Time was only an indicator of what the next meal will be, the need for clocks replaced by the tide's arrival. In a creaking wicker chair, I gazed out the window, trying to spot migratory birds gliding over the dense marshland, intermingled with shipping tankers and the odd fighter jet. A blissful feeling, watching the world go about its business as if I were a non-participating third party. Watching from the other side of the glass is a pleasure that never tires.

My job often requires many hours tethered to a computer. From sunrise to sundown, human interaction can be somewhat limited—don't get me wrong, as an introvert, this can sometimes be a welcome perk. Life in suburbia races through quickly. Seasons come and go, with most people only recognizing or appreciating their superficial appearance. However, birds flock to our shores in harmony with nature, sourcing food in preparation for their next migratory adventure. Before you know it, another year has passed, and we all embark on another cycle.

We were on the precipice of summer, clocking out for the year and ready for autumn to begin its shift. One of my favorite seasons: the essence of decay squeezing life from the landscape, gifting us a burgundy and yellow bliss, the nights becoming sneaky and growing ever so slightly shorter, a little chill felt in the wind.

When your occupation demands you work outside, it's said, "One can feel the change." A common phrase uttered by people with weathered faces—the sort who smell the air, boasting their ability to utilize mankind's least-used, recessive sense. They claim prophetic skills in their ability to foresee the imminent arrival of rain or inform us of an impending thunderstorm. I often anthropomorphize the weather. It's much like seeing an old friend who has been absent for a few years. You begin to remember their traits, readying yourself for their personalities and familiar nuances. For me, at least, the shorts are reluctantly put back in the wardrobe for another year as the season of warm, golden evenings are superseded by bitter, frosty nights.

As a filmmaker and photographer, being outside brings many challenges. We are always looking for the "Goldilocks conditions." Not too hot, not too bright, just the right amount of cloud, using the available light to sculpt our art. But we are mere guests in nature's house. We dip into the outdoors, only to retreat to our safe interiors, where we have the luxury of lounging in comfort. Working outside is a totally different ball game. You can't negotiate with Mother Nature—she's been around far too long to pay heed to our nonsense. Instead, you adapt and find harmony.

This story derives from a niche area of my life: one which, over the years, seems to pull me ever closer toward an alternative path. A path forcing me to socialize with our seasons, to abandon the comfortable office and on-demand lattes.

- Elliot Manarin, 2024

ONE
STJARNA
THE STAR

t was 3 am, Sunday, December 19, 2018, a time of the morning known as "The Witching Hour." In more modern times, it is the hour frequented by haunted creatives, "anxious Annies," and fully paid-up members of the existential dread club. I had countless thoughts about getting up and Googling a good luck spell. However, at that moment, I was pinned down by my morbidly obese ginger cat, Stimpy (Stimpy T. Cat, to give his full title), his gaze darting from one corner of the room to another, chasing ghosts. Of course, there was nothing there that I could see, but it was still pretty unnerving none-theless.

At his last checkup, the vet announced with much disappointment that he weighed in at a monstrous seven kilograms. I joked to the vet we should have named him Garfield. The vet wasn't impressed.

It was quite difficult to breathe with a dense, fluffy behemoth encumbering my chest, his paws neatly set side by side, nestled in the basin of my throat. Every now and again, he would exercise his claws, stabbing my skin like a pin cushion, purring with pure adulation. For me, sleep was never going to be an option. Stimpy was busy making biscuits.

I rarely get more than three or four hours of sleep each night, and this occasion was no different. My brain was working overtime, waking me up on the hour, every hour. The fear of sleeping through the alarm kept my anxiety levels bubbling nicely. At 5 am, the sickly pleasant Caribbean tune I had assigned as my alarm sounded. I'd chosen it in the hopes that it would ease me into consciousness, softly breaking the visage of the dream world, but now I resented it with the rage of a scorned Greek goddess. Sarah-Jane awoke and bolted straight into the bathroom. She is much better at getting up than I am. Even though I had been awake for many hours, I needed the harsh, unforgiving retina-burn of my phone's backlight light to really wake me.

Stimpy sharply followed Sarah-Jane out of the bedroom, hoping to get a snack. Not much was said between Sarah-Jane and me. In my mind, it was still the middle of the night. To be functioning at such an ungodly hour was, at best, trying, yet that wasn't the sole reason for the muted atmosphere. We were both burdened with nerves. There were so many things that could go wrong. Firstly, getting into central London from our abode in Essex can be tricky at the best of times. And we absolutely *had* to be on time! Live television waits for no one. Our reputation was very much on the line, but this was merely the tip of the "Fear Iceberg."

We headed toward my car. It was a particularly icy morning, and I remotely unlocked the doors with the key fob, the handle frozen stiff. After a few persuasive attempts, it cracked open.

We left suburbia, passing hungry street foxes, scouring the neighborhood for an easily accessible bin, and entered the silent, black countryside. The inside of the car was thick with frosty breath, like a fog machine at an '80s concert. But there was no music playing this morning, and the heaters struggled to fight the icy build-up on the inside of the windscreen. I knew the road well; nonetheless, I took it easy as we traversed the narrow, winding roads of the Lee Valley. I looked at Sarah-Jane, who was almost opaque, furiously rubbing her gloved hands together.

"Are you okay?" I said, not conforming on this occasion to the British weather-related stereotype.

"Yeah, just a bit worried," she remarked, the apprehension clear in her voice.

I tried to inject a bit of gallows humor.

"What's the worst that can happen?" I said with a wry smile. I knew full well what could happen. We didn't want this little jaunt to turn into an internet meme or a clip on a TV montage program. You know, the ones typically aired at Christmas where the family all laugh at misbehaving animals, much to the horror and embarrassment of their handlers. Admittedly, I was *bricking it* (a British term often used to describe total and utter terror). We tried to make a joke of things by running through every kind of devastating scenario we could dream up. Unsurprisingly, we managed to conjure up quite a few—some I hadn't thought of—which only led to compounding the anxiety and making the "Fear Iceberg" even more daunting.

We arrived at the farm, which was ridiculously eerie at that time of the morning, the sun still off duty as we navigated the cobbled walkway toward the center. The Barn Owls became alerted to our presence and screamed the song of their people: a blood-curdling screech, a complete juxtaposition to their beautiful, ethereal appearance. This, in turn, set off the Tawny Owl, who threw himself toward the front of the aviary. And like a set of dominoes, each area of the center became alive with sound.

Sarah-Jane opened up the office—a converted barn, which, before we arrived, housed pigs. Sometimes, you need to take what you can get. The barn is separated into three spaces. The middle chamber is the central hub, housing all the necessary equipment to run a falconry center: travel boxes, fridges, freezers, and various other falconry paraphernalia. The door on the left leads to a seating area for experience-day guests: a designated space to brief them on the day's agenda while also serving as a mess room for the staff. It's rough around the edges yet extremely functional. It has been the home of Coda Falconry since 2012, and every year, it gets a little more refined and upgraded, with each member of the team chipping in to make it somewhere they are proud to work. Much to our amusement, it was once described by a Tripadvisor visitor as "a shed," which still remains an in-joke between the team. On the right is the mews: a medieval conception built to house raptors.

As we entered the middle chamber, the raptor alarm system was immediately triggered, an ensemble of Harris Hawks, buzzards, and eagles activated to an intruder's presence. I entered, greeting them with weary eyes. They weren't used to humans in their room so early in the morning. When they recognized us, they settled down—alarm disengaged.

"Right, we are going to need the big box. Oh, and some jesses and a leash. Could you prepare some food and then go and grab Loki?"

Still in the early stages of the awakening process, my brain struggled to deal with what Sarah-Jane had said. I pretended that I understood the list of commands and headed back outside. If in doubt, pretend you know what you're doing—at least, that's what I was once told. I switched on my phone's flashlight, feet crunching down on the solidified grass. I approached the top three weatherings, situated on a short hill slightly left of the flying arena. I proceeded toward the door, only to be met by a giant, black, wraith-like cloud that shot up from the floor to eye level. It scared the life out of me!

"Morning, LoLos," I said, his beady eyes scanning mine, analyzing the situation. "You gave me a fright, mate."

Who is this? What are they doing here at this time in the morning? Why are they holding a light in my face?

All very relevant questions. However, there was no response to my panicked greeting, only silence. I decided to put my phone in my pocket, plunging myself back into darkness. I fumbled around in the black void of the morning, eventually freeing the padlock responsible for keeping the beast in its lair. I then made the calculated choice to enter the weathering.

Okay, so picture the scene: you are woken up by someone in the middle of the night, shining a light into your room. They make their way toward you: an unrecognizable, silhouetted being. What do you do?

This risk, I decided, would have to be taken. I didn't have a choice.

"Hey, Loki. Are you ready to be on TV? You've got to be a good boy today. I don't want to become an internet meme."

The silence was broken.

Loki responded with a welcoming chorus of purrs. He now knew it was me, and the situation had been demoted to Defcon 5.

Now, I was in his aviary. He sat in front of the glistening moon, allowing me to just about make him out: an obsidian-like shape cut out of the transitioning sky, now the darkest blue. The moonlight shimmered on the frosty grass. I stroked Loki on the back and gently ushered my arm toward his legs. He stepped onto my arm, and I gained control of his flying straps with my right hand.

"Let's go and get you weighed," I said.

We worked in silence but at tempo, the enemy constantly creeping upon us. A pseudo-telepathy kicked in as I finished weighing Loki. He came in at two pounds, eleven ounces (just over 1.2kg). I winced.

"How heavy is he?" Sarah-Jane asked with concern.

I told her, and even though he was considerably lighter than our super-massive cat, he was on the heavy side.

Sarah-Jane drew a huge breath and immediately came to terms with the prospect. "Well, he is what he is; can't do anything about that now."

I shared her unease. This could be problematic because heavier birds tend to be less obedient, and the scenarios we played out in the car were now starting to sound less funny.

We boxed Loki and put him in the car. The first part of the journey remained absent of sound. However, when he heard our voices, he began emphatically beating the door with his beak. We continued to sit in radio silence, contemplating evermore the horror show we were walking into.

The sun oozed all over the city. It was glorious. The streets were rightfully empty, and we arrived at the studio in central London with plenty of time. The car park was located on the roof of a huge complex. We took a moment to look over the edge and soaked in the triumphant winter sun, twinkling against the glass peaks of "that London." Pinks, yellows, and oranges glazed over the city, prompting the birds to warm up their morning voices.

"Did you bring the big glove?" Sarah-Jane said with a sharp tone of panic.

"Yes. Did you pack the creance?" I returned.

"Yes. What about the food?"

We exchanged a volley of self-doubting questions.

"Er...I think so?" I said. "What about wet wipes?" The butterflies rattled in my stomach like an angry swarm of bees. I felt queasy.

We opened the car and began to go through the checklist, pulling out all the essentials. Just as we'd finished, a young lady in her late teens or early twenties approached us with a headset and microphone.

"Are you the crow people?" she asked.

Sarah-Jane and I exchanged a glance.

"Yes, we are the *raven* handlers," I responded bluntly. Early morning, no food, and a severe lack of caffeine will considerably test the tolerance meter.

"Coolies. Follow me. The other guy is, like, already here. He was super early." Her happy-hipster ways were grating. I struggle with overly joyous people at the best of times, but at that time of the morning, it was insufferable.

I took Loki's box out of the car, and Sarah-Jane scooped up all his various necessities. As the lady walked us toward the studio, she barked, "Oh my god, is it in that box?"

And right on cue, Loki responded with two staccato clacks, *"BAH-BAH!"*

She had her answer.

We snaked through the maze of corridors, various production crew members rustling about, some with similar headsets, others with standard-issue TV studio clipboards.

"Okay, so you're just in here." She stood in the doorway, gesturing into the green room.

At this point, already aware of who was in the room, my heart felt a sudden surge of adrenaline. I entered the room and saw the impressive and imposing figure of Christopher Skaife, otherwise known as "The Ravenmaster."

He was on the phone.

I tried to look busy and popped Loki's box down, Sarah-Jane following like a pack mule inundated with all of Loki's things. Hanging on the wall was Christopher's official uniform, sublimely tailored in deep blue with blood-red insignia. The dress code of the Yeoman Warders, more commonly known as "Beefeaters," exuded royal class. For those unfamiliar with the Ravenmaster, it is a duty bestowed upon him directly from Her Majesty Queen Elizabeth the Second (*well, it was at the time of writing; now the King*) to protect the ravens who reside at the Tower of London, the home of the priceless Crown Jewels. When it comes to ravens, he is probably one of the most famous people in the land, if not the world.

He finished his call and marched over to us. "I'm so sorry about that. I've got a booking straight after this. I'm Christopher." He extended his mighty thick hand, and we shook: a firm and definite introduction. We knew who he was—both Sarah-Jane and I followed him closely on Twitter, often marveling at his collection of beautiful ravens.

For the next half hour, we happily conversed on all things corvid, exchanging stories and experiences of working with ravens. It was a real mutual meeting of love for ravens. Both Sarah-Jane and I loved hearing about his role at The Tower and the brood of ravens he is sworn to protect. It was a very refreshing and humble encounter. Any nerves we had started to melt away. Christopher was very down to earth and didn't emit an ego. He confessed that he is by no means an expert—yet has far more knowledge than I, it has to be said—and was genuinely intrigued by some of the methods we used.

But it wasn't long before *the star* had to be involved in the conversation. Loki banged on his door. It appeared that he, too, wanted to meet The Ravenmaster.

Christopher smiled. "Can I meet him?" he asked.

"Of course!" I beamed. I held the leash and opened his door. A swoosh of black feathers stormed out of the box, almost knocking me over. I sat on a chair next to Christopher, and Loki hopped up onto my lap.

"So this is Loki, is it?" he said.

I nodded.

Christopher was incredibly respectful and didn't try to stroke Loki —a sign of a pro. I offered some food to Christopher, who gladly obliged to feed Loki. They got on like a house on fire.

"Right, guys. Can I get you all to come through to set for rehearsal?" demanded another member of the production team. I looked at my watch; it was 9:15 am. *We were on air in forty-five minutes!*

We headed for the set. Loki decided *now* would be a good time to go to the toilet. The sound of splattering fecal matter horrified the production manager.

"Don't worry, we will clean that up!" I said sheepishly. *Thanks, Loki.* But he had no cares to give about my awkwardness and stood proud on my arm.

The four of us were escorted back into the convoluted production maze. As we tunneled through, various people stopped in their tracks to do a double-take. I tucked Loki close into my chest, massaging his throat to maintain a sense of calm. There were lots of new sights and sounds—all of which he wanted to explore, I might add. Yet, to unleash a roaming, curious raven in a TV studio was not a good idea in anyone's book. As we continued down the silent halls, he randomly barked, echoing incredibly loudly! I shushed him as best I could. He didn't care, barking again in an act of defiance. Both Christopher and Sarah-Jane both turned around and smiled.

"They certainly have a mind of their own, don't they?" Christopher joked while I tried to be as discreet as possible, wandering the corridors, hugging a nearly three-pound random noise box.

We eventually arrived at the studio floor. It was smaller than I thought: sets made from flimsy plywood, plastered with the charms of Christmas decor. The production coordinator asked Sarah-Jane to fill out a consent form. All the while, Loki was busy being papped by members of the crew who had spontaneously downed tools and swarmed over to us, eyes wide with bewilderment.

Sarah-Jane asked for another consent form allowing me to be on screen, too, yet was met with a firm rejection.

"Sorry, just you. We haven't got room for you both," the production coordinator stated. And before Sarah-Jane could respond, he and his clipboard had vanished into the nethers of the studio.

This was potentially a *huge* problem. I am Loki's primary handler. His buddy. His comfort blanket. He might get scared or, worse still, violent.

We didn't have time for a Plan B.

The floor manager ushered us onto the floor: The Ravenmaster taking center stage, Sarah-Jane to his right, out of shot, and me lurking in the shadows with the production crew. I handed Loki over to Sarah-Jane and stood as close to the set as possible. The presenters arrived to scope out the guests. The floor manager ran through the questions that had been prepared. The cameras were given their cues, and the rehearsal was underway. The problem was, well, the three-pound noise box, Loki.

Every time the questions were asked, Loki would bark over the top, going through his full repertoire of vocalizations at *fortissimo!* I could see the fear from everyone in the room, none more so than the presenters. *What had they done? Who thought having a raven on live TV would be a good idea? This could be carnage!*

One presenter became restless and interrupted the rehearsal. He demanded that they record a cutaway of Loki *now*: if he were to start interrupting while on air, the viewers at home might be confused. After a spell of flustered negotiations, the crew agreed to have Loki and Sarah-Jane in the shot right from the start. They prayed he wouldn't be so vocal.

The floor manager approached me and asked, "Will he be like this when we go live? Is there anything you can do to keep him quiet?"

No, not really. This is an animal with a pendant for causing trouble. His name is Loki, for Christ's sake! I thought. However, I responded by reassuring this quite concerned chap that Loki would be fine; he just needed to settle down and get a feel for the place. At this point, Loki took a shit all over the studio floor.

I wanted to die.

The rehearsal seemed to last forever, yet in reality, it was no more than ten minutes. Loki would not stop calling out. When it eventually ended, Sarah-Jane handed him back to me. He snuggled into my chest and wiped his beak across my sweater. More crew members came over for pictures, all absolutely blown away by how big and shiny he was and all sharing a cheeky laugh at the poop incident. At the same time, one of the runners vigorously scrubbed the soiled floor.

We weren't permitted to hang around and were promptly sent back to the green room. We continued talking with Christopher as he donned his official regalia. Meanwhile, Loki continued to parade around the green room, showing off and being a little menace, dropping more poo bombs, and attempting to steal all the biscuits. The Ravenmaster found it very endearing.

The list of concerns seemed to be growing. The top three were as follows. Coming in at number one—and perhaps the worst-case scenario—Loki would be freaked out by all the camera equipment and lights. This would result in him forging escape plans, followed by pure rage and aggression tactics, which would look pretty harrowing on TV. Secondly, he could be a little savage and bite anyone and everyone in reach just because he could. And finally—well, we didn't actually plan for *this* disaster scenario—the rehearsal had shown us Loki's fondness for exercising his vocal talents. It would be equally amusing and embarrassing for both us and the presenters. There would be no more time to ponder and brood on disaster scenarios, for the moment had come for us to find out how the cookie would crumble.

Now, for some of you who might be reading this, drawn into Loki's story from seeing how wonderful he is on camera, our fears might seem unwarranted. But there were legitimate reasons for our apprehension.

Loki's past was a very different story.

TWO
MIN BEGYNDER
MY BEGINNING

A s a kid of the 90s, I look back, feeling lucky that I didn't grow up in a time where every move you made was documented by a device that fits in your pocket. Without sounding like "old man river" observing the past through rose-tinted glasses, I spent most of my childhood outside, be it playing football until the street lights came on, fishing in the local streams, or building camps, creating fires, and terrorizing the village residents, doing the whole "boys will be boys" thing. We did things for fun—not for likes, not for popularity.

I grew up in a small village in Hertfordshire, a forty-minute train journey from central London. We were surrounded by golden fields, thick woodlands, and fish-laden rivers. As a kid, you take these things for granted. My dad taught me how to fish, and I began to learn all the native species of river fish in the UK. This naturally led me to butterflies and songbirds. My dad had a sharp ear: he could recognize the sound of a bullfinch and then quickly point out a goldfinch. I was hugely impressed: I, too, wanted to be able to identify birds just as quickly. On numerous occasions, we sat on the banks of the River Lee, waiting for the greedy perch to take our bulging bait of cheese or bread, and we would look out and listen for birds. As a kid, a crow looks like a rook, which looks like a jackdaw, but on closer inspection, looking at the finer details, you can finally appreciate they are nothing alike.

"Be patient and look carefully," my dad would say. Being patient as a kid, jacked up on sweets, is a real ask, but when I began to correctly identify the various songbirds, I felt empowered.

My thirst for learning about the natural world took me on an adventure back a hundred million years to the age of the dinosaurs. On a rare occasion as a seven-year-old, I got a day trip to the "big smoke," and I got to visit one of the world's most notorious collections of fossils. I'll never forget the feeling when I stood outside The Natural History Museum in London, nestled in the affluent district of Chelsea for the first time. I was in awe of its size and demeanor. It made our village church look small and pathetic, which, at the time, I thought was colossal. I'd never seen such an enormous structure in person. However, this sensation was quickly superseded. When I walked into the great hall, bearing witness to the remains of a T-rex and Triceratops for the very first time, I had a genuine "wow" moment. I stood frozen to the spot. I got as close as I could, and as all kids do, I really wanted to look at the bones with my *hands*. I made a tepid effort to reach out before being scolded by a strict, stuffy museum steward. After reeling away, I struggled to fathom how such a creature could have existed. And also, how did they piece it all together? Must have taken ages!

At that time, I was an only child, and my days were spent in the company of many plastic toy dinosaurs recreating epic battles between carnivorous super lizards and their plant-eating prey. I was dinosaur-mad. I spent hours glued to videos of great paleontologists like Jack Horner, unearthing these godlike creatures bound in their rocky tombs. It was a magical world. Pages and pages of brightly colored animals of all kinds, animals that used to rule this planet, and I was totally captivated by it. I was often sad that I could never see one in real life or own one as a pet. What kid didn't want a pet T-Rex? Perhaps it was just me…

I wasn't an academic kid: I did okay, but nothing exceptional. I loved sports and played a lot of music. First came the cello. The beautiful melancholic drone made me fall in love with it instantly. I then incorporated drums, guitar, and piano into my repertoire. I was a good all-rounder. Music came relatively easy for me since I had a good ear and developed strong improvisational skills. I found the other subjects a chore, but never music.

My dad was a landscaper, and often, I got to go and work with him. It was a good opportunity to learn about plants, trees, and general horticulture. As I got older, my skills developed, and I discovered how to wield chainsaws and other lethal power tools. Sometimes even safely.

I started to germinate ideas for a career working with or alongside nature. I found it difficult to be motivated with normal curricular teachings, but this really got my full attention. My parents suggested a vocation in the veterinary field, and from there on in, at the young age of perhaps six or seven, my dream of being a vet constantly lurked in the back of my mind. It was a job that came with respect, money, and a benefit to the animal kingdom.

Like most schools, the mandatory work experience week rolled out in our fourth year of secondary school. We were each given a long and uninspiring list of potential placements. Most were admin-based. Some kids opted to go and work with their parents, but I didn't fancy cold November days with my dad. Besides, I had worked with him on weekends and throughout school holidays since I was a kid.

I ran my finger down the list and, buried amongst solicitors and insurance brokers, was a spot at a vet. It must be a sign. I put my name down and was fortunate enough to be the only student in over 150 who wanted that placement.

Day One. I arrived punctually—I'm not a fan of being late, it is rude!—and I was introduced to the team of vets, nurses, and reception staff. The smell of disinfectant hit me like a slap in the face; it lingered on my tongue, biting and sour. The vet's consultation room was spotless, and it was my job throughout the week to maintain this level of cleanliness. The bottle containing a pink cleaning solution was to be holstered on my person at all times. After the introductions and briefing, I was asked to accompany the vet on an emergency home visit. I wasn't told where we were going or the reason.

Once we arrived at a house in a small residential estate, we were ushered in by a lovely, polite, middle-aged lady. I remember not one word was spoken by the owner of the house all the time we were there —which, at the time, I thought was weird.

We were led through the house out into the garden. I had a bounce in my step, happy to be doing some real work, but my jubilance was not shared. *Maybe they have a pond and some expensive carp that need checking over*, I thought. Herons were known to be canny thieves in the area. *Perhaps one of their fish has been injured in an attack by a modern-day pterodactyl!* I could hear the cutting sound of a spade digging into the grass. It was devilishly warm and bright for November, I realized, and I should have probably left my coat in the car.

I turned to see a man with his back to me, resting on his shovel, taking a brief minute to rest. Now, there was complete silence.

The vet called me over for assistance. I approached a crowd of people kneeling down, and standing behind them, peering over their shoulders, I finally saw the subject of concern. A very old golden retriever lying on his side, resting on his favorite blanket. It was red tartan, tatty, and well-used.

I took up position next to the vet, and as I looked up toward the family members, I saw the tears sliding down their cheeks. Despite their best efforts to be strong, the emotional tidal waves battered down their defenses. Only at that moment did I realize the reason why we were there.

The vet opened up his dark leather briefcase and handed me a large tube. He then pulled out a very large syringe. My heart was pumping so fast I thought it was going to smash through my chest. I had a fluttering of intense emotions: fear, sadness, confusion all swashing around in my stomach. My mouth dried up, and the ability to speak was now a disabled function in my operating system. Bright blue liquid filled the thick plastic tube, reminding me of the tall glass of Barbicide used in the barbershop to disinfect combs. I'd rather be there having a number three all over, but alas, I was in someone's back garden assisting in euthanasia.

The sound of digging continued.

The vet, with a warm smile, asked me to hold the dog's paw and stroke his head. The dog was an old chap, graying around the muzzle but still happy to lick my hand and show unconditional kindness to a complete stranger. It's as if he was comforting me rather than the other way around. Man's best friend, right to the very end. The family couldn't watch and quickly escaped into the house. This left just me and the vet to share the dog's last remaining moments.

I didn't even know the dog's name.

At the time, I was happy to help, but now, I look back with a deeper sadness and maturity. I completely understand why the family couldn't bear witness—after all, they were losing a member of their family. Yet part of me feels they should have stayed. That dog had been their loyal companion for many, many years. Every day he would have looked to them and offered infinite amounts of affection and love, but in his most desperate time of need, he was left with strangers, weary and confused. Within seconds, the tube was empty, and the pooch silently drifted off to the Big Sleep. I continued to stroke his head while the vet packed up his bag—stuck in some kind of trance, trying desperately not to cry. The vet asked if I was okay; the best I could do was nod, eyes refusing to make contact.

The sound of the family's sobbing grew louder as the pounding of the shovel stopped.

Over the course of the week, I assisted in a horse castration—which, by the way, if you've never had the pleasure to experience, it's quite something. The crunching sound haunts me to this day—an operation on a cat's eye and the futile task of trying to save a baby deer hit by a car. The shock was too much, and it ended up dying in my lap before the vet could prep for surgery. Added to the list were half a dozen cat and dog neutering operations.

My week with these amazing and talented people had taught me a lot. I saw animals in their most vulnerable state. Their eyes look at you with bewilderment and absolute terror. They are at our mercy, counting on compassion, expertise, medicine, and sometimes, luck. It was an emotionally hard week, but I strangely enjoyed it. The experience reaffirmed my desire to be a part of this benevolent and caring community.

As I progressed through school, we were encouraged to decide what we wanted to do after compulsory education had ended. I dared to look up the requirements for vet school.

I shut the brochure and abruptly put an end to that dream.

It was a feeling I didn't shake for years. I'm not sure anyone ever knew how disappointed I was or even knew that's what I really wanted to do. I felt worthless, knowing I would never be smart enough to pursue this vocation. I tossed away my childhood dream in the blink of an eye: I was foolish and naive, thinking I could possibly get into vet school.

In 2007, I met Sarah-Jane, a bright and infectious character who joined our team at a studio I was working at. A fellow musician and a genuine animal whisperer, she was destined to go on to do amazing things. She headed up to volunteer with her friends who ran the prestigious Galloway Falconry Center in Scotland. They had been invited to display and perform raptor demonstrations at the illustrious Royal Highland Show—a massive annual event catering to all things rural. She asked if I wanted to join them, but I knew nothing about modern raptors, nor did I fit the Barbour jacket-tweed brigade. However, it sounded like it could be a lot of fun—a good excuse to be out in the open and learn about some cool birds.

I made the long, monotonous drive up the A1. The humdrum of endless tarmac and average speed cameras gnawed at my desire to volunteer—this was a long way to travel for volunteering! Caffeine and podcasts on megafauna ensured I made it to my destination in one piece. Once I arrived in Edinburgh, I was immediately greeted by the team—a jovial and warm bunch who, within minutes, kitted me out in their company colors. They provided me with a pair of hunter wellies and a snazzy green flying jacket. If you have ever seen the popular meme of a dog in human clothes titled, "I don't know what I'm doing," this aptly summed up my situation. This is probably where I learned that sage piece of advice once: if you don't know what you're doing, then pretend that you do. At least I looked the part.

They sat me down and gave me a large leather gauntlet—a robust glove to protect me from the razor-sharp talons of the birds. Amongst the menagerie of raptors were owls, falcons, hawks, buzzards, and a very impressive and quite intimidating, white-tailed Sea Eagle called Murray. My first duty, bearing in mind I hadn't been in contact with a bird of prey since primary school—a bizarre British tradition of having your school photo with a barn owl perched on your shoulder—was to hold this behemoth of a bird. While Sarah-Jane got ready for the public show, Grant, the owner of Galloway Falconry with his then-wife Ffyona, picked up Murray and put her on my glove. It all happened so fast. I didn't know who Murray was, but I found myself with a four-foot-tall, one-stone-weighing (fifteen pounds), eleven-foot-wing spanning eagle on my arm. The best part was that she was still a juvenile!

"Whatever you do, don't look directly into her eyes. If she starts to stare at you, just ignore her," Grant said with a smile. This kind of precautionary instruction would have been nice to know before he put this monstrous and, quite frankly, terrifying eagle on my arm.

"She wants to intimidate you; don't play her game. If you do, she will try to dominate you and lash out," Grant continued.

Amazing. That is just what I wanted to hear. Murray's beak was inches away from my face, and I could see her attempting to eyeball me, cocking her head, trying desperately to get my attention. Thankfully, Sarah-Jane returned with her headset microphone. She scooped Murray off my glove and headed toward the packed arena. Murray was probably on my arm for two minutes tops, but the burning stare and the deft weight made it seem eternally longer.

The good news was I had passed the first test: both eyes were still intact.

Sarah-Jane introduced Murray to the audience—she raised her arm and cast the eagle into the wind. It was a truly magical moment watching Sarah-Jane and Murray dance around the arena. Murray would soar up into the sky, then, on command, drive toward Sarah-Jane and claim her reward. The relationship between the bird and the falconer was mind-blowing. I experienced the same overwhelming feeling of sheer awe when I was in the Natural History Museum. I had never seen this talent of Sarah-Jane's: back home, we both worked in a recording studio, and I never realized just how well she could command an extreme force of nature with such ease.

Later that day, when I was allowed to help out with the other birds, the team mentioned how well the birds took to me as if I was on some kind of trial—at the mercy of the court of raptor judges. They regaled stories of how some birds just don't like some people. Sometimes for good reason, sometimes for nothing apparent. I honestly thought they were just being nice to me, the trademark West Coast Scottish kindness.

The litmus test was truly complete when, at the end of the day, I was asked if I could put Murray back in her box for the night. I happily and rather naively agreed. After all, I was a natural, right? I took Murray, crouched down, and slowly backed her into the box—a four-foot by four-foot cube with its own separate road trailer! She stepped off the glove and onto the perch located inside, and I closed the door and locked the bolt. I stood up and looked at the team, all watching. They were all slightly surprised. The surprise —which I later became privy to—was that Murray hates going back into her box. Even the staff have difficulties putting her away. On occasion, she had been known to cause a bit of a ruckus. When they assigned me bedtime duties for Murray, they were expecting a much rougher ride for me, which I was glad didn't come to fruition. The fact a newbie just rocked up and put her away with no problem gave credence that I was okay. The verdict had been passed: I'd been accepted by the raptor and falconer community.

At this point, you must be thinking, have I bought the wrong book? Where are the ravens? Just like winter, they are coming. I think it's important to get this bit out of the way first, as it gives the rest of the story a bit more context.

THREE
NYR HEIMILI
NEW HOME

A few years after helping out with Galloway Falconry, Sarah-Jane set up her own bird of prey center. The ethos was to educate and give urban communities a chance to see and participate in the lesser-known, ancient art of falconry. The center's popularity and good reputation grew rapidly. There was obviously a demand for such a niche sport, coupled with owls being rather *en vogue* at the time, and people from all walks of life came to see what was on offer. Usually in the form of a quirky birthday or Christmas gift.

In the early days, the center consisted mainly of hand-me-down birds. Birds who were surplus to requirements and were no longer needed at other centers. Some were old, others just "weren't very good" and couldn't be used for displays or experiences. Or so we were told. We were a sanctuary for the outcasts, which was more than okay. A lighthouse for the unwanted and excluded often likened to their human guardians.

In a short amount of time, the center grew. The need to have more room for new birds, birds we could raise from chicks, became paramount. An opportunity to work with juvenile birds and the thought of training chicks was like an artist looking at a blank canvas. It became a fresh and welcoming challenge.

One of the first birds we got from a chick was Logan. Now, anyone who knows me will know my relationship with Logan. Logan is a Eurasian Eagle Owl—*Bubo bubo* to his Latin friends—and one of the largest species of owl in the world. Some females are known to weigh up to eight pounds, possessing skills that allow them to catch rabbits, foxes, and, if desperate, baby deer.

I was at work when I got a phone call from Sarah-Jane. "If you are free at lunch, pop back to the house. I have something to show you," she said. I obliged and went to her house for lunch.

I walked into the kitchen, and in the middle of the room stood a cardboard box, lid closed but not sealed. Sarah-Jane was smiling, and I could tell something cute was in the box. I went over, knelt down, and opened up the lid. Two huge orange eyes fixed in a perfectly spherical head peered back up at me.

"Whhhheeeeepppp!" the sphere of gray feathers yelped.

I immediately burst out laughing. He was the cutest, angriest-looking ball of fluff I had ever seen. I picked him up and put him on the floor. He struggled to stand initially, but soon enough, he found his feet. He looked around and bellowed another angry, *"Whhheeeepppp!"*

"You look like Chewie," I told him as I gently lifted him out of the box and onto the kitchen floor. His big, clumsy feet were treading air, paddling an imaginary boat. He looked straight at me and began working those big Yeti feet of his. He picked up a bit of speed and then leaped onto my lap. I stroked his head and rubbed the top of his cere. He shut his eyes and basked in his impromptu massage. When I stopped, he slowly opened his eyes with contentment as if demanding to know why the massage had stopped. I sat on the kitchen floor for the remainder of the hour, cuddling and playing with the gigantic fluff baby.

I went back to work and persistently watched the clock, which never seemed to make any progress. When it hit five, I was out the door, ready for another baby owl fix.

I fell madly in love with that bird, and not long after, Sarah-Jane officially signed him over to me for my birthday. I was now his legal owner, his parental guardian. Best birthday present ever!

Over the years, my bond with Logan—aka Chewie—continued to blossom. I would visit the center to see him and spend most of my time with him. With other people, he could be...quite *naughty* and somewhat contrary, but with me, he was different, and I proudly wore that sentiment.

Sarah-Jane taught me how to be a falconer: everything from husbandry right through to coping of the beaks (filing and creating new shapes). When the center got too big for the premises, it moved from its urban location—a petting farm in the middle of a town—to the heart of the Lee Valley. Nestled in amongst lush rolling hills and woodlands, it felt more like home. The center stood on a working farm, open to the public: a place for children to learn about animals and a place for parents to meet and let their kids burn off surplus energy on the various outdoor climbing equipment.

In its new location, the center continued to expand quickly, and I found myself helping out as much as I could. I had set up my own business at this point—a film and television production company— and this gave me a great degree of flexibility. Every weekend and every spare minute I had would be devoted to working at the center.

I stopped playing football—soccer to some—partially through injuries but also because I actually preferred being with the birds. This was not a decision I took lightly. I loved playing sports, and giving it up was not a throwaway decision. As my love for contact sports dwindled, my knowledge and desire to work with raptors grew exponentially. Like anything, if you do something enough, you learn quickly, absorbing tricks of the trade like a sponge. You can absorb so much in a short space of time if you enjoy it, and I had well and truly taken the bait. I took to reading up on different species and delving into the etymology and biology of birds—understanding their history and their biomechanisms. This eventually led to me gaining a National Diploma in Zoology.

At times, I was an almost full-time member of staff, and I found myself working late in the evenings to keep my own company running. When you are good at something, you tend to want to indulge in it as much as possible. Working with great people who share the same values and ideologies toward animals is why I believe Coda Falconry is so successful. The passion and selflessness you need to work and care for these animals should never be understated.

When we run Experience Days, which involves taking guests out to the woods to fly our owls or hawks, I take great pleasure in running through every detail about the birds, answering any questions they have. I truly revel in the guests enjoying the birds, getting a chance to witness first hand their magnificence and grace. More often than not, the guests have never had any experience with a raptor and are shocked to learn that this isn't my actual job. I do this voluntarily. I happily tell them that for me, this is not a job—it's a privilege. Being able to wield a bird of prey and have it return to you of its own volition is an incredibly addictive experience, an experience that still leaves guests feeling flabbergasted once they get to enjoy it for themselves. The very concept of a winged animal capable of flight, who could leave at any time but rather chooses to return on its own accord, blows people's minds.

Over time, much like with people, you can build bonds with the birds. You learn their personalities: you learn body language, subtle signs, and indicators. We need to form a bond with each other without the luxury of spoken communication. For all intents and purposes, birds of prey are flying killing machines. Their core drivers are food and safety. There are always exceptions to the rule, but on the whole— again, like most people—food is king, and those who provide it are gods.

Before being under the strict ruling of a zoo license, the center, on occasion, would get wild birds brought in by the public. Often, buzzards and peregrine falcons too weak to fly, succumbing to nature's cruel hand. We did our best to rehabilitate and re-release, but it's not that easy. These cases are pretty much formalities, and without wanting to sound heartless, survival chances are slim. That's how nature likes to play. They're her rules, not ours. When we are given captive-bred birds to rehome, again, it's not always so black and white. Mainly because people like to *embellish* the truth.

———

In the summer of 2014, Sarah-Jane received a phone call from a man who had a bird he needed to be rehomed. The man was a bird breeder and had sold the animal in question to a private buyer, not a specialist or a bird zoo/center. In the UK, this is completely legal and not uncommon. However, after a year, the man who had purchased said bird passed away. The bird was then returned to the breeder, who had no room or reason to want it back. Sad, but a reality of the industry.

It's always really upsetting when we get these kinds of calls.

"I'm off to see a man about a bird."

Oh, right, is that some secret code, a modern version of heading out to see a man about a dog?

"No, this guy has a corvid that needs rehoming."

I pondered what Sarah-Jane had said.

Why are you looking at rehoming a corvid? They're not birds of prey. What are we going to do with it?

In truth, none of us had any experience working with corvids. Perhaps she would just go and see the man and offer some advice, perhaps help him find an owner?

I came home from work around eight in the evening. I had been on a commercial studio shoot all day and was weary from the 4 am call time. I went upstairs and heard the sound of the shower splattering against the tiles. For some reason, the spare room next to the bathroom was emitting a warm, dim glow. My intuition twitched, and like a cat, curiosity drew me inside for a gander. Standing in the middle of the room was a bow perch, a water bath, and a large black bird. I stood there pegged to the spot.

Once again, I was hurled back to the museum. The intense feeling of wonderment froze my entire body. Like the fossilized Tyrannosaur, my gaze was utterly fixed, glued to this creature who was staring back, cocking his head, trying to look at me from all possible angles. His body looked to be formed from the blackest onyx: he was so black light couldn't escape, and neither could my interest.

I attempted to gain some ground and get a bit closer. My curiosity burned stronger, and there was a desire to look with my hands.

23

However, a slight turn of the bird's body indicated to me he was ready to bate away from me (bating is when a bird attempts to fly from a tethered perch or glove, usually because something has scared them or they can feel a gust of wind under their wings, giving them an incentive to get up into the air).

I could see he was tethered to the perch. The bird turned its head side-on to me, beak slightly agape. The light in the room was faint, making it hard to see anything other than a large, solid black shape. I turned the light up a bit, which triggered another twitch of the body. It can see me, and I can now fully see it. Its eyes frantically rolling in all directions, rapidly calculating all possible scenarios and escape routes. Me, I'm just staring like some sort of dribbling bemused man-child.

I towered over it. Slowly, with precision, I sat down on the floor around five feet away and got at its eye level. I didn't want to add more reasons for the bird to feel anxious, but I did want to get close to take in all its shimmering beauty. We just looked at each other, both of us trying to work out the other's story. Was I a threat to him or her; was he or she a threat to me?

The shower came to an abrupt halt. The silence was heavy. The bird looked toward the sound of the shower room, acknowledging the absence of running water and questionable singing. The door began to open behind me slowly: Player Two had entered the game. The bird became more anxious: its gilded black feet pivoted on the perch as it pensively turned its back on us. Still, its eyes locked on our movements. This was just in preparation, a cautious maneuver.

Sarah-Jane came and sat next to me. "It's an adult male," she said softly.

"Okay, why is he here?" was my blunt response.

"He's ours now," she responded.

At this point, it's worth mentioning that spontaneous bombs like this can sometimes spin me out—it's a character flaw I'm very much aware of. The spontaneity of it all makes me jittery and agitated. Not having time to process and analyze the pros and the cons, devise a strategy. *We hadn't had time to think anything through! Where is he going to stay? What are we going to do with him? How do we train him? Does he even have a name?*

After I stopped having a little internal tantrum, Sarah-Jane, over dinner—which is, without doubt, the best way to negotiate with me—explained her decision to take ownership of this bird and divulge some of its origin story. The bird, an adult male raven, was bought by a man in Oxford. The man had unfortunately passed away, and the raven had been left to fend for itself, all alone and without any knowledge of how to survive, albeit in an aviary situated in the man's garden. He was eventually returned to the breeder after a few weeks of torturous solitude. Through some act of divine fate, the breeder got our details and made inquiries. I asked Sarah-Jane about his temperament. Apparently, he was a "well-trained" and a "nicely mannered bird." Well, that at least sounded promising.

Chores, I believe, are a good way to allow the brain to think. The monotonous act of having to carry out a task with little cerebral input allows me to process and gain clarity. I usually find vacuuming very therapeutic and also quite cathartic. Personally, I find it helps discover solutions to many of life's problems, as does a cup of well-brewed tea (dash of milk, no sugar). On this occasion, I sought clarity and wisdom in the form of loading the dishwasher. It gave me the perfect opportunity to mull over the situation. My autonomous mind carefully placed the plates into the slots, leaving the logical, rational side of my brain to work out where this raven would fit into the bigger picture. Sarah-Jane, like most nights, was illuminated by the glow of her laptop, sorting out Experience Day bookings for guests and attending to the mountains of admin that had piled up over the course of the day.

I felt a powerful urge like a tractor beam pulling me upstairs, away from the unwashed dishes. While Sarah-Jane was engrossed in her work, I softly ascended the stairs. I carefully opened the door, half expecting the room to be empty, but there he was, sitting bolt upright, cutting an imposing figure on his perch, as if to say in true Bond villain style, "I have been expecting you."

Once again, I sat opposite him, as far away as possible, not out of fear but more of a courtesy gesture. He continued to watch every move I made: scratching my head, getting out my phone. His eyes tracked my every movement with fastidious motion. He was building a database of information, making a case folder on me, and I on him. *Was this warfare?*

Like most animal owners, I guarantee I'm not in the minority here —here's hoping—I unashamedly speak to my animal friends all the time. It's something most of us do subconsciously, and I engaged in a one-sided dialogue with the raven. I asked him questions about his past while I scanned a few books we had on birds, looking for some information on corvids.

It's fairly common knowledge that ravens and other members of the corvid family are incredibly intelligent. But just *how* clever they are is somewhat a mystery to the general public. As I spent the night learning as much as I could, I felt we had spent enough time together for me to further the relationship to the next level. I know what you're thinking: I hadn't even bought him dinner!

I put on a leather falconry glove, and like the moment in the museum, I went to look with my hands.

I stretched out a curious fist, but what followed was utter chaos: a series of mad crashings with water being swept up onto the walls and ceiling. The raven sent himself into a crazed panic. You never really appreciate how much water a vessel can hold until it is tossed around a room in a mad frenzy.

I backed away, and he slowly calmed down. I quickly returned to my seat on the other side of the room like a naughty schoolboy. The raven was panting, standing on the floor, its wings spread half on the perch, half in the empty bath, riddled with shock. After a brief stare-off, he dusted himself down, jumped back onto the perch, and fired off a few rounds.

"Bah-Bah-Bah!" His response was short and staccato, but it was a simple instruction. The tone was explicitly clear, but was I clever enough to interpret the message?

"Okay, no worries, I'll just sit here, no problem," I replied softly, not wanting to cause further angst as I watched the water drip from the ceiling walls. The raven cocked his head as if he was surprised *I* could talk and weirder still, that I could understand.

I sat up with him until just after midnight. I talked to him about the center and all the other birds there, and all the time, he watched me, listening intently, making detailed mental notes. I eventually got up. Pins and needles permeated my legs after sitting still in one awkward spot for so long. I bid him goodnight. Just as I was leaving the room, the raven decided to speak.

"Ahhhh-Ahhhh-Ahhhh." Three equally spaced, slow, purr-like calls.

I turned around and looked at him. The raven had a suggestive look in his eyes. Exactly what that truly meant, I had no idea, but it seemed too coincidental that he would call out at *that* exact moment. *Was he pleased I was leaving?*

I took the day off work to help get the raven sorted into his new digs. We only had the dilapidated cardboard box he arrived in, so I sat in the passenger seat with it on my lap. Out of the tiny crease in the lid, a little glimpse of the jet-black beak emerged. Like a shark fin, it would suddenly appear, bobbing in the air, then slowly dipping out of sight. And like a shark, he was deathly silent. I became anxious, forcing myself to double-check to see if he was okay. I cautiously opened the lid, but not too much in case he jumped out. The last thing we wanted was to instigate a repeat of last night's ruckus, but this time, in a moving vehicle. You think driving with a bee in the car is bad: imagine this unit of a bird terrorizing you as you try to avoid oncoming traffic. I caught a glimpse of a beady little eye looking back. He looked full of fright.

I assured him we were close and there was nothing to fear, but there was only silence.

This poor bird had no idea what was happening or any clue about our good intentions. He just had to trust us, which is quite a lot to ask, considering.

Upon arriving at the center, his new enclosure was cleaned and ready for him, complete with a lovely thick tree stump for perching and a clean, fresh bath. But first, we needed to replace his leather equipment. This consists of his anklets—a leather strap that goes around the bird's leg containing a brass ring to allow flying and mews jesses to be inserted, which are also made from leather. We had never made a set of equipment for a corvid before, so this would be interesting.

I put my glove on and put my hand in the box. Immediately, the raven began to attack my hand impetuously. Even through the tough leather glove, I could feel the full force of his beak. A frenzied melee of stabs, grabs, and twists. In amongst the fury, I managed to get a hold of his equipment and get him to stand on the glove. However, the violence didn't stop there. Like a jackhammer, he continued to mercilessly attack the glove with his beak, furiously raining down on it with all his might. He looked at me, realizing I wasn't reacting to his brutish assault. He changed tact and began to work on the finger joints, and my god, it was excruciatingly painful. He made this horrific, blood-curdling shrieking sound, which prompted him to try and bate off the glove. He so desperately wanted to escape.

I held his straps firm, and we cast him. Sarah-Jane threw a big, soft fleece over him and wrapped him up like a newborn baby. We do this to subdue birds and stop them from stressing themselves out and potentially causing injuries to them and us. I held onto him tightly with all my might, doing my best to brave Odin's storm. I could see his long, black scythe of a beak just peeking out of the gap in the wrapped fleece. Sarah-Jane snipped off the old, brittle anklets, and she began to work on quickly forging some new ones from a sheet of kangaroo hind.

At this point, the onus was on me to keep this raven tight. If he managed to break free, there would be no way of us controlling him: he could fly off into the wilderness, where he would more than likely die a slow and drawn-out death. I held him close and taut, speaking to him the whole time. He croaked and uttered quite little murmurs, and I'd get a slight glimpse of his eye as he threw his head back into my chest, his beak millimeters from my face. I could feel his racing heart through the fleece, and I wished for this to be over as quickly as possible for him. Once again, I assured him over and over that we were not going to hurt him and we were working as fast as possible.

Sarah-Jane loosened the fleece so she could have greater access to his legs, shiny black with overlapping armor, and the raven squirmed. I instinctively bound tighter like a python. Within thirty seconds, Sarah-Jane had put both anklets and flying straps on the raven and slotted the straps through my hand and into the safety position.

"Release him on my count. One, two, three!"

The veiled fleece removed, the raven flapped his large, thick wings, bashing me in the face. He squawked with purpose, and when he realized he couldn't fly away, he hung upside down like a bat. I quickly cupped him by the chest and lifted him back onto the glove. He found his legs, and like a flash, he bit my exposed thumb hard and then began hacking away at the glove. There was unfinished business. He managed to split the glove at the finger joint! Bear in mind, this was an eagle glove, tough enough to withstand the talons of some of the largest birds of prey on the planet. I yelped in agony, which only served to alert him to my weakness and provide him with an area to attack.

From thereon, the raven deployed precise attacks to further breach the glove and dish out the maximum amount of punishment possible. The pain was electrifying. I rushed him back to his aviary, and once inside, I opened my hand, but he wouldn't let go. His beak clamped down on my thumb joint, hanging like a rabid dog. I shook my hand, but no luck. His vice-like grip refused to be denied his vengeance.

In the end, I had to pry his beak off with my naked hand—in hindsight, this was an incredibly risky gamble, which thankfully had the desired effect. The beast relinquished its grasp. He landed on the floor and then jumped away to a suspended branch at the back of the aviary, partly cloaked in shadow. I backed out and away from the monster, keeping a visual on him at all times. My heart was racing, forehead beading with sweat, but the raven posed a different stance—his hunched-down body morphed into a sleek arrow formation, bitterly shouting at me once again, *"Bah-Bah-Bah!"* He wasn't happy, and he sure as hell wanted me to know.

Back in the safety of the office, we all looked at each other, breathing deeply. Eventually, we could inhale freely now that the subject had been confined to his quarters. What the hell had we let ourselves in for? My thumb had been opened up, blood dripping down my arm—a steady, warm stream like a raindrop on a window. A most delicious blue-purple bruise was forming on my gloved hand by the knuckle on my index finger. The glove went in the trash, and I went for some medical treatment.

Why was he so aggressive? One minute, he was snug in the box, calm and silent. The next, he was possessed by the most heinous demons of the underworld. Some of the lore I had read the previous night began to make sense, which was a tad worrying.

Could this raven be the *actual* harbinger of doom? Because after its most recent outburst of rage, I'm not even sure Odin himself could tame this potent and vicious creature.

Throughout the day, I would walk past the raven, shooting shady glances at him, my hand still throbbing from the attack. Observing from afar was my new tactic—a subtle, covert reconnaissance mission to glean intelligence on him. Every time I innocuously floated by his aviary, he would be sitting on the exact same branch where I left him, just glaring. Perhaps he was gathering his own dossier of what these strange humans were getting up to. Was there a war of attrition brewing? I could feel his stare following me each time I walked past. He was ultra calm—suspiciously calm and eerily calculated as if he was eyeing me up for round two. He obviously hadn't forgotten our last encounter and was lusting for more blood now that he had a taste for it. For the first time since having Murray the Sea Eagle on my arm, I felt nervous and totally intimidated by a bird. A bird a fraction of the size of the eagle.

Many people ask us about how we train birds of prey, and perhaps one of the most common questions is: how or why do they come back? I always like to use the analogy of any good relationship. Be it bird or human, success is quite often based around food. If you look after them and keep feeding them, then they will keep coming back. A comparison I like to draw is that birds are very similar to male lions, by which they spend a large proportion of their day belly up, bathing in the sun and sleeping. The rest of their day is spent eating, hunting, and a dash of…well, I'll let you fill in the blank.

Before we can fly birds of prey, we need to know what their weight is. This is the absolute fundamental of falconry. If you try to fly a bird that is "too heavy," they will be utterly unresponsive and, more often than not, sit up in a huge tree and look at you with discontent, much like a cat. They will not move until the next day or, in some cases, many days after. Equally, if they are underweight, they will struggle to fly. Forcing them could put them into a critical state, potentially killing them due to their lack of energy to survive the night.

Out of the twenty-six birds at the center, guess which bird had not been weighed yet that day?

"Okay, well, that's all the birds weighed. Just leaves the raven…" The silence was deafening, and unsurprisingly, there was little sign of any volunteers coming forward to wrangle with our insidious and calculated corvid. Considering I had already been mauled that morning, I thought, and perhaps in hindsight rather naively, I could somehow try and salvage the day by restarting our relationship. I picked up another glove, but this time, I went in armed with food.

Sarah-Jane and I, along with Emily, a part-time falconer and volunteer at the time, all went together *en masse* to where the beast resided. There he was, reminiscent of that early scene from the film *Ghostbusters* when Ray, Egon, and Venkman head out to hunt their first ghost in the library. The intrepid ghost hunters approach in anticipation, scared and amazed in equal proportions. We see the spectral figure of the ghost flicking through a book. And like the ghost, our demon was inches away, not paying us any attention, seemingly minding its own business preening his tatty matte black feathers. Similarly to my '80s heroes, we neared our target while whispering the best mode of attack.

"Just grab him!" one person mumbled.

"No! Don't do that; you'll enrage him," someone else chimed in.

The options were bleak and somewhat limited. Thankfully, unlike the Ghostbusters, no one opted to shout, "Get him!" Instead, I elected for a more placid ploy. I gently opened the aviary door, which Sarah-Jane quickly closed behind me, the sliding sound of the bolt lock sealing my fate. *Great, now I'm locked in with this savage.* I'm pretty sure they didn't need to lock the door, but hey-ho, better be safe than sorry.

I slowly began my approach. The raven stopped cleaning his bill and grew still, his eyes piercing as if to say, "Hello, Clarice." I edged closer, but still no signs of movement. I reached up to grab the jesses dangling inches within my grasp. I lunged and locked onto them. Phase one complete.

A voice from behind me decided to offer some advice, just like the excitable teammates in the 90s hit TV show, *The Crystal Maze.* I pray this game doesn't have an automatic lock-in. "Slowly raise your glove up," uttered Sarah-Jane.

As I did, the raven stepped cautiously up onto the glove. This was good progress. Phase two complete.

Then, the violence began.

With the same routine as before, he smashed his face-knife into the glove again and again. Plunged into survival mode, I reached into my jacket pocket and quickly pulled out a deceased day-old chick, which he snatched from my other hand with lightning speed. The attack was temporarily paused while the soft and fluffy chick hung lifelessly from the creature's mouth. My team quickly opened the door, and I dashed to the weighing scales. En route, the raven drops his yellow bundle of fluff onto the floor, but there's no time to go back and get it—we are on a mission! Remember Adam West in the old Batman films running down the street, holding on to a bomb with a lit fuse? This was my current predicament.

I reached the scales that sat on a faux-marble work surface, roughly four feet high. The scales have a basic LCD screen with a T-bar covered in astroturf coming out of the top, which is where the birds perch. The raven stepped onto the scales with little fuss, but he kept fidgeting, causing the scales to fluctuate. I was getting a reading of 2lb 5oz right up to 2lb 10oz. Why wouldn't he stay still? The longer it took, the more chance I had of getting hurt again. He stopped for a second—*brilliant!* The scales read 2lb 7oz.

The raven decided he'd had enough and barked in my face. I took heed of his instructions. I invited him back onto the glove and hurried back to his aviary, grateful for a long fuse. Sarah-Jane and the team waited by the door, sucking themselves thin to create as much distance from me and the ticking incendiary device on my glove. The door swung open, and I released the flying straps from my grasp. He retreated back to his spot in the corner and began to preen his dark feathers. We shut the door and locked the bolt. We had earned one crystal.

Over a cup of tea, we all had a chat about the raven beast. Emily rightly asked the million-dollar question, the one we'd all been thinking. "Is he staying here, or will he be going to a new home?" The tone of her question implied she was hoping for the latter.

Sarah-Jane confirmed somewhat hesitantly. "He is staying." Her response was met with silence.

Eyes down, I gently sipped my tea.

Over at the office table, Sarah-Jane was in the process of completing all the necessary paperwork for him to be permanent. We all shared the same look of woe and dejection. I looked down at the fresh wounds on my hands and contemplated what this was going to mean.

Great natured, the breeder had said!

At this point, it was easy to see why the breeder didn't want the bird and perhaps told a little white lie, but the underlying feeling that plagued my thoughts for many days was, "How are we going to work with this bird?" Admittedly, this was quite a selfish question. Firstly, I'm not at the center all the time. It's easy for me to bail out and let someone else deal with the problem. But that is exactly the kind of attitude that got him, and a third of all the other birds in the center, here in the first place. I will openly admit that when Emily asked the fatal question, I was kind of hoping the answer would have been different.

Over the next few weeks, my availability meant I was unable to be at the center apart from weekends, and in all honesty, I was relieved. It was a strange sense as being at the center had always been such a joy, but I feared my haven of solace was now tarnished by a destructive tar. Sarah-Jane persevered with the raven during the week, and I picked up the slack when and as I could.

We found that every time we entered the aviary wearing a glove, the raven would run away. He would try to get as far away as possible —you had to literally catch the flying straps mid-flight or chase him on the floor, making a dive into the shingle to get hold of his flying jesses. I've since learned that most people who work with or keep corvids have a tendency not to put anklets on their birds, but as it turns out, it was the best decision we could have made. If we hadn't, it would have been impossible to handle him.

Once the flying straps were *under the thumb* and into the safety position—yes, some reading this will know all about this phrase and may be surprised to learn that this is its origin—well, that's when the beatings would start up. And much like before, he showed me absolutely no mercy. We did discover that we could get him on the scales more easily if we brought them into his aviary. Perhaps now that he had bedded in, he would feel a bit more at home. This seemed to work well, and again, progress, however small, is still progress.

The frantic and hectic schedule of the summer was coming to a welcomed end. This means as a team, we were generally less busy and, therefore, allowed the luxury to wind down operations in preparation for the winter.

One Saturday morning in September, I was examining the weight sheets. I went through all the birds, checking that the data had been filled out correctly and cross-referencing the weights from the previous day to see if there were any anomalies in weight change and associated flying behavior. I got to the bottom, and it struck me: we still hadn't given the raven a name. On the weight sheet, we had the bird's name and species. Here, it just said "raven." He wasn't part of the family yet, more of a guest and a burden at that. He was completely unassigned, just as he had probably been his whole life. My stomach felt a swirling sadness; my heart pierced with pathos. It was time we changed this.

Sarah-Jane and I decided it was time to give him a name since, after all, he would be here for the long haul. Without thinking, I blurted out, "Loki!" She looked at me, and on the spot, we one hundred percent agreed—which is rare. That would be his name, but were we tempting fate? Naming an already ferocious bird after the Norse god of trickery and mischief might be playing with fire.

FOUR
HRÆDDR
FEAR/AFRAID

rummaged through our big blue trunk of gauntlets—big ones, small ones, some sporting epic gouges, deep battle scars from various engagements with raptor talons. Naturally, I picked out an eagle glove. It's larger than the regular gauntlets—a thicker, more robust garment that extends up to the elbow, and in this case, it was brown (unlike our other gloves, which are mostly green). I donned my armor and headed over to Loki's aviary.

"Hi, Loki. That's your name now, by the way. It's time to get you weighed. I beg of you, please don't bite me again."

As I entered, Loki cocked his head and looked at me. It was different than before. It wasn't aggressive; it was more guarded. The feathers on his head inflated like a fan. As I continued deeper into his lair, he turned his body away from me and made these very cute, innocent pips. The sounds he emitted were a clear indicator to me that he was apprehensive.

"It's okay, Loki. We are just going to weigh you."

I picked him up, and he nervously stood on the glove, still cooing. *Shit! I'd forgotten the scales!*

"Okay, mate. I'm going to take you outside. No biting, okay?" I opened the door and walked him to the office, keeping an eye on him and making sure that his beak was at a safe distance from my face. Something was very different with Loki. He craned his head down and fluffed up the feathers on his head, his eyes permanently locked on mine.

I sat him on the scales, took a reading, picked him back up, and returned him to the aviary, but this time, it was different. Instead of running down the street clasping a volatile explosive, it would appear the touchpaper hadn't been lit. I locked the aviary door and returned to the office.

He didn't attack me. Not even once. I was more shocked than relieved as I was beginning to feel accustomed to mid-morning savagery—no signs of aggression, no barking, no stabbing. I asked if anyone else had had similar experiences, but they all point-blankly refused to go in, and I couldn't blame them. I double-checked with Sarah-Jane, who was immensely pleased with the progress. She asked if he tried to run away as per usual. I was happy to inform her that he didn't. In fact, he sat beautifully. But this got me thinking. *Why, all of a sudden, had his behavior changed?*

I returned to the office and picked up another glove, not the eagle glove, just a normal-sized gauntlet. I ventured back into Loki's aviary with a bounce in my step, dressed in a veil of improved confidence. Before I could get inside, he dropped down from his supervillain-perching branch and ran straight to the furthest corner of his aviary. He buried his head in the shingle and sang an ensemble of bizarre, distressing noises. Normally, my go-to analogy for birds is a human teenager. However, in this case, what I witnessed was more of a fear-stricken child running from an abusive parent. I was awash with an overarching feeling of pathos and a desire to quash his feelings of anguish. It was awful to see him like this. Was it something I had done? As I cornered him, I leaned in and picked him up. The result was an all too familiar fight or flight reaction, which kicked in immediately. He lashed out like a deranged wild dog, doing his utmost to hurt me as much as possible. Like a switch, he went from fear to ultra-violent.

The only conclusion I could come to was either the glove's size or color was spurring him into having fits of rage. To test this theory, I went back in with the brown eagle glove from before. Surprisingly, he was okay and very submissive, scared but not violent. I switched back while in the aviary to the regular green glove, and he went ballistic. Now we were getting somewhere. I rooted around in the glove box, and I found an old brown glove. No one used it because it was very stiff and uncomfortable. It also had a clear hole in the top of the thumb. This might have been asking for trouble. I put the old, damaged brown glove on, which was also regular-sized, only coming halfway up my forearm. I tentatively offered it to Loki, who exhibited the same timid, non-violent behavior as with the eagle glove. I thought I'd cracked it! It was all down to the color. Loki didn't like green gloves.

Over lunch, I chatted with the team about my intrepid test and conclusion. I found the results fascinating; the others were confused as to why I kept returning to his aviary, expecting to get hurt. I was theorizing on why this might be the case. Why be scared of a color? This kind of behavior is not seen in any of the birds of prey. They do not care what glove you use as long as there is a sumptuous lashing of raw meat on offer.

That night before I went home, I got one of the green gloves out of the trunk and took it over to Loki. Within seconds, he clocked it and, like all the previous times, hastily retreated to the floor, sobbing in the corner. I opened the door, left the glove on the log beside him, and ran out to watch from a safe distance. It felt like I had just pulled the pin and chucked in a hand grenade, curiously observing what the result would be.

After a few moments, Loki was consumed by a fit of rage. He made a move and lashed out, jumping on the glove and attacking it vigorously as if his very life depended on it. He was relentless. He grabbed the glove in his beak, growling and grunting, then with his feet, he clasped one of the fingers, causing him to roll off the log over onto his back, glove between his feet and beak, tearing away at it tooth and nail. I left him to it for a few minutes before returning to try and retrieve my hand grenade. However, Loki wasn't finished with it. He wanted it destroyed. I ran my hand over the newly healed scars on my hand, a good reminder that there was no way I was going in to try to pry it away from him in this heightened state. I left the center to the sound of a deranged corvid mutilating a glove.

The next morning, I was awake earlier than usual. Normally, the sound of unwilling children fighting their parents' efforts to go to school rings throughout the concrete jungle of our estate. I'd much prefer the sickly Caribbean alarm on my phone to bring me into the real world. My sleep was a disruptive storm of ominous and brooding ravens: a whole conspiracy of them stood over me, staring menacingly with judging glares. I felt as though the dream was perhaps some kind of subconscious test. Was that it? Was Mother Nature testing me, deciding if I was capable of persevering with this serendipitous task? With the fuzzy, warm blur of sleep softly fading and all the unruly children finally battened in for the school run, the unsettling experience of standing in a corvid court left a sour taste in my mouth. Today, I decided to take advantage of my urban alarm clock and head into the center early.

The fifteen-minute drive through the valley is the perfect way to cleanse the mind, think clearly, and ease oneself into the day. My subconscious thoughts are finally allowed to filter into my mainstream thinking before my brain can achieve full functionality and begin its logical sorting process. The mist hovered over the fields as if suspended in time, the sun gradually warming up, ready to burn it all away, putting an end to the hard efforts of the night. Only the early risers are privy to this exclusive and beautiful scene. I consider it a treat.

I strolled through the farm, gliding over the cobbled path, ensuring my feet didn't slip on the glassy stones. I plotted a course to where the tyrant resided, but before I got anywhere near, I heard him. A bizarre, rasping call I've not heard before: *"Eeerrr-eeerrr-eererrr."*

It's not threatening; it's calm but deliberate. I paused, rooted to the spot. He paused his song, too. Then he started again, the same call. It had a lovely, deep, warm sound, similar to the effect my Italian relatives produce when they roll their Rs.

I strolled up to his aviary, and again, he stopped his song. He held his position firmly at the back of the aviary with an air of pride, his beak slightly raised with one eye on me. He knew I had been listening. He watched and analyzed my reactions, predicting my next move. I looked down at the log where I had left the glove the previous night. It was no longer on the log. I surveyed the floor and saw it in the corner, beaten and left for dead. It had taken quite a hammering over the night —no wonder he looked so proud of himself. I opened the aviary door and entered with extreme caution. I kept an eye on Loki as I crouched down and shuffled slowly over to the glove. The damage was fatal. I pronounced the glove dead at the scene. As I finished my examination, Loki fluffed up his onyx crown. He watched intently, expecting a response from me, but would it be praise or scorn? I decided to further the experiment and leave the glove in there with him: after all, it had no use to me now.

The day went by, and as I was flying the other birds, that urging pull, the invisible tractor beam, drew me back to the shadowy figure in the aviary. He stood in there motionless, observing everything that happened around him, quietly biding his time. I finished up and headed over to see him. I slinked inside his base and deliberately sought out the lifeless and devoured glove, which had been untouched since my first inspection. I picked it up and put it in the left side pocket of my flying jacket. I took out another green glove, the one I had been using to fly the birds, and straight away, Loki noticed it. His hackles flared up, and his body started to pivot: battle stations!

I walked in and slowly approached, glove down by my side. He was watching, itching to make a move. I softly spoke to him, whispering safe and calm vibes. I raised my glove and gently took his flying jesses. We maintained eye contact; so far, all was well. I edged the glove toward his leg, inviting him to step up, wanting to go at his pace and convenience. What I got was another torrent of abuse. I rode the storm, pretending it didn't hurt, but every strike on my thumb joint sent bolts of intense pain shooting up the length of my arm. I whipped him out of his aviary and ventured out into the fresh air. I took a seat on a rustic bench that lives in the corner of the flying arena. Like most birds at the center, the bench is a hand-me-down, weathered, and a bit broken, but it was still full of functionality and charm. I sat with him on my glove. He eventually stopped beating me up for a minute and just stared at me. My hand was aching, and I could feel my joints swelling inside the glove. I was pretty sure I was bleeding, too.

We spent half an hour staring at each other. I reach into my pocket and pull out a hobnob, a classic British biscuit and a treat most often enjoyed in accompaniment with a nice cup of tea (again, a little bit of milk, no sugar). I took a bite and offered it to Loki. He snatched it out of my hand with full petulance, managing to get a bit of my thumb at the same time: a not-so-subtle way of telling me he was still mad but also somewhat thankful for the treat. I didn't want to push my luck and concluded that was probably enough raven time for today. Was this progress?

The next couple of weeks were a frustrating blend of petulance and stubbornness, with very little, if any, developments being made in taming Loki. I convinced myself there must be some literature on the subject, so I turned to my savior, the holder of all knowledge, the custodian of secrets, everything mankind knows and beholds as true all in one place: the internet. I spent my evenings desperately trying to understand the cause of this kind of behavior. I combed through hundreds of corvid forums, bird of prey forums, message boards, Wikipedia articles, and YouTube videos, frantically looking for advice from other trainers, trying to find the secret formula to cracking this nut. But ultimately, my search for the Holy Grail of corvid behavior secrets was barren. The most common results yielded were with pied crows and getting them to do tricks. I wasn't anywhere near this stage or indeed in the market for gimmicks. I needed to find the root of the anxiety. Was it specific, would it ease with time, or is this behavior now baked in? On this occasion, the internet provided little help on the subject, and I felt somewhat dejected and void of hope. It was totally and utterly demoralizing.

I desperately wanted to persevere with Loki. There was something about him—it was magnetic. Was it because he was a challenge and something new? Perhaps I was subconsciously on an ego trip, wanting to conquer the beast that no one would dare battle with. Whatever it was, the will and desire were intense, burning strong as a dwarven forge. Whenever I was at the center, I made sure to sit with Loki at some point during the day. I would chat with him just like that first night. In fact, it was quite therapeutic. I imagined that he was listening, and much like a good therapist, he wouldn't interject, instead opting to let me work things out for myself. I did wish he would give me a clue as to how I could help work out his issues, but he opted for a mute stance. Like the ravens in my dream, I felt I was under strict test conditions. Loki's aggression cooled slightly, but it still reared up. He was, at times, completely unpredictable. I was insistent on persevering with the green glove. I would prove to him it's not a threat.

Stubbornness has always been my worst trait.

Within the first eight months of Loki being in our care, he had put me in the hospital three times. In that time, he had opened up my left forearm like a can of sardines, pulled out clumps of hair and scissored my ears, savaged every knuckle and joint on both hands, taken chunks of flesh out of my calves, thighs, and head. He inflicted devastating blows to my arms, causing swelling and bruising covering the circumference of a tennis ball. He had bitten my nose and hung off the underside of my bicep, refusing to let go. On one occasion, I had to physically rip the flesh out of his mouth. It was a riot.

I would sit in the accident and emergency waiting room thinking, "When they ask me how I have injured myself, what will they think if I tell them the truth?"

After my third excursion to one of the NHS's finest establishments, I opted to explain to the medical teams that my wounds were trivial mistakes. "Yeah, I cut myself on some gardening shears...caught my ear on a barbed wire fence...hair got pulled out in a bar fight..."

It was easier for them to comprehend, but it wasn't that simple. Deep down, I wanted to protect Loki and the raven image. I felt somewhat obliged to hide his darkness, and comparable to victims of Stockholm syndrome, I didn't want to propagate the evil omens and connotations of my abuser. I constantly toyed with this duality. I knew there was good in there, and I didn't want people to be scared of ravens. They had been persecuted enough, and I felt that Loki was a chance to break some of these myths. I knew folk might not understand because, in reality, I didn't either.

Most nights, I would sink my torn and scarred hands into icy water, then into hot water, and back again into icy water, the entire time asking myself if it was really worth it. Why the hell was I doing this? Maybe I was wrong. Maybe ravens *were* just malevolent lunatics. There is enough lore that pointed to it. Scratch that. Maybe it wasn't the ravens. Maybe *Loki* was just an evil lunatic.

FIVE
FÓLCVÍG
BATTLE

Stubbornness runs strong in me: Sarah-Jane, my friends, and my business partners will happily corroborate that. My dad says I got it from my mother, and he'd be correct. My mum was your typical stereotype Scot: patriotic with a fierce, fiery temper to match her burning red hair. As I grew up, I looked more like my dad but inherited a scorching stubbornness from north of the border, which would often clash quite spectacularly. My mum and I could wage war on each other, conjuring arguments of epic proportions that could last for hours. It wasn't unusual for these battles to drag on for days and sometimes weeks: ugly, brooding atmospheres forcing neither of us to concede out of pure obstinance. Apparently, to some people, at times, it's a good trait to have, often interchangeable with being driven and goal-orientated. However, it's often hugely detrimental, aligning more with inflexibility and inability to submit. I hate being wrong, and I hate losing. I saw Loki as an opposition similar to my mum, and similar to when I was a bullheaded teenager, I didn't want to lose under any circumstances. This was mistake number two.

I chased Loki around the aviary as I couldn't find the golden glove of peace. Eventually, I grabbed ahold of his jesses, and like many times before, he began his assault repertoire. This routine was becoming exhausting. I had to mentally prepare to go into his aviary each and every time, and the worst part was knowing it was causing him stress.

I really hate to see animals suffer. On various social media platforms, there are numerous videos being shared to highlight the horrific mistreatment of animals all around the world. I understand the shock tactics, but I just can't stomach them. Just knowing it exists is enough to bring a tear to the eye.

The frustration of seeing animals unable to recognize our good intentions made me question whether or not what I was trying to achieve was really for the best. Was my stubbornness counterproductive?

On this occasion, Loki showed signs that he was learning. The glove I wore in this instance reached halfway up the forearm. Loki changed tact, and instead of hammering the glove with all his might, he opted for a new line of attack.

He had been studying me.

Biting down on the glove, although painful, was just manageable enough to hide any signs of discomfort. My lack of a visual reaction forced him to up his game, so he diverted his efforts and went for the forearm. He grabbed me and tore deep into my arm like a pair of scissors. He sliced through my skin as if it were paper, peeling the flesh right off. I panicked and grabbed his beak with my other hand like before. I forced my thumb and index finger into the joint of his mouth, trying to pry it open. The strength in his beak was incredible. I eventually managed to force his clamped beak off of my arm, and instinctively, he snapped his neck around and razored the palm of my exposed hand.

Thankfully—small mercies—this all happened in the confinement of Loki's aviary and not in sight of the general public. I dropped the glove and exited with haste. I closed the door and clutched my arm. Loki stood at the back of the battlefield, bolt upright. Motionless and silent. He didn't look shocked or proud or ashamed but stood with an air of complete tranquility as if nothing happened. Was he a sociopath? *Can birds be sociopaths?*

I looked down at my arm: I was leaking blood all over the floor. My work shirt was smeared in deep ruby red. I looked back up. Loki did a rouse—when a bird ruffles its feathers—an indication he was comfortable and relaxed. The sun hit the spot on his beak, brilliantly reflecting back to me my glistening blood. I'd lost this battle, and badly. One to nothing, Loki.

I needed to discuss with the rest of the team to see how they felt about Loki. All the full-time staff agreed they didn't like going in with him, and they just got in and out as quickly as possible, wearing as much protective clothing as they could find. We didn't allow any volunteers at the time to pick Loki up, only falconers. Weeks went by with little improvement. My hands, however, boasted a trophy cabinet loaded with glorious scars.

We decided to change tactics and welcome a new challenge. We needed to fly and exercise this bird: maybe that would ease the aggression? We *hoped* it would ease the aggression.

Considering the unique situation, we took Loki's training right back to the start for two reasons. The first issue became clear after a much closer inspection: we discovered he didn't have a fully formed tail. The most likely reason for this not to develop is stress. Sadly, we've seen it a few times in owls that have found themselves in our care after a less-than-great start to life with humans. It was possible his poor condition was due to his past living conditions. Had it been before or after his previous owner died?

In the past, with rescued captive-bred birds, it had been common to receive birds with a missing or poorly-formed set of tail feathers. We allow them to fully molt out a fresh new set. This process requires us to ground the birds and then overload their body with the richest food we have. A delightful selection of rat, quail, duck, mice, and goose will usually see results within a month, depending on the species. The bird's body, after a few days of no flying, realizes it doesn't need to allocate energy for flight, so it pushes out new feathers much quicker.

Loki had been with us for a few months and already had a plethora of rich food. He was weighing in at around two pounds, ten ounces. Having never worked with corvids, we didn't know if this was what a raven of this age should weigh. We knew for sure he wasn't starving, as the only way he would cooperate was with edible bribes. We decided to continue with a rich diet and introduce some light training.

With all new birds, training is short with an attractive reward, pending, of course, that the bird has cooperated in a positive fashion. We can't just set the bird free: it's a death sentence. If we do that at a young age, they are unable to hunt for themselves because they haven't been taught how to. Instead, we tie a long piece of string called a *creance* to the bird's anklets (which translates roughly to "line of little faith"). The first few training sessions only require the bird to jump a small distance to a glove—around a foot—and they need only do this at least once. Each day, the distance gets farther, provided they completed the training successfully the day before. Finally, after a few weeks, once the birds are flying twenty feet to the glove on command, we can then start to remove the creance and prepare for a completely free flight.

Obviously, Loki was at no point to be set free because let's face it: a potential psychopath of a bird with a pair of devastating scissors on its face just hankering for some more human blood wouldn't go down too well on a children's petting farm. Our initial concern was if he would return; the more worrying question was, would he attack someone? There wouldn't be much reason for him to return to us because, for all intents and purposes, we hadn't really bonded. If anything, he was still very anxious in our presence. Letting him loose would be a Daily Mail headline waiting to happen. In other words, career-ending.

We picked him up on the eagle glove, and Sarah-Jane quickly tried to fasten the line to the swivel—a metal device that allows us to join the two flying jesses together. However, his nimble beak attacked her every which way she tried, and she couldn't get close to his feet without being nipped by his laser-guided sensors. I raised my hand in front of his face to divert his attention, which worked amazingly well. What's another bite to add to the list? Sarah-Jane managed to thread the line through the swivel and engaged the falconer's knot (this is a quick and easy knot you can do with one hand, which tightens the more it is pulled).

The only downside to my cunning diversion tactic was that Loki didn't just stop and look at my raised hand; he chomped down on it. He lashed out and grabbed the second knuckle on my index finger. His grip was fierce and as powerful as ever. I winced in agony before I shouted at him to let go. I'd never raised my voice in anger at any of the birds in all the time I had worked with them. It's an absolute no-no. They can't understand us, and we don't use aggression as a communication tool, not even as discipline.

However, Loki did understand. He read my annoyance loud and clear. My outburst left him in shock, and even Sarah-Jane was slightly taken aback. He had never been scolded like this before, and it put him in his place. Perhaps he understood what he was doing was unkind; maybe he would realize *his* place in the pecking order. My rage gauge immediately faltered to a more level-headed disposition, allowing me to speak to Loki in a calm, more respectful manner.

"You can't keep biting me, Loki. It bloody hurts, and we are only trying to help you."

His body illustrated a figure cast with remorse, his head lowered, and his eyes seemed softly apologetic. He was silent. We all were.

"Okay, he's now ready to go," said a confident Sarah-Jane.

I walked him to one of the perches in our arena. The perches are solid wooden posts roughly four and a half feet tall, with a two-foot-long wooden bar covered in flexible astroturf sitting on top of it. I placed him on the perch with ease. Sarah-Jane gently unwound around six feet of slack on the creance which would allow him to easily fly to me before coming torque. I put a few day-old chick legs on my glove, raised it up, and called him.

"Loki! Loki! Come on, mate."

He point-blank ignored me and started to preen. It was a total act of defiance, the kind often exhibited by teenage children deliberately disobeying a parent. He would rather clean his feathers than come to me for food. I decided to move three feet closer. I held my hand up. Same result. In fact, he started to angle his body so his back was facing me: the absolute cheek of it! I moved in closer still—six inches from his feet. Close enough for him to hop on with the absolute minimum of effort. Like lightning, he rotated and swooped his neck down, stealing the food without moving off the perch. *The little bastard!* I could hear giggling in the background.

Next to the perch is a small, three-foot fence that separates the public viewing area from the arena. People come and lean on the fence to watch the birds. Along the fence are plaques giving information on various raptors at the center, exhibiting lots of interesting facts that I'm certain they don't read. I put one chick leg on the fence. As soon as I removed my hand, Loki leaped off the perch straight onto the fence, snatching up the offering in no time. He stayed put; I looked at Sarah-Jane. I put another leg on the perch he had just vacated. Quick as a flash, he was back up there, chick leg quickly gobbled up.

Okay, this was good. Loki was complying, kind of. He wasn't jumping to my glove, but at least I wasn't bleeding or wrestling with him. Once again, I was grateful for these small mercies. I walked roughly fifteen feet to the next perch. I checked over my shoulder to make sure Sarah-Jane had a firm grip on the creance—I was riddled with paranoia. Visions of Loki hurling himself like a mortar into a pack of unsuspecting children raced through my mind. I faced the perch, back to Loki, and put a chick leg on the astroturf. I heard the sound of flapping wings race upon me, and he landed and swallowed the leg.

"Good boy, Loki!"

I continued to walk and fly Loki to the other six remaining perches. He was as good as gold. I showered him with praise, cementing that this is good boy behavior. A small gathering of the public looked onward—I could hear them chatting amongst themselves. "Look at that crow, he's massive!" They headed toward the viewing area to get a closer look. Loki had an audience and found himself performing in an impromptu show, but how would this act end?

We finished his flying for the day with a crowd of pleased children and two intact falconers. In total, he had ten legs and three day-old chicken heads—quite the feast, I'm sure you will agree. I would feed him the bodies these heads once belonged to once back in his aviary. This was our insurance policy in case a disaster were to strike, and we would need bartering currency.

As I walked past the crowd, the children gasped in awe, and the mothers recoiled.

"I think they look evil," one of them scorned.

Just wait until they bite you, I thought with a chuckle.

Sarah-Jane untied his creance with utter ease. Loki was completely unfazed this time around. I popped him back into the aviary, and he hopped back to his favorite perch, turning around to face me. As I put my hand into the pocket containing the remaining rations of his food allocation, his head adjusted immediately. He was anticipating what I was about to pull out. I paused. Like him, I studied every movement of his. I slowly raised my gloved arm, partly in protection, anticipating an attack. His lingering gaze was firmly fixed on my hand, still rooted deeply in my pocket. He totally ignored the precautionary glove I offered up. I slowly pulled out the jackpot, and within a fraction of a second, he leaped onto my glove and yelled in excitement, *"Bah!"* He snatched the food out of my hand and bounced back to his safe place.

We had made actual, tangible progress today. I always wanted to end our sessions on a positive note, so for the benefit of fairness, we would call this one a draw.

SIX
UNDRASK
TO MARVEL

Growing up, my parents have always had big working dogs in the family home: a German Shepherd, a Bull Terrier, and two hefty Bullmastiffs. These kinds of animals need to be worked. They need to burn off their intense energy and fully use their power to prevent them from becoming boisterous and destructive hellhounds. We would take the dogs on long walks and spend hours in the garden wrestling and playing with chew toys. I love dogs, and, in my opinion, we humans don't deserve them. I tend to subscribe to the notion that if a person doesn't like dogs and dogs don't like them, I'm going to be siding with the canine. I've been surrounded by them all my life.

Kai, a stout and proud-looking German shepherd, was an incredibly smart and well-disciplined dog. My dad, who at the time was coming to the end of his martial arts career for which he taught for twenty years, used Japanese commands to communicate with Kai. Our pointy-eared pooch was an expert swimmer but also had a highly aggressive tendency toward certain dogs and people. Sometimes, he'd slam into a state of rage, full-on protection mode. Other times, he would be totally fine with other dogs, so it was paramount to be able to maintain full control of him at all times. I was only a toddler when

Kai was around, and my parents, as you can imagine, erred on the side of caution with him whenever he was around me. However, that dog would never leave my side, assigning himself as my sworn protector. There were even a few occasions when he snarled at my dad when I misbehaved and angered him. In retrospect, it feels good to know that I had my own personal bodyguard looking out for me.

As I got older, we adopted a beautiful, stocky bull terrier called Charlie. He was a rescue dog who had suffered from some pretty bad brain damage. A side effect of this was an unpredictable personality, a real Jekyll and Hyde-type affair. But, like Kai, this dog allowed me to ride him like a pony and play with his ears without ever showing any signs of malice or aggression. There definitely seems to be an innate ability infused into their genetic makeup, a sense that we as a species seem to have chosen to relinquish. Spoken communication, specifically the use of words, makes up only 7% of effective communication. According to some studies, tonality makes up 38% and body language takes the largest slice of the pie with 55%. So, is it any wonder why animals haven't evolved communication based on words? They seem to be doing all right, but humans, on the other hand, struggle with effective communication. As evidenced by the self-help section in any library, we as a species are generally pretty terrible at it. This inherent trait, I believe, is real and very much exists. I've seen it for myself with birds of prey.

The story I always like to draw upon comes from an experience I had with my own bird, Logan. One of the excursions Coda happily volunteers their services for are visits to hospices. In particular, dementia wards. On one such visit, Logan was given the opportunity to have a day out. He doesn't get too many outings because at times, Logan can be quite *bitey*, but only if you put your hand near his face, so it's completely understandable. He is in no way comparable to Loki on the violence spectrum. On this particular visit, Logan sat on my glove, and I gave a talk to a mixed group of people. There were approximately twenty dementia sufferers and a dozen caregivers all huddled in the day room. Apple green paint covered the walls, the room incredibly warm with radiators cranked to the max and blazing rays of sunshine colliding through the huge French doors. The residents sat in a circle as I waxed lyrical about my boy, who let out a random loud *"Wheep!"* every so often, which people thought was rather cute and somewhat hilarious.

"It's like he knows you're talking about him!" one of the caregivers said.

Maybe he did, but then again, owls are not known for their intellectual capabilities, so I highly doubted it. I thought, I do love Logan, but he is by no means the sharpest tool in the box.

There wasn't much conversation happening in the group, mainly because everyone was just so fascinated by his size and those enormous orange eyes, which were just spellbinding. You could see the look of awe in both the residents and the caregivers. I walked Logan around the inner circle so people could get a closer look. One lady, roughly in her mid-forties, extended her arm toward Logan, who was around five feet away. I took a risk and brought Logan close so she could experience his silky, soft plumage. He didn't mind at all. In fact, the lady fearlessly began stroking his head. My heart leaped into my throat. I was just about to block her, but she landed a pat on his head and, with grace and delicate respect, gave Logan gentle strokes. One of the staff realized what was happening and suffered a brief moment of lapsed concentration. She snapped to and headed over to intervene, but by then, it was too late. She looked at me with panic, but I gave her a smile, letting her know everything was under control. Logan sat there proudly while this lady, with pure joy splashed all over her face, continued to stroke and tame this colossal oaf. She was having a wonderful time.

We got a call the next day from the hospice. The duty manager called to thank us for coming to see the residents, who all seemed to really enjoy the experience. She continued to explain that the lady who stroked the owl had a very severe form of dementia. Her memory was limited to seconds. She didn't recognize her own children or even her husband of seventeen years and pretty much started every day fresh, anxious, and in a state of panic and confusion. The reason for the call was to let us know that the lady over breakfast had told the carers every single detail about Logan, from his weight to his crepuscular hunting tendencies. The manager was in tears over the phone. Her voice began to break, choking with emotion. It was the first time in decades she had ever seen anything like this and she was completely dumbfounded. The staff couldn't stop talking about it.

There is absolutely no doubt in my mind that Logan was able to sense the poor lady was unwell. He knew his surroundings and behaved accordingly. I would bet my house that if one of the care-givers were to do the same thing, the outcome would have been much different. A subliminal, celestial bond is woven throughout the fabric of the natural world: it exists, and it always has, but we as a species have chosen to forget the language and how to speak it. Instead, we have turned our backs and annexed ourselves, in turn, making humanity the self-proclaimed kings of the planet. A sad case of us and them.

But nature does have a thirst for balance. Charlie the Bull Terrier knew I was a member of his pack, and in his mind, I needed to be protected. But there was the odd occasion where he would turn on the hand that fed him. Thankfully, I was not the custodian of the food. Perhaps Loki saw me as a threat. What was it he could be protecting? Was I emitting body language or an energy that made him pensive and anxious in my presence? Was I perhaps similar in stature to his previous owner? There had to be a reason. Ravens are supposed to be pretty smart, right?

They, whoever *they* are, say animals can smell fear or at least sense it. Maybe this could help me try a new strategy and elicit a different kind of bond with Loki. Like working with big-pack animals, there needs to be a leader. The leader can't show fear or weakness—they need to dominate. It was time to put the green glove back on.

The car radio acted as a comfortable and welcome distraction. I snaked through the valley, listening to the trivial issues surrounding self-important, million-dollar football (soccer) players. They likened the London Derby to going into battle (the London Derby is a football game between Arsenal and local arch-rivals Tottenham Hotspur). It's hyperbole at its finest. However, they had never had the experience of walking into a raven's lair with a green glove on. I pulled up to the center and turned off the ignition. I took deep breaths—lots of deep breaths.

I walked past Loki's aviary, and he saw me straight away. No surprise there. I bid him a good morning and told him I'd check on him soon. I had a coffee with the rest of the staff and, as I hadn't been in for a week, wanted to get a bit of an update on the state of play with regards to the "antics." Apparently, he'd been fairly well-behaved, flying well just as he had done previously, and his violence was controlled and kept to a minimum. Maybe, just maybe, today wouldn't be such a big deal.

I grabbed the green glove and ventured over to our dark lord. He stood up with perfect posture, with his head slightly cocked to one side. I opened the door and closed it behind me. I stopped, and like the police about to embark on a drug raid, I clearly stated my intentions. I walked over and picked him up, and…he resisted arrest and fought me, working the glove over with his beak, then switching to my lovely, soft, fleshy forearm, stabbing deep. Luckily, he didn't get a chance to lock on.

I retreated and exited the aviary. I got out of sight and checked my arm. The bruising had started to swell immediately. I closed my eyes and inhaled deeply. I remembered the radio chatter about the London derby. I exhaled, "Once more unto the breach, dear friends, once more," a flashback to my A-Level English lessons—perhaps Henry V's speech *was* worth learning.

Once more, I headed straight back into the lair. Like before, I stated what we would do and tried again. And like the definition of madness, the exact same result happened as nothing had changed, with me retreating with fresh wounds. The pain was excruciating, and this time, Loki had cut me open. I could feel the blood skating down my forearm. On the outside, I tried to remain unfazed, but on the inside, I was hurting. I was here on my day off. I was supposed to enjoy this.

The match was still poised at one-all. I couldn't let today be the day he edged in front. Two-one to him would leave me at a huge disadvantage and a mountain to climb. I hovered outside his aviary. After dabbing up the excess blood on my arm, I took a breath, exuding an air of nonchalance, knowing that he was watching me. I checked my phone, looking at dogs doing stupid stuff and super fat cats—one ginger cat reminded me of Stimpy, which raised a smile. I saw one of the volunteers outside flying a Harris Hawk, and it oozed fun and harmony. This was the bond I was desperate to forge with Loki. I was getting quite bored of being physically mutilated by his beak-like machete.

At least ten minutes passed. My arm was throbbing from the beating I received, but I had things to do, so it was time to suck it up: round three, *ding-ding!*

This time, there was no messing about, no pre-game warnings, just straight to the point. I walked in, strode straight up to Loki with real vigor, grabbed his jesses, and forced him onto the glove. I opened the door and marched him to the scales. I showed him the scales, and he jumped on.

At this point, I assumed that I might be winning this little skirmish. I looked at Loki on the scales. He looked back, blinking his eyes, a volcanic glass-black. More importantly—he wasn't biting. "Well, that wasn't such a big deal now, was it," I said with authority and seriousness.

He immediately responded with a very staccato, very sure, *"Bah-Bah!"*

Later on in the day, I flew him with the help of Chris, a full-time member of the team at the time. Chris wasn't too keen on Loki after the damage he did to my arm and was always on his guard. Loki zipped around the arena on his creance—this was actually fun. He had a very clumsy flying style due to his incomplete tail. He lacked the dynamism of a falcon, the grace and elegance of an owl, and the power and guile of an eagle, so what was his special trait apart from the ability to efficiently tear apart human flesh?

After all his flights, Loki was tired out, panting. He could not continue doing full lengths of the flying arena, so instead, he utilized his sassy corvid strut to waddle to the perches. Chris removed the creance, and I sat with him for another counseling session on the bench. I chatted away, giving him my thoughts on the impending football game, and without thinking, I stroked him on the back. I'd never done this before, and I don't know why I did it. It was risky and a brash move, but fortunately, I didn't get bitten. I got away with another three strokes before I got a little peck. Nothing serious this time—it was more of a swatting action, but I recognized I had gotten my money's worth. It would be foolish to push my luck. Was I starting to finally get somewhere? Did I need to adopt a more authoritative approach to Loki? Do ravens need tough love and order?

I escorted Loki back to his aviary and popped him back on his perch. I took the green glove off, and as I did, I passed the glove close to Loki. The reaction was astonishing. He flinched, running away to the corner of the enclosure, and began to sob.

Much like a dog when a rolled-up newspaper is raised, Loki reacted the same to the green glove. Was it possible that a corvid could associate an item to past trauma, even down to such details as the exact color? This was a real light bulb moment—a moment of extreme clarity. As absurd as it seemed, it did seem like the most logical explanation and would certainly go toward explaining his lashing out. From that day on, I never went anywhere near that raven with that specific shade of green glove. He had suffered enough physically, and now salt was being rubbed into mental wounds with my obnoxious persistence. I finally realized that my stubbornness on this occasion was most definitely inimical.

If Loki had been forcefully disciplined with a green glove when he was a baby, then there was no way he would ever bond with me if I had continued to remind him of his horrid past. To him, at least, I was no better than his previous tormentor—this bird has real human emotions, which I was too naive to recognize. This was a real breakthrough moment and a lot for me to comprehend.

We constantly discourage people from anthropomorphizing raptors. They are not like us: they don't love; they don't need luxury. What they do need is food, water, exercise, and safety. But Loki wasn't a raptor—he could feel, and knowing this completely changed everything. That night, I danced with a really mixed bag of emotions. On the one hand, I was ecstatic to be making some real progress—understanding the psychology of the raven and uncovering their closely kept secrets. But on the other hand, my heart broke knowing this poor, beautiful creature had been the victim of physical abuse by human hands. No animal should ever suffer mistreatment by man, ever.

As usual, I found it difficult to sleep. My arm was pulsing with pain, and the bruising doubled in size. Like the shiny, glossy corvid, my skin shimmered an unnatural black and blue. My mind boarded a train of consciousness that took me on a soul-searching journey. I imagined what other traumas Loki had endured. It was hard to picture him suffering physical and mental abuse. I just couldn't comprehend why someone could or would want to inflict suffering on an animal. Was it because he was aggressive? Surely, his current behavior was the consequence of violence. At first, I felt sad, but then came anger. Humans can be the worst this planet has to offer. He was so much more complex and sensitive than I could imagine, and it was at this very moment I stopped looking at him as a bird.

SEVEN
SÍÐASTI SÉNS
LAST CHANCE

I t was a busy week. I had been on another long shoot, pulling a few fourteen-hour days. I was groggy, tired, hungry, and all together, pretty irritable. Toward the end of the week, I got a call at work from Sarah-Jane. The only reason I'd get a call during the day was if something bad happened, so I braced myself for the news. One of the falconers went in with Loki to weigh him, and he went berserk, savaging the falconer's ear. Apparently, "Loki made a right old mess…" I was so disappointed and annoyed. *Loki, why?*

Later that evening, when I got home, Sarah-Jane gave me the "we need to talk" eyes. After dinner, we began to discuss the progress of the other birds. I used diversion tactics, like asking how my boy Logan did, but the conversation ultimately steered back toward the inevitable: the giant, raven-shaped "elephant in the room." We talked at length about whether or not we could keep Loki. We couldn't risk another episode where one of the staff was seriously injured again. Luckily, the damage had been surface-deep, but next time, it could be worse. He could do some serious damage—he could potentially blind people.

I explained my theory about why he was lashing out to Sarah-Jane. I told her how I had been watching and critically examining his body language, but the conversation swung toward the fact that I wasn't there all the time to work him through it. To be honest, I couldn't argue —which is very much unlike me: I can have a heated discussion in an empty room. But Sarah-Jane was right. I was in complete agreement that the safety of the staff was paramount, but that deep-seated feeling returned. The tractor beam, that desire to stick with it, the good side of my stubbornness was refusing to give up.

I somehow convinced Sarah-Jane to stay the course. She agreed, confirming she would spend extra time with him in my absence. It would be difficult with the already incredible workload—Coda, after all, is a small center with limited resources. I had bought Loki some time—not much, but hopefully enough.

That weekend, I raced to the center, determined to be the first one there. I had a weird dream involving Loki escaping his aviary and being reported on national news, terrorizing the local town. A crazed, shimmering lunatic on a rampage, stripping the flesh off innocent passers-by in an attempt to quench his insatiable thirst for human suffering. I whipped the flying jacket on and loaded up with the essentials: one brown glove, a creance, and a box full of mealworms. I opened his aviary to find him in his familiar stance: sleek, weaponized beak raised and on guard, ready to duel. I was deep into enemy territory and took up my position on his log. The wooden vantage point was around the height of a bar stool, and there was a slight wobble. I carefully placed myself down. I solemnly looked down at the floor and explained to Loki he was in the last chance saloon. With a sprinkling of pathos, I confessed that I kind of understood why he did what he did, but it absolutely under no circumstances could ever happen again.

He looked at me and replied. *"Ahhh-Ahhh-Ahhhhhhh!"* Two short crotchets followed by a longer, sustained note. He was normally quiet in the enclosure, so this was a little off. That call was the exact same vocalization he did at my house on the first night in our custody.

Equipped with my new theory, I would scrutinize everything he did, be it vocalizations or changes in body language. There would be a reason for everything, and I needed to decipher his code to determine whether it was a positive or a negative reaction.

I put my hand into the pocket containing the food, and his eyes snapped onto the target. He remembered what resided in that pocket. I pulled out some mealworms.

"If you come here, you can have some," I said, my tone gentle and playful. He looked at me, high up on his perch at a comfortably safe distance.

"*Ahhhh-Ahhh-Ahhh,*" he croaked at me like a teenager moaning about doing the simplest of chores. He wanted them but wasn't willing to move.

I conceded and approached him with a smile.

"*Bah-bah-bah!*" he exclaimed.

Was he getting defensive, or was he pleased knowing he could train me? I opened up my hand with the mealworms and offered it to him. He gobbled them up. The surgical precision was amazing. The mealworms are around 10mm long, and he picked them up one by one without making contact with my skin.

"Good boy!" I said.

I returned to the wobbly log and sat down. I pulled out a few more mealworms and gestured my hand toward him. He seemed a little unsure, but this time, he was willing to concede. He nervously shuffled slowly down the perch, making his way to my outstretched hand. Once again, he gently took my offering, craning his neck to reach my hand. I deliberately kept it a distance, which meant he was leaning at his maximum reach. My surreptitious intention was to get him to jump to me. When my hand was totally devoid of snacks, he quickly scooted back up the perch, caution still written all over his face. We did this for around an hour—a positive game of give and take. All the while, I talked to him constantly, and occasionally, I got a response.

I was having such a good time chipping away at Loki's defenses, and to be honest, it was nice to spend some time with him without being sliced apart. As a consequence, I had completely forgotten to weigh him, meaning one of the team would later that day have that pleasure. I was outside cleaning one of the aviaries when I heard one of the falconers let out a loud shrill, "Loki!"

I turned to see Loki flying out of the office, immediately followed by the panicked falconer. He was completely free! No creance, no radio transmitter. The center went into red alert.

He landed and proceeded to strut right through the middle of a patch of ground occupied by six very capable birds of prey, all tethered to their perches. The birds flared up in a crazed fury, lunging at him with their feet, trying to get at him—it was total chaos. To Loki, it was a game, albeit an incredibly dangerous one. He was smart enough to realize they were tethered and bowled through with a cocky air of confidence, laughing in the face of danger. I grabbed the nearest glove and dashed toward him.

One of the birds—Griffin, a fifteen-year-old Harris Hawk—thrust forward toward Loki with his bright yellow feet. Talons splayed out, he missed him by millimeters. Another falconer tried to help and thwart an attack but, in turn, became the target. Loki sprung up to attack the other falconer, but luckily, I caught him mid-air—and *chomp!* He locked onto my hand. I wriggled free and cuddled him like a burrito.

Loki looked up toward me, neck bent backward, and softly cawed. I'd spoiled his fun, and he was totally unaware of how I had potentially saved his life.

As I cradled him away from the frenzied hawks who were still jumping toward us, eyes burning with blood lust, I had a deep, sickening feeling germinate in my stomach. Would this be his third and final strike? We escaped yet *another* close call, but how long before something serious happened? This question kept getting asked, and I feared this would be the last time.

Not one of the staff wanted to work with him, which was understandable. I could feel their scowling eyes shooting looks of distrust and fear toward Loki. They are our family. I understood the feeling of angst within the group—I was pretty mad, too, but I tried not to add my feelings to this already well-stoked fire. I had convinced Sarah-Jane to keep him, so I felt partly responsible. However, this latest installment in the Loki chronicles now added further cadence to his potential exit. Not only were the falconers brimming with discontent but now the birds had it in for him too. *Was it too late to rename him?*

As the day drew to a close and the dust slowly settled over "Griffin-gate," I closely studied Loki's behaviors, trying to gauge how he would emotionally respond to the aftermath of his little journey into the pit of raging hawks. The result: cool as a cucumber. I went into his aviary a few times throughout the evening and exchanged mealworms without fuss. But just like the time he attacked me, he showed absolutely no remorse. It was scary to see him so calm. Perhaps it was just another day at the office for Loki. "Wander in and fuck shit up" was his motto.

Toward the end of the evening, I gave him his dinner: a prime chunk of quail on the bone with apples and blueberries for dessert. *Would this be his last meal with us?* I went back to the office to take care of some admin, but it wasn't long until my attention was once again needed.

A loud commotion rang through the center. I heard one of the owls making an obnoxious racket—sounds of frantic flying and wings slapping against the aviary wires. A lot of defensive beak clacking and some delightful ear-piercing screeching. Of course, the source of the agitation was all too obvious. I slowly crept along the mews corridor and peered around the corner. Loki was teasing his neighbor, a powerful Snowy Owl named Freya. Loki was taking his quail and parading it as close to her as he could. She would swoop down, trying to get it off him, through the dividing aviary mesh. Loki would then run away with the food in his mouth. I observed him doing this repeatedly.

Owls aren't blessed with intelligence. It's a stark, honest truth I often have to explain to adults and children alike who are enamored by our stealthy murder-birds. It shatters many hearts, but I'm adamant we can't live in ignorance forever. Freya was no exception and no match for this cerebrally-shrewd raven. She was being toyed with like a child. Loki, her intellectual superior, took to stuffing some of the food through the mesh toward Freya and backed away. It looked like he wanted to end his game of fun and torment and finally share. As she came over to collect her prize, Loki quickly dashed over and stole it away from her, waltzing around the aviary floor like a matador. It was absolutely remarkable.

It's true: ravens are known for being nature's pranksters. There are many anecdotes of ravens pulling the tails of wolves, dogs, and even eagles just for fun. Even within their own social packs, ravens will tease and taunt each other in the name of banter, often pushing their siblings off ledges and downslides. This characteristic is inherent within corvids and shows just how complex their brains have developed. Their ability to form social constructs and openly develop and present emotionally-based decisions puts corvids on par with chimpanzees, dolphins, and, dare I say, us.

Was Loki finally finding his feet? It was coming up on a good few months now since he'd first arrived. Perhaps he felt more comfortable, finally accepting that this was his home. The behavior I had witnessed was just another sign of how this bird kept on surprising me. He was entertaining himself, finding pleasure in jostling with another animal, knowing full well he was safe and that there was no way she could get the food. I needed to tap into and harness this natural tendency. I had to stimulate him differently than just offering food for flight. Maybe this was my way in, a new avenue to bridge a connection with him on a more intellectual platform. It's not uncommon to see humans, when frustrated, resort to anger and violence, so maybe the same applies to ravens? If I could challenge his emotional and intellectual capabilities, the potential to be unlocked could be huge. And hopefully, it would go some way toward placating his frustration and anxiety. Perhaps with certain activities, I could keep him emotionally and physically satisfied so there would be no need for physical outward violence toward myself, the staff, and the other birds. I felt a bit like Professor Xavier from the X-Men Series, convincing myself I had a plan to recognize and tame the Wolverine. He had so much potential to offer—we just needed to find that common ground and mutual trust.

Armed with yet another theory of attack, I had to have *the chat* again. It's hard to defend the undefendable, but true to my flawed character, my stubbornness told me I had to, so I locked horns again with Sarah-Jane. Was Loki really worth the effort? Besides, I supposedly didn't even like corvids. Deep down, I knew the answer.

EIGHT
FRISK BLOD
FRESH BLOOD

At this point in Loki's story, I feel it's necessary to add another ingredient to the already colorful mix. Due to Loki's rowdy and unlawful behavior, he had built up quite the rap sheet, meaning it was mainly Sarah-Jane and I who handled and flew him. Loki burned bridges faster than I could rebuild them. However, there was one other member of the team who tried exceptionally hard to woo and befriend Loki.

Emily came to the center when it was in its infancy, and to be honest, she was still pretty green. Back when Coda Falconry was Harlow Falconry, we had six birds and operated in a tiny pig pen. It was a small but ambitious outfit striving to be different, seen as a stain on the sport by the chauvinistic, established members of the falconry community. Sarah-Jane and her young new ways were not welcome into this ancient, regal sport. Being a woman also didn't help, but being damn good at falconry was the real thorn that lodged in the tired lion's paw. Apparently, opening the sport up to a more urban clientele watered down their heritage and the true identity of falconry. The old boys brigade hated it, but all falconers have a duty to keep the sport alive. For it to survive, we need to bring in fresh blood and spark the interest of people who would otherwise never be able to access this amazing and hidden world.

Emily, like many kids, didn't do well in school. How she was wired meant that she was a square peg being forced into a round hole. Emily dropped out of mainstream education and was cast aside from the educational system. One of the many different community programs Sarah-Jane worked with in the area gave teenagers an opportunity to work with the birds one day a week. As long as the kids turned up and cooperated, they were allowed to remain on the course. For some, it was a treat, and for others, a chore, a forced tick in the box.

We were assigned Emily. She arrived in her dark hoodie, ripped black jeans, Doc Martin boots, and bright pink hair. Emily had the unique ability to wear thick beanie hats even in the height of summer. It was a permanent fixture reinforcing a strong, personal identity. When I first met Emily, she was incredibly quiet—she hardly said two words to me. I guess I have that effect on people.

On the flip side, Sarah-Jane is fantastic with people. She can connect with almost any kind of person from any kind of background, which is a rare skill, in my opinion. She worked closely with Emily and taught her the basics of falconry. But working with teenagers isn't plain sailing. What's the old saying about working with children and animals?

In the early days of the program, Emily often didn't bother to show up, giving credit to the stereotype held by many baby boomers of the typical teenager: "They're all the same: poor attitude and unwilling to work." Sarah-Jane was asked for progress reports from the program leaders, and on numerous occasions, Sarah-Jane had to reluctantly explain that Emily was, more often than not, a no-show. This was in stark contrast to the other side of the story that they were given. I guess sometimes, where there's smoke, there's fire.

I'm unsure what eventually happened or what was said between Emily and Sarah-Jane. Personal conversations between Sarah-Jane and her staff have always been confidential. Trust is a virtue that is hard to find and one that Sarah-Jane values above all. But something had been said, and a connection had been made because Emily's attitude changed. She arrived on time every week after; she worked hard and got stuck in. She had a focus. You could see she was enjoying what she was doing. It's difficult to hide genuine happiness, and perhaps for the first time in her life, Emily knew what it felt to be happy and, more importantly, valued. But, like all good things, the program ran its course and came to an end. Emily turned sixteen and needed to opt into a full-time college course or find employment.

I think it's fair to say that most people go through life not ever fulfilling their potential or even knowing what they want to do in life. I've been told by many people, much wiser than me, that there will be some monumental moment in life, a phase or a sudden flash when you just know that what you are doing is what is congruent with your true values. That moment when you realize exactly what you want to do with yourself.

Sarah-Jane told me Emily asked if she would employ her full-time —she didn't want to go to college; she wanted to be a falconer. From a stroppy urban teen to wanting to be a falconer, a job she didn't even know existed two years ago! It's amazing what a bit of guidance, support, and respect can do for a kid. The girl had been transformed, and maybe she was lucky enough to discover that mythical turning point in life. I must admit that at thirty-two and three-quarters, I still find myself asking what I want to do, and I think if we're honest, most of us still do.

Emily was adamant falconry was her destiny. She didn't want to work with horses; she didn't want to work in a zoo. It was raptors and only raptors—very loud and very clear—but here's the kicker. Sarah-Jane had invested a lot of time into Emily, who, in the end, had dutifully repaid her faith. Now, Sarah-Jane had the unpleasant job of telling the rejuvenated, newly inspired, and motivated young woman that there was no job for her and that she wouldn't be able to accommodate her request for business reasons.

Shattering anyone's dream is heartbreaking. Life can be so cruel— to build someone's confidence, giving them the thinly veiled visage of hope is all well and good, but the road doesn't always take us where we want to go. Emily, as you can imagine, was utterly devastated. Naivety is a cruel card to hold, and we have all had the displeasure of its bitter effect on our hearts. The hurt and embarrassment it brings can only be given a silver lining by the experience we gain...not that it offers much salvation at the time. It's particularly damaging to those who actually discover their dreams because most people never will. Be it uncertainty or apathy, a large percentage of folks are dragged into the whirlpool of triviality and the mundane; we build ourselves a warm, secure prison born out of doubt and the fear of failure. The saddest part is that we are happy to possess the key and then throw it away.

Sarah-Jane thought about it long and hard and convinced Emily to go to college where she could study animal management. As a compromise, she would, in turn, offer Emily a Saturday job.

Emily blossomed into one of the most loyal and enthusiastic people I have ever had the pleasure of working with. The center has seen staff come and go. Some have let us down by betraying Sarah-Jane's warm, hospitable nature. But Emily quickly became an integral member of the team. As of now, she is a huge contributor to the company's success as a full-time falconer responsible for weddings, outside demonstrations, and Experience Days. She has never let us down and continues to train and build strong bonds with all the birds. However, even to this day, there is one bird that refuses to be won over.

Emily was unfortunate enough to experience early on the full force of Loki's petulance. She had been bitten on the arms for no reason numerous times. He would chase her in the flying arena and strike at her shoes and ankles. He even maliciously pecked at her ear. And yet, she still tried.

On one such occasion, I watched her approach him from a distance. Her body language portrayed unease: her neck was rolled, her eyes fixed to the floor—everything about her poise subconsciously screamed fear. Loki glared at her as she grew closer to his aviary. With perfect posture, he articulated himself to look as intimidating as possible. His body language painted a different picture to Emily's—confident and preemptive.

Emily bravely entered his aviary to change his water. She scuttled in with her back to the wall, not letting him out of her sight. A smart move. The moment she deflected her gaze away, he seized the opportunity, shooting down toward her feet. Loki launched a barrage of targeted hammer blows to the ankle. Eventually, Emily suffered enough and manufactured a drastic exit. Loki escalated the offensive and chased after her, delivering another expert strike on the back of Emily's calf just before she could seal shut the enclosure door. He had mastered the art of guerilla warfare. Loki jumped up close to the enclosure door, pleased about seeing her off. Like before, he showed zero signs of unease in her presence and, as a parting gift, shouted a few bullish jibes into the wind as Emily sheepishly retreated to safety.

The hierarchy had been long established. Loki placed himself at the top and viewed Emily as his inferior. He identified her as a weaker sibling. Loki was fully aware he intimidated her, and he enforced it with vigor and absolute zero tolerance at all times. Legendary football/soccer manager Sir Alex Ferguson spoke at a conference on what made his Manchester United team so successful. He once eloquently said, "Put your foot on their neck and keep it there." I wonder if Loki has Sir Alex's autobiography?

I went in to help.

After six months, Loki and I had a shaky but amicable relationship. He didn't attack me, but he still showed caution in how he held himself, and he was still not a fan of the glove. I prepped him for flying, and Emily nervously helped change his falconry equipment. I'm glad she chose to persevere because if I can win Loki over and prevent him from attacking her on sight, then perhaps there will be another person able to work with him—potentially another aid in our quest to try to tame the currently untamable, and maybe another troop in my rank. He took food from her hand but nipped her fingers with belligerent content. It was one hundred percent deliberate, especially knowing how gentle and precise he could be.

"All I want is to be your friend, Loki! Why are you like this all the time?"

Although Emily had said it in jest, I could feel the undercurrent of frustration and despair. I tried to explain the status quo to Emily and how he saw her in the chain of command. It was going to be hard to undo and reset the mindset Loki had created for himself. I'd fought on through it in the early days, losing a lot of blood and gaining a lot of scars to get to this point, which, in the scheme of things, still didn't seem very far. What I didn't want was for Emily to endure any more pain. This was her job, and although working with raptors does come with its dangers, this kind of hostile treatment was guaranteed every day from Loki. She admitted that the relationship would be, at best, non-hostile, and I admired her will to continue with him because most wouldn't. This was and still is her dream job, and I never want that to change.

On another such occasion, a few months later, Loki woke up in a bit of an *off* mood. He seemed uninterested in cooperating, probably because I gave Emily the reins to try to dictate the order of play. I stood by her, giving her pointers and commenting on various subtle hints projected by his body language. He was completely despondent, and when he had enough mooching about, ignoring Emily's commands, he took to attacking my boots—a sign of his unwillingness to be directed by a perceived subordinate. I was glad he chose to take out his objections on my boots rather than on Emily. He made quite a mess of my shoes and eventually tore through, breaching the thick brown leather and spitting out the chunks as he vented his frustrations.

Over the course of the following weeks, if he "got the hump" with me—by which I mean if I didn't reward him quickly enough or feed him for not doing anything in particular—he would continue his campaign of retribution on my boots. The total and utter destruction of my footwear became another of his little side projects. Eventually, he destroyed them, penetrating right into my exposed foot. Like a game of Battleships, he had scored a direct hit and knew exactly where to fire his next shot. I needed new, better armor!

Emily left the battlefield with dejection but was also thankful that Loki's assault on my footwear prevented her from acquiring extra bruising. Her legs bore the blue and purple reminders of past skirmishes.

I rounded him up and took him back into his enclosure. At the end of a training session, the norm was for him to fly to the glove for the marquee reward. This time, I decided to mix things up. I placed the food on the roof of his aviary, stuffing it through the wire grid.

Loki watched from his perch with an intense curiosity. He called out *"Ahhh-ahhhh-ahhh"* as if to say, "Why are you doing this, human? This isn't part of our routine!" And he was right. It wasn't—it required him to adapt.

My initial thinking was that he would have to improvise, forcing him to use up some of that energy. He'd need to climb on the side of the aviary, hoist himself up to the top, and procure it that way. Instead, he did something quite different. He quickly scanned the environment, his eyes darting all over the enclosure, making quick-fire calculations and plotting his mode of attack, then *whooosh!*

He flew straight at me.

I covered my face with my hands by instinct, but he wasn't aiming for my head. He landed on my shoulder, ripped down the meat, and flew back to the perch. The task was executed too quickly and too easily. He had worked out the path of least resistance and, interestingly, used me as a tool. In that split second, when he was on my shoulder, I had been truly terrified—terrified he would exact his onslaught and tear my ear to bits.

Admittedly, there is a fair bit of repetition, and although it may not be that interesting to read, good habits form from good practice. I repeated this task for many weeks, and Loki was one hundred percent compliant. He would take his food and use me as a perch.

Then, one day, after a few months of this repetitive regime, he decided not to fly back when he gained access to his food, opting instead to stay on my shoulder. I tried as long as I could not to move my eyes into striking distance, but I caved and nervously gazed up. He had the food, a day-old chick minus the head in his mouth, dangling down a mere inch from my eye, the yolk sack oozing onto my neck. *This meant my eyes were safe, right?* He stood there, towering above me, boasting his spoils. He casually scanned the area to see if anyone was around to see his prize.

Generally speaking, if you see a sign saying, "Wet paint—Don't touch," most people obey, knowing full well the consequences. And then there are the others. My brain said, "Don't do it; don't do it!" over and over again, but I couldn't resist the urge. I reached up and stroked his black, prehistoric-looking feet.

He didn't react. Not a flinch. The feeling under my touch was a weird sensation—hard and callous but smooth like plastic, similar to having a gloss paint finish. It is a design that has been perfected and refined over millions of years.

He eventually made his way back to his safe spot to tear up the meat, gorging on what was left of the splattered yolk sack. I stayed inside his quarters for a while and watched with a keen interest. He wasn't bothered that I decided to linger. I witnessed his definitude as he surgically tore the meat into smaller chunks, using his feet to keep the meat secure while ripping the flesh with ease, courtesy of *that* beak —the matte black scythe of pain. He kept a chunk in his mouth, hopped onto the floor, and headed to the corner of the aviary. He swept away the stones and offloaded his food, all the time keeping one eye on me. He placed the stones one by one on top of the meat, completely concealing it. Only he and I knew it was there. What was the significance of him sharing this information with me? Was I considered part of his circle of trust now?

Loki and I continued to play this game every time I worked with him. He was consistent in his behavior, which allowed our relationship to develop without further incident. I tried to always end training on a positive note, and he knew that after playtime in the arena, the good stuff would be brought out. Not only had we established routine and rapport, but we were establishing hierarchy.

I approached the entrance to his kingdom and coolly cruised through the door. As soon as I was inside, he launched up from the ground like a dark surface-to-air missile and sat on my shoulder. I didn't even see him on the floor, so it took me by utter surprise. To tell the truth, at that moment, I thought I had taken our civil concord for granted. Was I about to be dominated and put down in the power pyramid? He loomed over me and spoke. There were four knocks and then a *"Gwah"* sound. It was eerily human sounding—*was this him trying to mimic me?*

I laughed nervously. "That's a new one. What are you trying to say?"

He responded—another four knocks followed by a *"Gwah."*

I chuckled again, this time a little nervously. Surely, if he were going to bite me, he would have done it already? As I laughed, he cocked his head, keeping eye contact at all times. Did he find my laugh funny? He definitely reacted to it, as I could see his pupils dilating in response. I asked him kindly to jump down and pointed to the perch with some thinly veiled optimism, wondering if he'd actually listen. And wouldn't you believe it, he did!

"Good boy!" I yelled with shock.

He had obeyed without dispute. Perhaps he wanted to jump there anyway, and it was merely a coincidence that my command came before his action. I quickly reached into my pocket to bring out the food, and as I did, he excitedly leaped onto my shoulder. I fed him directly to the mouth, and he remained on my shoulder, taking the food from my fingertips with deftness and kindness. I pointed back at the perch, hoping the first time wasn't just luck, and like before, he happily obliged. Once again, I rewarded him with both food and audible praise. We did this for ages: constant repetition with suitable rewards. We were bonding with absolutely no sign of aggression and without the need for a glove. It was really fun, and my body erupted in a hive of goosebumps. Like an over-excited kid, I couldn't wait to tell the others!

I think it's important to note that even though I may have sounded like a madman and probably still do, talking to a bird in a positive tone is a massive benefit to building a constructive and healthy bond. If these creatures have the faculties to distinguish between colors and be able to mimic, then perhaps they can also gain context from tonality. I made sure every time Loki complied, he would receive a joyful "well done" phrase. When he was naughty, however, the tone used was just as important.

Physical punishment is unthinkable. Even though in the wild, many animals establish order through power and assault, I believed Loki had already been down that route, and I refused to discipline him physically. Even after all the times he shredded me and scored gorges of pain into my arm, I could never return a hand in anger. When he did misbehave (getting frustrated from not being rewarded when he demanded it), he would begin to utter a grunting noise, which usually led to him biting my shoes or pulling my shoelaces— then moving up to the ankle and then the leg. I would deliver a stern

"No!"—a deep, sharp, and loud indicator reinforced by complementary body language. I would impose myself over him with a frown and direct eye contact, or I would turn my back on him and walk away.

In hindsight, this was a massive risk, as I was inviting myself to a sucker punch. But what was interesting about this haphazard experiment was that I realized Loki was acute to my body language. He learned that I had two sides: a benevolent food-giving side and an authoritative, stern side. When reprimanded, he would scuttle around by my feet so I could see him and then issue an apology call. He'd bow his head in submission and make the cutest, most delicate little sobbing noise. It was hard to believe this butcher could be so dainty. This marked another crucial point in our relationship, as we now had developed a communication channel whereby Loki could understand my feelings, but more importantly, it reinforced that I was at the top of the pecking order. *Did this mean I was winning?*

For the first time since this black cloud of animosity entered our lives, I was enjoying my time with him, and I think Loki enjoyed my company, too. It felt like we had got the worst out of the way, and a lot of choppy water had gone under the bridge. I was also pleased my hospital visits had stopped. It begged the question: had he finally learned to trust me, or had I done just enough to deserve his kindness by simply rolling with the punches and not giving up? Regardless, we were working well together and progressing in the right direction. His vocalization repertoire also grew. He offered more differently pitched croaks and a delightful *"Ah-bwah"* sound, which I interpreted as a playful expression.

Toward the end of one winter's evening, the sky was fading from a rich red to a deep, sultry purple. All the staff gathered in the office to huddle around the oil heater, which was cranked to the max. With brews in hand and an assortment of cookies and biscuits being passed around, we mused over the day's events, making jokes about who had been asked the most ridiculous question of the day by the general public. The contenders were: Do birds lay eggs? Do falcons have three legs? Are they real or just fancy animatronics? I kid you not—the last one was a real question. From an adult!

73

After a slurp of tea and a bit of a biscuit, someone made a joke, which I found funny, and once the laughter died out, we fell silent.

However, my laugh was played back to us.

We all looked at each other in silence and confusion. Once again, my laugh rang throughout the center. Had someone recorded it on their phone by accident? We all got up and went outside.

"Loki, was that you?"

He did it again, chuckling away to himself. We all looked at each other with sheer amazement. He continued to laugh after we laughed. His eyes widened and brightened when he saw how we were all positively reacting to his antics. He looked so pleased with himself, and it was the first time the staff smiled because of Loki, not reeling in pain or fear.

I secretly did a little fist bump inside. *Good boy!*

As I trotted up to his aviary, he continued mimicking my laugh. The pitch and intonation were perfect; he had mastered it. I went inside his enclosure, and he fluffed up his glorious head feathers—a magnificent display that had since given him the moniker "microphone head" as it looks almost perfectly circular. I had a "Dr. Pepper moment" and thought, "We are on a roll here; what's the worst that can happen?"

I stood over him and gave him a head scratch, and he began to purr like a cat, dribbling joy from his beak. The staff could not believe it. To be fair, *I* couldn't believe it. I could hear their jaws thudding on the ground behind me like giant comedy cartoon characters. What the hell was going on?

Ravens are hugely complex. When you see it firsthand, you are forced into a cryptic game—one I had never played before, but I think I was *finally* getting to grips with the rules. This was the real progress I pined for in the very early days, but the journey was still long. I needed to keep the positive momentum going.

I ordered *Mind of the Raven* by Berndt Heinrich. It's an inspiring account of Heinrich's fascination with ravens and his staunch testing regimes on ravens he caught in the wild. The research and findings were an eye-opener and actually strengthened some of the theories I developed while pontificating on Loki (albeit Henirich was much more scientific with a tried and proper systematic approach). I learned an enormous amount from Heinrich's accounts and conclusions, which gave me the confidence to take Loki's training to the next level. I was no longer completely stumbling in the dark: I had found Asgard on my own. Now, I was equipped with the weapon of knowledge, and it was time to head deeper down the rabbit hole and unravel the real secrets.

NINE
METODEN TIL SPIL
THE ART OF PLAY

P lay and stimulation feature as a prominent social device within both human and raven behavior. In fact, I'd go as far as to say it's incredibly influential in the development of both species, but with ravens, it also helps determine status within packs. I conjured up a few games that Loki and I could play together to add a different dimension to our relationship. I crafted a crude-looking Kerplunk device from a large plastic Coke bottle and used wooden kebab skewers to create an interlocking matrix I could put food inside for him to see.

The other game I devised was simpler still. I took a long, wooden rectangular box containing a lid that could slide out. In its previous life, before it became a raven toy, it housed a very fine single malt. I wrote "Loki's Box" on the lid in thick black marker. In the box, I put a large rubber Kong toy, the kind you buy for dogs. When I first showed Loki the Kong, he looked it up and down, creating detailed blueprints he could file away in his mental database. I tossed it on the floor beside him, and his instinct was to run away immediately. Ravens, by nature, are quite cautious of new items. In the wild, they learn what to be afraid of from the teachings of their elders. As Loki was missing this initial and vital step in his upbringing, he would now need to rely on me, but this did mean almost everything new to him would be ultimately feared.

I picked the toy up and brought it over to him to investigate. He looked at me and cawed. He didn't like it and pleaded with me to take it away. Instead, I pulled out a block of cheese. Now let me tell you one thing: cheese to Loki is like catnip. He goes crazy for it. I put a little block of cheese in the Kong toy, and he jumped onto my shoulder to investigate. I held it up, and he rotated his head, peering into the dark hole. With his beak, he motioned into the hole, but nerves ultimately got the better of him, and he teetered like a rocking horse. I softly breathed words of encouragement, keeping my body incredibly still, not to startle him or rock his balance. He plucked up the courage and stuffed his beak in to claim his prize.

Okay, so now we have established that the Kong is safe. In fact, the Kong is a most wonderful thing, especially if it yields the gift of curdled milk. I put another piece of cheese in the Kong and threw it on the floor. Loki leaped down to the ground and began to circle the rubber toy. He made pensive lunging attacks but jumped back at the last minute. He continued to circle the toy for a few minutes and looked up to me for help. I got onto my hands and knees and picked the Kong up.

"See, it's okay, mate. It's not going to hurt you."

I threw it back on the floor a few feet from him. The noise it made landing on the shingle made him jump, and he backed off. I stayed on my haunches and ushered him toward the toy, like a parent encouraging their kid on a bike. However, he's firmly lodged at the far side of the aviary, the apex covering his six.

"Come on, Loki, you can do it! Come on!"

He eventually edged closer and went for it. He made a quick grab but dropped it, his lack of confidence and conviction clear to see. I picked it up one more time to show him that it was perfectly harmless. He cawed at me—that beautiful bass, croaking sound—a fine blend of music to the ears and emotional unease. He wanted me to hold it because he was too scared to take another shot. He continued to call, still begging for help. I agreed to help and kept the stout, rubbery toy in my hand. He waddled over, bobbing his head, and peered inside from a safe distance. Within seconds, he seized the moment, lunging in to skewer his cheese. "Good boy!" I said. I had one more bit of cheese and wanted to finish this little game on a high. He's already done really well, but I know with a little bit of persistence, he can crack it. Talk about a pushy parent, eh?

I stood up and placed the last mature, yellowy cube of goodness inside. Loki studiously watched my every movement, and like in a magic act, I showed him the cheese inside to prove it was really there. I wasn't tricking him because if he thought I was, well, that wouldn't end well, would it?

"Right, I'm going to throw it on the floor again. Ready?"

He looked at me excitedly, his head bobbing in sync with my hand.

"One, two, three!"

I let the Kong roll out of my hand onto the floor. He flinched slightly, but not as much as before. He shared with me eyes of vulnerability. I saw he wanted to trust me, but he was still so nervous. I couldn't let him down. He placed one foot in front of the other and softly approached the uneven shingle. As he grew closer to the target, he looked up at me for guidance. I smiled at him and buoyantly nodded my encouragement. He cautiously nudged the Kong a few times with his beak, and it rolled in a circle. He danced a bizarre tango, aiming a few more tactical prods on the Kong. I also prodded it with my finger, rolling it back the way it came. He gained confidence and stuck the tip of his beak into the small hole at the top. With ease, he lifted it up, gave it a little shake, and out rolled the cheese. He saw his prize, dropped the Kong, and gobbled the cheese up in a flash. He looked back up to me with bright eyes, beak wide open.

Instantly, I could tell by his body language that he was super proud of himself. Loki really felt he had achieved something special and had overcome a huge obstacle that day. Once again, I, too, basked in his success. I was the proudest dad that ever was. Such small wins felt like major victories—the feeling of doing it together meant the world to me. Him, the fearful and nervous corvid being coached by me, the ignorant ape, also with a veiled sense of fear when it came to my feathered burden. We were slowly managing to fumble through this whole process, but the important thing was that we were doing it together.

It was after this point that I introduced the box. I sat on his log with the box on my lap, and Loki shuffled over on his perch just above my shoulder. He watched me slide open the lid—its dry scraping sound made him twitch, but not enough to induce a full-on retreat. I placed inside it a fully loaded Kong, but instead of cheese, I opted to put in a few grapes because even ravens need to have a balanced diet. I closed the box and set it down on the uneven shingle floor. He cawed at me. I was pretty sure it was laziness rather than fear on this occasion. I deduced this from his aggressive body posture. He wasn't cowering or meek in stature like when he first saw the Kong: he leaned forward, puffing his chest out. Loki had fully observed the box from all available angles; he understood it wasn't a threat, and he remembered seeing the prize contained within. I sat and waited for him to interact, but nothing. I decided to leave the box and Loki alone to see if he could figure it out.

After a short while, I could hear the distinct sound of a beak smashing down on wood. I swung by to see how he was getting on. Like any angry teenager when they don't get what they want, Loki's full-on tantrum mode was activated. He hammered the box from all different angles, even standing on it. This wasn't like the glove: this wasn't fear—this was his frustration. He was trying to get into the box but couldn't work it out.

I walked in to try to help him.

He barked at me: *"Bah-bah-bah!"*

I showed him how the lid slides by pulling gently on the string affixed to the lid. He shuffled around and came next to where my hands were. He gripped the lid and pulled it toward him. The box opened slightly. He saw an opening and clambered on top of the box. He squeezed his beak in the slender opening, but it was no use: the gap was too small. I tapped the edge of the lid as a reminder, gently giving it a tug. He shot back around and yanked on the lid. After three or four consecutive tugs, he pried off the lid. Loki leaped up, feet in the box, took out the Kong, and emptied its contents in the corner of his lair.

I removed the Kong and the box from the aviary and took it to the office. I put some treats into the Kong and laid the toy back in the box.

I slid the lid back on and returned to Loki. He saw the box, and the strangest thing happened. He started to wag his tail, just like a dog. He was vibrating at such a rate I thought he was going to take off—he was so excited! He was ready for more playtime, but what I thought was more incredible was that he actually enjoyed our little games. I couldn't believe my eyes. Never had I heard that the omen of death could produce an emotion such as joy! I was spellbound by the sound of his tail feathers clacking against one another—it seemed so bizarre. Loki, the terrible, the slayer of staff, was trembling with glee.

That evening, instead of putting the box on the floor, I hung it upside down from under his perch. To gain access, he would need to pull the lid down. I briefly showed him just to refresh his memory. However, in true Loki style, he ignored my instruction and hopped up onto the perch.

"What are you doing? I just showed you how to do it; you need to be on the floor."

Little did I know that I hadn't completely closed the lid—there was roughly a 10mm gap at the top. Loki had obviously seen this and, from above, pushed the lid down, which saved a lot more effort than tugging from below. He then swooped down, and with one jerk on the frayed twine handle, the lid slid off with ease. He jumped up and, in mid-air, pinched the Kong and snuffed out the treat. Clever boy.

I began leaving the box in with Loki for his amusement every night I worked at the center, and the next morning, it was always empty. The game had well and truly been mastered. It didn't matter if I hung it upside down, changed the orientation, or put a cloth on top—the result was always the same. It had become apparent to me that not everyone in the team used the box, so the box became a game that only he and I would play. When Loki saw me in the morning, that tail would begin to wag like a child on Christmas morning, buzzing and brimming with happiness. I was now being associated with more than just a provider of food and now considered a co-conspirator in games and play.

Loki's playful character toward me was a sure sign of a new-found trust. He didn't play with everyone: you had to be chosen. I would never have imagined the same biting, shoe-destroying Loki I first met would ever enjoy the company of another. Back then, peace had never been an option. The gratifying sense of achievement that I was allowed to share games with him meant I now trusted him more, too—enough to attempt flying.

As mentioned in the previous chapter, Loki's flying sessions were controlled by him being on the creance, or the "good boy line." For trust to blossom, you must let them go completely free—I have no doubt birds are completely aware of the difference. Every time we remove the creance on a bird while still in training, the first thing they do is fly toward us as normal, then, at the last second, divert their trajectory. They climb high and fast, scouting out a perfect place to perch, and more often than not, it will be the tallest part of a tree.

One such instance of this rebellious behavior was with Logan the Eagle Owl. When he was ready to be initiated into the big boy club and fly without the aid of his line, Logan did exactly this. He pushed off from the perch with his giant, fluffy but deadly feet. The perch was stationed approximately twenty feet away, and he pumped his massive wings, flying head-on directly toward us with power and guile. He had a devoted look of concentration as he maintained sight on the target, which was our gloved hand. Suddenly, his giant burnt orange eyes snapped away from us. He gained speed and engaged in an evasive maneuver, flying directly over the top of our heads and landing halfway up a giant oak tree.

"Well, he's your boy…" muttered Sarah-Jane, which, reading between the lines, meant I had to go and find a ladder because it didn't matter what we did, he wouldn't come down. We offered three times the amount of food. Hell, we even put down a whole rabbit, but would he come down? We put food on the glove, we put food on the floor, we chucked food into the air, and we even tied food to a piece of string and ran around the paddock pretending it was alive. Nothing got his attention. He was not coming down because Logan is a big, stubborn baby and is bizarrely afraid of heights—which makes two of us.

As I extended the ladder, the clanking of the metal against wood was a sound Logan hadn't heard before and caused a few nervous twitches. *Maybe he would come down on his own accord?* Nope, false alarm. He stayed put, calling out to us with his high-pitched *"Wheep!"*

The ladder only extended so far—it was a good start, but the tree is old, bearing witness to many cycles of the sun. It's both tall and wide, and scaling the rest of the journey would be a treacherous task. I was nearly at Logan's position, and as I turned around, I made the silly mistake of looking down at Sarah-Jane. She was joined by a few onlookers who were having a gawp and taking much amusement at my current predicament.

"Wheeeep!" Logan cried as I slowly offered an olive branch—an answer to his plea to be rescued. I extended my arm as much as I could and took his leather flying straps in my hand. Slowly, I picked him up, now very unbalanced, holding this four-pound winged baby up a large oak tree. Sarah-Jane offered up some food from the ground and whistled for his return: nothing. I pulled my arm back and attempted to cast him out of the tree, but his zygodactyl feet locked on to my glove with an immense grip. It was no use. He wasn't coming down voluntarily.

It took me nearly forty-five minutes to reverse and climb out of the tree holding *my boy*, who, as soon as we hit *terra firma*, flew straight to the perch, completed a rouse, and then demanded feeding. Welcome to the secret life of falconers.

But this is why we do the training—the birds need to fly free, and Loki was no different. He would need to be given his chance. All the line training and all the bonding would be put to the ultimate test: we were now at the mercy of his choice to return to us. We'd come to love him like a family member and put months of literal blood, sweat, and tears into nurturing and bonding. We wanted him to feel a part of our feathered family. But would he choose to stay with us? Or would he choose a different path on his already colorful adventure and seek his future in the wild as a "free bird?"

We fixed the GPS radio tracker to his anklet and shuttled him to the flying arena. I stood in the middle of the arena, which seemed to look incredibly small all of a sudden. I was conscious of my nervous disposition and hoped he wouldn't pick up on it. *Would he fly off and never come back?* Although he had a tracker and we could find him, it would feel like he didn't want to live with us anymore. I really hoped he felt some kind of emotional attachment to us and his home—at least the same attachment I felt toward him. When birds opt to go on a little unscripted adventure, I must admit to lacking much of an emotional response other than frustration at the impending discord. We know we can find them; it's just a pain in the arse to have to traipse through fields, woodland, and people's gardens to recover them. With Loki, however, it was different.

I tentatively opened up my hand, giving him the opportunity to explore the world as he saw fit, but he just sat there cleaning his feathers and enjoying being present in the moment. I encouraged him to take flight by swinging my arm toward the perch. The momentum and the lift generated made him take flight, and he flew to the intended perch. He spent a few minutes on the perch examining the radio tracker. He'd never seen it before, so he was instantly curious. Upon careful inspection, he had evaluated that it was not edible, nor was it a threat, so he got bored. I raised my gloved hand—balanced on top was a juicy chicken leg. Loki swooped down with a formidable presence and graciously accepted my offer.

We did this back and forth for a good fifteen minutes, and he was in no way interested in leaving the confinements of the arena: it was like there was an invisible screen that he could see around the perimeter. He wasn't curious at all about what existed outside of the arena. It was strange, really, given his nature and personality, but I was totally okay with that, and it helped me to relax and enjoy our time together. After around half an hour of flying to the glove and perch, I was almost out of food, with only a few bits left to give him. Before I could present them, Loki had decided he'd had enough and walked back to his enclosure and put himself in. I was gobsmacked.

He was clearly done for the day and ready to go home—how remarkable! The fact he chose just to go home ratified my hopes that he loved it. The raptors would never do this, and I was in total shock. But if you think about it, it makes perfect sense. He trusts us and feels that this is his forever home. He feels no desire to go anywhere else, and that realization alone made me a little bit emotional if I'm telling you the truth. From those small acorns, we were starting to see the fruits of our labor.

Over the next few months, Loki's flying and stamina increased: he was getting stronger and fitter. He did, however, start to get up to his old tricks again. Loki decided that, for some reason, he no longer wanted the telemetry attached to him and broke it off into little pieces. These things aren't cheap, so we were a bit cross with him, and as usual, he gave no concerns to our disappointment. He was not going to wear it—he obviously felt it invaded his privacy, so what were the options? We could put the creance back on him and therefore limit his flight, or fly him without any telemetry, *completely* free but not free of risk. This was the ultimate test, the time for us to trust him: could I really do this, and should I be doing this?

The answer was a strong no. Not attaching any form of tracker is completely irresponsible and puts him at huge risk—all that hard work would be for nothing. If he were to fly out of our visual range, for example—if a strong gust of wind forces him off course, or if he gets spooked by a dog or some other unpredictable variable, it would be catastrophic for him. It would almost certainly be fatal, and that would be on me and me alone. But here we find ourselves again, on the precipice of taking another risk: *nothing risked, nothing gained, right?* How much was I willing to risk, and what was the gain?

If he did choose to fly off, there would be little chance of ever finding him. My only clue as to where he could be is if the local neighboring gang of corvids—of which we have a plentiful ensemble of jackdaws, crows, and magpies—would, without doubt, gang up and bully him. Loki, being the largest of the corvids, would stick out like a sore thumb to them, and he would not be tolerated. I have found other birds this way. Harris Hawks and falcons can gain a considerable amount of distance very quickly, and sometimes, even with the tracker, it's best to look to the skies and observe nature. The corvids are merciless and will attack pretty much anything: they are after all an equal opportunity offender, a different breed of villain.

I held him in my hand and stroked his neck, getting right under those soft, shimmering feathers. "Now, don't you leave me, okay? You be a good boy!"

I headed to the aviary door and prepared to depart. I opened up the aviary and released my hand. He didn't fly. I walked him ten yards to the perch and encouraged him to transfer from my hand. He does kind of reluctantly—why fly when you can be taxied everywhere? I eventually get him going, bopping from one perch to the other and back to the shoulder. He's still not overly keen on the glove and prefers the safety of being nestled on my shoulder close to my head. He was perfect so far, with no inclination whatsoever to fly off, and after a good twenty minutes of flying, I had totally forgotten he didn't have his telemetry on! His focus was on me. I had his complete, undivided attention, and he had mine as we danced from perch to perch. I thought this was what it was all about: he left his fear and anxiety somewhere else and managed to truly be free. Free from abuse, free from worry. It was just me, him, and a pocket full of protein.

From here on in, I flew him almost every single time with telemetry. On that first occasion, I had a feeling deep down he wouldn't disappear, but it was reckless and irresponsible not to put a tracker on him: the risk wasn't worth it. I knew what we were doing together was positive and progressive. Perhaps this was just my naivety or an over-estimation of our relationship. I believe it boils down to the fact that he knew his home and knew me. Both had become beacons of trust and safety, plus I had a pocket full of food. If I were him, I wouldn't go far either.

Loki does like to throw the odd wrench into the works, just to keep us on our toes. In the off-season when the farm is closed to the general public, we utilized the children's play area for the birds. Our arena can get boggy underfoot in the winter periods, so we try to not overload it with footfall. We fly the hawks and let them sit on top of the climbing frames and wooden tractors. In the off-season, it becomes an avian play park where we can test the birds' acrobatic abilities and dynamism by flying through all kinds of child-friendly obstacles. It really is spectacular to watch. The area is at least double the size of our flying arena, so I thought Loki would love this: think of all the things he could interact with!

I rushed over to him with child-like excitement. I opened his enclosure door and let him out, and I realized as soon as I did this that I hadn't yet put his telemetry on. *I'm sure he'll be fine*, I thought. He ran across the floor next to me and glided up to the perch closest to me. He was happy and expecting a treat, and I handed him a cat biscuit for his troubles. I opened the gate to gain access to the play area and made my way in, expecting him to land on my shoulder any second.

However, what I got was an angry set of caws. I turned around and saw him still on the perch—shoulders up, head down, looking annoyed because I left him. I called him over with some food, but he firmly resisted. He couldn't get past the invisible barrier! I trotted back over to him and rubbed his shiny black feet. He barked in a slightly less aggressive tone, pleased I had returned but still miffed I was on the wrong side of the fence. I tossed some cat biscuits on the floor, and he ignored them. He was too scared to enter this new territory. It was perplexing to me, as he saw it every day: he watches people eat and play; he even keeps an eye on us flying the other birds in there, so why won't he make the leap? His confidence is so slight, and he is so wary of everything. It's only when you understand this that you can start to really develop an idea of exactly how insecure he is.

My teasing smile turns to one of sympathy. I picked him up onto my arm and gave him an ear rub, which he highly approved of—changing from barking to purring. I walked him incredibly slowly throughout the play area, letting him see all the nooks and crannies that this new area has to offer. I showed him that there is nothing here he needs to fear, and that I am by his side for protection. It took a good half an hour, but it was worth it. Surprisingly, he sat calmly like a good boy. I stood in the middle of the play area and opened my hand. After a series of erratic head glances, he completed his reconnaissance and plucked up the courage.

He left the glove in a puff of black smoke. I expected him to land on one of the many children's climbing apparatuses, but he didn't. Instead, he picked up pace and bypassed everything! Full fight or flight mode engaged: instant panic!

He yelled a series of loud, brash *kronk*-ing sounds—a call I've not heard from him, but one similar to wild ravens I have heard in Scotland and Iceland. Experts say these calls can be heard up to 2km away, such is their power and ability to project. He left the children's play area and headed over to the trees that border our center. He has disappeared completely out of sight.

My stomach dropped like a lead weight. I panicked and ran back toward the arena, calling him. I was beginning to forfeit to hysteria. I had properly messed up here. The risk was too great—what kind of idiot doesn't put telemetry on their bird? The brain has a canny ability to batter itself with a quickfire assortment of high-octane anxiety mixed with a variety of pessimistic '"what ifs" and "should haves." What I really needed was a cool and calculated head. I needed to plan toward a beneficial solution, remedying my incompetence and stupidity. Like any disappearance, the next few minutes would be critical to a successful retrieval.

I stood on the highest mound in the arena and surveyed the area in a full-frenzied three-sixty sweep. Out of the corner of my eye, I saw behind the trees a large black bird circling: it was him! He swanned over the conifers, swooping back into the arena, *kronk*-ing the whole time. I held out my arm with desperation, hoping he would just simply return to me. He made a beeline for me, but at the last second, he diverted and flew past me back into the play area. I continued calling him, but he seemed oblivious to my call. Like a child learning to ride a bike and gaining too much speed, he had worked himself into a state of alarm and confusion. He circled back around, hidden by the huge ash trees that give our center a natural barrier. I lost sight of him again, but I could hear him: my heart was racing, but I was powerless to do anything. I should have put that bloody telemetry on him!

I stood in the middle of the arena, glove up, offering a generous protein prize, but it was to no avail. I rotated slowly, looking to the skies and looking for clues. There was nothing: not a single *kronk*. Just the sound of my own heart furiously beating wave after wave of dread against the inside of my chest. I bellowed out Loki's name once more in desperation, hoping he hadn't gone too far. I prayed he could still hear me, but there was no reply.

While staring into the horizon, trying to hone my hearing to the faintest calls of the wild, I was struck in the back. The thick thud caused me to lose my balance, scaring me half to death. I felt claws trying to find purchase on my shoulder, which lightly grazed the flesh on my neck. Then, out of nowhere, that all too familiar beak appeared. Dripping with raven joy, droplets pattered onto my palm. The beak cleaned up the prize, and my heartbeat began to return to normal. The sound of Loki panting was deafening as his fluffy body nestled up close to my ear. I admit to giving him a little nuzzle, knowing he was back safe with me. He'd never flown that far or for that length of time in one hit before. He was absolutely shattered but ultimately very pleased with himself, if not a little scared.

After the adrenaline and panic wore off, I, too, was able to share pride in his aerial stealth, praising him for coming back, but in the same breath, lightly telling him off for leaving me like that. His new disappearing act soon became a frequent trick in his magical reper-toire, and each time he did, I was totally at ease. Every time he went soaring, skating high in the sky, pirouetting like falling confetti, I knew he was having the time of his life. It was so important for me to let him do this. We now had a high level of mutual trust, which meant we were getting the best out of each other. When he was ready to come down, I'd find him sitting on top of his aviary door, waiting for me to formally welcome him home. I always did, gladly, with the obligatory and expected treat. Loki was totally satisfied and enjoying life to the full, the life he deserves and the one we always wanted for him.

However, it wouldn't be a Loki story if there wasn't a mischievous anecdote that accompanies his newly found desire for exploration. It had been mid-morning on a Saturday, and the farm was already open to the public. I could hear from afar the sounds of children stomping around the cobbled paths and pushchair wheels rattling the uneven walkways. I was cleaning Loki's aviary, which happened to be particu-larly messy that day, but to my surprise, he had left me an offering of regurgitated quail on top of his perch. As much as I recognized his generosity, I was in no way prepared to eat it. He sat in his aviary, watching me ignore the food.

Loki was silent, but I could see the look of excitement on his face, hoping that when I had finished cleaning, I would take it. I was scrub-bing his log, which was coated in various dried fluids, when he lost patience with me. He went over and picked up the raw quail meat. It was food I had given him the night before, and he brought it to me. He stood on the floor looking up, beak full of meat, lightly cawing for me to take the food. I offered an empty palm, and he dropped the food. I caught it and placed it on the floor next to me. He looked at me, confused. Why didn't I eat this most wonderful gift? Quail was gourmet and should not be sniffed at.

Disgruntled, Loki went around the other side to where I knelt and picked up the meat. He jumped up to the log, putting him at eye level. He barked at me, pushing the food toward me in his mouth. "Take it! Take it!" he seemed to say. I did and put it down on the log. *Nope, you're doing it wrong, human.* He scooped it up and, this time, cut out the demanding phase. He took no nonsense and pushed his beak toward my face, smearing my cheek in quail juice. He was trying to force the quail into my mouth!

"Loki!" I yelped, the smell of decaying meat suddenly hitting my nose. I appreciated his intentions, so I took the food and pretended to eat it, keeping it cupped in my palm. My slick, sleight-of-hand skills seemed to work. Satisfied, he hopped out of the aviary into the arena to let me continue my cleaning.

After I finished cleaning up, I headed out and called him back. A nice fresh, clean home, ready to be pooped in as soon as his royal highness returns—but there was no sign of him. "Loki? Where are you? Come on; time to come back in!" Nothing. I looked in the usual places he liked to explore, but I couldn't see him or, worse, hear him.

Sarah-Jane came out of the office clutching a walky-talky all members of the farm staff carry, with a confused look on her face. "It's Reception. They are saying there is a large black bird in the canteen. It's stealing food and scaring the customers and canteen staff."

Uh-oh.

"Is Loki in his aviary?" she asked.

At this point, I was already on my way down to reception to be greeted by utter chaos.

Loki, with a packet of chips in his mouth, was hopping on top of all of the counters, putting fear into all of the kitchen staff. One of the cooks, the bravest of the group, wielded a tea towel, using it to shoo him away while the rest huddled behind their chosen warrior.

"He's stolen one of the sausages!" one voice screamed.

The public gave him a wide berth. Parents dragged their children to safety, taking cover behind tables, as the devil bird administered unsparing carnage by eyeing up loose food and threatening the desolation of all mankind. Strutting along the serving counter, he unashamedly knocked over display stands. The sound of reckless vandalism bellowed throughout the cafe walls.

"Loki!" I exclaimed in my best stern and official voice (in reality, trying to hide how incredibly funny this whole escapade was).

He stopped dead and cawed, the sound muffled by the packet of ready salted lodged in his gob. I confidently approached him and carefully extended out a hand to try and reclaim the stolen goods. He made a tepid attempt to resist me, and I managed to grab the chips still locked in his beak.

"Let go!" I stoutly commanded, but he wasn't interested in letting go.

He pleaded with me, voicing soft caws.

"If you let go, I will give you something better."

He cawed again with an amicable defiance.

With my other hand, I gained control of his flying straps and picked him up without contest. I wriggled the chips, but still, he refused to relinquish his loot. But now I had control of him, which allowed me to escort him out of the cafe, which was then returned to a civilized place to dine.

Once back in the comfort and safety of his aviary, I let him go. I half-expected him to drop his loot, but he didn't; instead, it was locked firmly in his beak. I delved into my pockets and produced an assortment of grapes and apple slices. Golden rule number one: never enter negotiations with a raven empty-handed. I gave him a few apple slices, and he barked. I took that as a no. *Okay, what about grapes?* He looked at them for a second, cocking his head and evaluating the pros and cons of the deal. It was deemed favorable in his eyes, and he dropped the chips in exchange for his grapes. Since this incident, we are happy to announce that Loki has never been back to the canteen, much to the delight of the kitchen and reception staff.

TEN
DIGR HJARTA
BIG HEART

At the age of twenty-six, I was in the fortunate position to buy my first house. I owned my own company and was on the verge of getting married. Like most people, these landmarks coincide with the inevitable stages of growing older and, similar to most of my peers, children are, more often than not, the next step. The cliché of attending various networking events, family outings, or social gatherings spawns the unavoidable and most predictable of questions: "So, when are you going to have kids?"

It's still a surprise to me in this day and age that people are totally shocked when they learn of my intention not to add offspring to the already saturated pool of miniature people. Some have even accused me of being selfish. And as night follows day, the inevitable and most vintage of phrases rolls out from seasoned parents: "Oh, you might not now, but you definitely will someday," topped off with a compulsory all-knowing wink. The icing on the patronizing cake. The problem is that the cake is stale, and I'm not eating it.

For me, it's quite simple, and to be fair, those people are correct. I am selfish. There we go: that wasn't so hard. I'm aware enough to realize that I enjoy doing what I want when I want. Do I fancy going into the office today? Shall I stay out for a few more beers? Shall I go and tour Europe with my band? All these trivial pursuits are often not possible when you are responsible for another human and for good reason. When you make the choice to bring a life into the world, your priorities have to change. I don't want my free time to be a luxury. I want it to be a mandatory outcome of my life choices. Don't get me wrong: I absolutely adore kids. I love playing with them, teaching them, and spoiling them. It gives me an excuse to play with Lego, which, in most scenarios, is deemed socially unacceptable for adults. I absolutely do not judge anyone for having children. It's a life choice I think should be taken very seriously, but one we should all be allowed to have.

At twenty-seven, I became a parent to a child I didn't really want—a decision that was thrust upon me without a chance to decide if this was right for me. People say, "You can't understand what it's like to be a parent until you are one." Well, I reckon I've now got a good idea: it's just my kid has feathers. Yes, the irony certainly tastes delicious, and for once, I agree with the parent mantra, "There isn't a right time; you'll never be ready." Aligning my way of thinking was phasing on a new path. I was beginning to make progress with Loki quicker and with better results.

One day, Sarah-Jane and I needed to pick up some emergency food from a local pet shop. The birds are served only the finest cuts of meat: normally, they gorge on "chicken *al fresco con yolk sack*," which still bemuses me when children and adults alike squirm and recoil with disgust, yet still love a "dippy egg and soldiers" (U.S. friends, I'm aware you don't believe in egg cups, so this British delicacy will be lost on you; however, Google it).

On this particular occasion, we were picking up a batch of quail, mice, and rats, or what we call "good food." While in the shop, Sarah-Jane did the adult thing and scouted for what she needed and negotiated payment. I, on the other hand, reverted back to a ten-year-old child. I wandered off, touching things I shouldn't, playing with the dog toys, and it was in this section of the store where my eyes lit up. I had absolutely no idea about the vast range of entertainment you could buy for your animals.

"Where the hell have you been?" barked a voice from behind me.

I spun around to see Sarah-Jane marching on my position. I looked at her silently; in my hand, I held a shiny box, and I was grinning like a Cheshire cat.

"What's that?" she said sternly, looking at the offending article within my grasp. She carried the worried "mother losing her child in the shop" look.

I showed her the front of the box. "Can I have this?" I said, like a pensive child asking a parent for a toy when they have been bad.

Sarah-Jane looked at me utterly puzzled, partly because I'm a fully grown adult who can afford my own things. But it was my intentions which puzzled her.

"What for?" she asked, the cogs turning in the mill.

I was still grinning like a loon, playing out my plan in my head. "It's for Loki."

Sarah-Jane rolled her eyes. "You and that bloody raven."

I took this as a yes, so I scampered to the till and made the purchase.

The next day, we got to the center, and I quickly said my token *hello* to the staff, eager to see my boy. The staff looked at me the same way Sarah-Jane did in the pet shop—mystified as I zipped past them with my newly acquired purchase. As I put distance on my mere mortal colleagues, I heard Sarah-Jane explain with rolled eyes, "It's for Loki."

This was quickly followed by a resounding, "Ah, that makes sense."

I gleefully arrived at his aviary door, buzzing to show him what I had, and of course, he was already there, ready to greet me. As soon as he heard me say *hello* to Emily, well out of eyeshot, he knew I was here. He barked in excitement, tail wagging furiously! I entered his area, box in hand, and he jumped straight to my shoulder, intrigued to see what I had. I sat on the log and began to open the box. He cawed the inquisition, curious. He stuck in his beak, nudging the flaps of the box, trying to get a better look. I summoned him to the floor and tore open the flap. I gestured to the weakness in the box, and it didn't take him long to take advantage of an opportunity. He grabbed the lid and began to yank the cardboard, tearing it at the joints, and together, we abruptly ripped open the box. Team work!

The item fell to the ground, making a god-awful crashing sound. Loki jumped up in shock and yelped, provoking him to scatter back to the perch toward the back of the aviary. It wasn't just the thud of the item on the ground but the various other sounds that also came from the item—sounds Loki had never heard and was instantly terrified of. Emily, Sarah-Jane, and Chris all hurried over to see what the commotion was.

"Oh my god, why have you bought him a xylophone?" Emily shrieked with a raised smile.

Just like in the pet shop, I grinned ear to ear.

This newfangled idea of mine didn't start off with quite the impact I had in my head. For some reason, I imagined Loki would love his own xylophone and would tickle the (plastic) ivories like all those cool cats from New Orleans. However, it was in fact the complete opposite. Still reeling from the initial sound of the colorfully decorated keys clanging in a chaotic crash, Loki looked at the device with suspicion and terror. Beak open, head cocked, panting—that all too familiar defensive stance. I sat in his aviary for a good forty-five minutes, and it felt like an age. He staunchly watched me with that meticulous beady eye. I didn't want to scare him, but I did want him to see it was nothing to fear, just like the Kong toy.

I began by just softly pushing each key, slowly, in linear order from left to right, purple to green, ascending in semitones. The xylophone has four keys, roughly an inch wide each, and the metallic *bing* has a fast and playful decay. I fumbled around, trying to make recognizable melodies, all the while being surveyed with extreme caution. I tried to coerce him with some gentle, reassuring reasoning, but he wouldn't budge. So I decided to take the fight to him.

I stood up and headed over to Loki with the portable piano.

He nervously rotated his back toward me. His body language was easy to read as he cawed gingerly at my advances.

I softly serenaded the tetchy corvid by playing the keys in front of him. He was twitchy but had not made an evacuation attempt just yet. Nervously, he looked over his shoulder, a perfect seven-eighths turn. I practiced my composition in front of my cautious audience member. The owls next to me paid no attention to my impromptu symphony.

Perhaps they were as devoid of class and taste as they are wisdom, or perhaps they just knew what they liked.

I entered the creative flow stream, experimenting with different rhythms and variations of notes. Some were quite catchy, even resembling popular songs, and Loki began to thaw out a little. He swung his bum around and faced me. This was a positive indicator—either that or he was gearing up for a spectacular full-frontal attack. I watched him closely as I continued to play. He watched me play the notes, then looked me directly in the eye. He did this after every time I played a key, looking for some kind of cause-and-effect correlation. He angled his neck toward me and the musical device—a sign his confidence was growing. Either that, or he's really digging my mad xylophone skills. With trepidation, he pecked the top of the xylophone, a metal rectangle piece that provides the resonance and the source of the *bing*. He jerked back immediately: was it the texture of the metal or the sound of his beak clanging against it that caused him an issue? With a wariness, Loki edged back toward the device and tapped the metal key again, but this time, he stood his ground.

I rotated the toy around so the button keys were facing him.

He recoiled, pulling his head back. *"Bah-Bah!"*

He wasn't too sure about it. I played a few notes, and he cocked his head. Just like before, he whacked the key. It binged with full amplitude, and this time, he didn't recoil. I bestowed on him praise as if he'd just played Pachelbel's Canon in D. He looked me in the eye, and his crest inflated in reaction to my admiration; the tone of my voice decoded to insinuate a positive appraisal. He took the initiative and struck the key again, earning him more "good boy" coins. He picked up some momentum and launched into a jazz improvisation, tapping each note at random. Some he played *fortissimo*, while others he played more serenely, with delicacy and grace invoking light and shade to his first-ever ensemble.

It may seem fairly frivolous that a corvid, a bird known for being naturally inquisitive and intelligent, can hit a key at random. What's the big deal? But it *was* a big deal, especially to me. This wasn't any old corvid. This wasn't a corvid that was raised by its parents to fully develop acute cognitive abilities; he wasn't shown what aspects of life needed to be feared. He wasn't instructed on the art of curiosity. He was instead mistreated, bullied, and tormented all at the hands of my species.

This broken bird was trusting a human—trusting me! He was showing positive signs of rehabilitation, realigning him back onto a path whereby he could learn, adapt, and overcome. Could it even be possible for him to forgive? That would be an incredibly tall order and one I wouldn't expect from him, but one I would always hope for.

I genuinely believe that *we* as the most powerful, resourceful, self-avowed, and intelligent species on the planet, often show huge levels of arrogance and naivety toward the capabilities of other animals. Take, for example, the Staffordshire Bull Terrier or those in the USA, a breed on a par with the Pitbull. They are one of the soppiest, most loving dogs a human could possibly own. The negative stigma is, for the most part, obnoxious propaganda, a negative smear campaign devised by ignorant and heartless people wanting to disassociate themselves from a once-proud working dog. The fighter, the aggressive child-mauling killer, the dog-assassinating brute. The image is propagated by the media, which loves to exhort the stereotype, but at the end of the day, the ones that "go bad" do so at the hands of humans. The hard truth is that it's all our fault: *we* have done that, and we need to take responsibility for our actions.

These animals are bred in droves. They are beaten, and they are physically and mentally broken down so humans can watch them tear each other apart for "sport." The self-awarded top of the food chain species still takes pleasure in this barbarism. The dogs certainly do not want this. All this breed of dog wants is the most basic of desires: they want to be warm, they want to fend off starvation, and they desire to be part of a family unit. These animals excel at loving and protecting their pack.

If I wasn't talking about dogs, one could easily assign these wants as virtues that define the basic needs of humans. It's no wonder that people—the ones that go to the rescue centers, the ones that take the dog with the scar on its face, the one with missing teeth, the one with a perforated eye—all end up saying the exact same thing. These dogs will love you unconditionally even after they have been mistreated.

They will look at a human without an ounce of revenge. How many humans can do this? Is it because they don't have the prerequisites to remember or associate negative experiences with specific species? I strongly disagree. What I think it comes down to is the size of their heart. I often find myself wondering: *does Loki have a big heart?*

It was lunchtime at the center. The children were in the play area dipping into their picnics before exploring the various climbing activities, and the parents were taking full advantage of the gift of a play area. While the Coda team ate their lunch, I decided to bring Loki out and start by flying him to the perches. He did very well, considering he still didn't have much of a tail. He flitted toward the perches in a clumsy flight, landing without any grace. The Harris Hawks looked on with disdain. I imagine when all the birds are in their muse at night, they like to poke fun and make jokes at the resident corvid: he's common in name and uncouth by nature.

As I walked between each perch, I jingled—a cluster of random notes seeped out because I was carrying the xylophone in the back of my flying jacket. Loki prefers flying to my shoulder for his treat, and for some reason, he feels safer up there. Perhaps having a high vantage point to better detect threats or just a way to avoid being on the dreaded glove? Either way, I don't mind him being up there, but I am always a little conscious that if I don't present the reward quickly enough, he will dine on my ear. I called him to the fence, which he did without hassle, and sat about two feet below eye level. I reached to my back and pulled out the xylophone. He looked and cawed at the children's musical instrument with a deep, burly croak. The children behind him paid no attention: just another generic black-colored bird, probably a crow. The parents continued to chatter, picking at their kids' leftover picnic.

I pressed the red key and looked at Loki, and he looked back, puzzled. "C'mon, now you press it," I prompted. Nothing. I pressed it again, but still no response. I delved into my pocket and gripped a few cat biscuits between my fingers. Loki spotted them immediately and begged for the food by extending his head toward my hand. I showed him the cat biscuit, pressed the red key, and let him eat the biscuit. He gobbled it and produced a quaint, delicate retort that I took to be a *thank you.* I showed him another biscuit, pressed the key, and fed him once again. He stayed fixed on the spot. I showed him a third biscuit, and this time, I held it up but refrained from pressing the key. Loki croaked: he wanted the food. I remained strong, and with my eyes, I suggested the keys. *Bing bing bing!* He blasted a set of triplets, for which I immediately rewarded him. I pulled out more biscuits, and instantly, he played a random assortment of keys, hammering indiscriminately—perhaps we have a jazz prodigy in the making. He was rewarded, and the game went on.

"Mummy, look! That crow is playing the piano!" a child called out.

My initial mental response was a typical British internalized tutting: *He's not a crow!*

The children decided that something of interest was happening and waltzed over to watch Loki. They sat in the dedicated seating area nicely and quietly. Loki's size quickly became apparent: from afar, he's fairly inconspicuous, but only when you are up close can you really appreciate the stature of this amazing bird.

Loki wowed the children. As his beak danced among the musical notes, people were drawn over to watch this spontaneous musical recital. Children and adults alike watched him fly from perch to perch, playing with his new favorite toy for cat biscuits with the excitement of a child who had just learned to ride a bike or mastered a new skill. There's a new breed of busker in town, cawing to a venue near you!

Loki's newly identified talent for music started to become notorious. Every time I led him out to showcase his musical prowess, out came the mobile phones, everyone wishing to capture a piece of Loki to show their friends. Even the staff at the farm would stop their chores to grab a video memento. Loki took it all in his stride, and I was immensely proud of him.

One evening, just after the farm had closed, I was unexpectedly approached by a young lady, her boyfriend in tow, jaded with exhaustion. You know the look—go to any shopping center at the weekend, and you will see them in the wild. Disheveled males plonked on seats, leaning against pillars withdrawn from the world, praying for the pain to stop. Waiting, begging for their significant other to finish trying on "just one more" garment. You can instantly tell which people come to the farm and which people come to the falconry center to see the birds. The dead giveaway is an absent child, so on this occasion, I knew this couple—more so, the woman in the relationship—was here for a specific reason.

"Excuse me, do you work with the birds?"

Uh-oh, was I about to be berated (again) over how cruel it is to keep birds in captivity? It's the most common grievance uttered by the uninformed public—ultracrepidarians aplenty!

I cautiously admitted to working with the birds, and in my mind, I was preparing my defense rebuttal.

"Do you ever get Loki the raven out?" the lady inquired.

How odd. I'd never been asked that before. What was even more perplexing was that she knew his name. I assured her I did, still apprehensive of a cruelty to birds dressing down. I positively confirmed that he is flown numerous times throughout the day, as are all the birds. I started to gain momentum into my battle speech, but she switched off and spun around to her boyfriend and then back to me, wide-eyed and bushy-tailed. My offense was momentarily halted.

"Okay, so this might sound a bit weird, but I really love ravens. I saw Loki playing a toy piano on YouTube and wondered if we could see him."

The magic of viral video marketing.

I chuckled and happily agreed to let her watch him in action. I headed over to his aviary, and he stood to attention, vocally welcoming me to open his door. I opened his door, but he didn't fly out. I walked back over to him and asked him politely if he wouldn't mind showing the lady his musical skills. He spluttered a few stoic barks. I gave him a single mealworm on the house. It did the trick. As I turned and left his enclosure, he came swooping out and, without prompting, put himself on the perch closest to the lady. She beamed with joy and instantly became absolutely besotted with him. She snapped hundreds of photos and took plenty of video footage of Loki flying and playing his musical renditions. She went on to tell me she'd traveled up from south London just to see him—roughly a two-hour drive. Loki's magnetism and tractor beam seemed to be having an effect on others.

I'll happily spend as much time with anyone who wants to learn more about our birds. If someone shows an interest, I'll do anything I can to satisfy their curiosity. It was at this point I decided to take a bit of a risk. The boyfriend was slumped in the seating area, happily watching his girlfriend enjoy herself, but he was in no way interested in the subject matter. His girlfriend, however, was full of beans and excitement, and after all, she had come a long way just to see Loki.

I reached into my flying jacket and felt around. I probed the glove and confirmed to myself, due to the size, that it was an eagle glove.

I opened up the gate to the flying arena and invited the couple in.

"Would you like to hold him?" I asked her. She looked over at her boyfriend, the sparkle of joy and light unmistakable. She seized the opportunity with all the excitement of a kid on Christmas.

I pulled out the glove and picked Loki up from the flying perch. He stood on the glove nicely and was silent as a rock. In fact, the whole farm was calm. There were no more children running rampant, and all of the animals had been ushered home for the evening. It was just us and the faint tweeting of the midsummer evening chorus.

I put the flying straps into the safety position and removed my hand from the glove. The lady casually slid her hand into the rugged, oversized gauntlet, complete with a perched, proud raven. She was stunned, completely speechless. She tried to utter a word—her lips moved but they made no sound.

Her partner perked up, seizing his opportunity. He snapped away, and all the time, she was totally unaware as he flitted around her, getting multiple shots from as many angles as possible. He'd obviously done this before. Her eyes were transfixed on Loki: nothing else mattered at this moment in time. He had her complete attention, and all it took was for him to be him. A tear ran down her cheek, and with a break in her voice, she confessed she'd always wanted to see a raven close up. I asked her to hold out her hand, and I dropped a few biscuits into her palm. She instinctively raised it to Loki, who, with surgical precision, ate them one by one. He was on point with the script, playing his role perfectly, and once again, I believe he could sense the energy the girl was projecting. It was obviously something he could appreciate and felt compelled to reciprocate.

By now, I recount these memories with the benefit of hindsight—

once again, concluding it was another risk, but it just felt right. I'm glad I trusted my instinct because, for a brief moment in time, two souls made a connection that crossed species. A positive meeting of energies that brought so much happiness to someone's life and at little cost. His energy was soft and relaxed; he made no sounds and even produced a rouse while being held. I had an innate feeling that he would behave and not let me down, and he did me proud. The boy did well!

"You've made my day. No, actually my year! I can't believe it; I've actually got to be this close to a raven!" She continued to cry and to be honest, I felt quite emotional, too. The overwhelming contentment this young lady was experiencing gave me goosebumps and reiterated how incredibly lucky I was to be Loki's friend. He had shown a big heart that day, as this was the first time I had let a member of the public hold him. He was a true gent and played the moment with perfection. Honestly, I believe that the authentic energy and emotion the lady radiated empowered Loki, giving him a grander sense of purpose and an environment in which he felt safe and empowered.

It's safe to say she fell in love with Loki instantly. Never have I been more convinced of love at first sight than on this particular day. Perhaps much to her boyfriend's displeasure, but Loki does seem to have this ability to draw people to him: people are fascinated by him. There also seems to be a thirst that needs to be quenched by those fixated on the lore that surrounds ravens and their well-documented cerebral competencies.

When I got home, I did a quick internet search on Loki and right enough, there he was—numerous videos all over YouTube and Facebook of him zipping about, playing with his new favorite toy, completely unaware of his rapid rise to fame. The only way was up, and his short rise to fame wouldn't stop there.

ELEVEN
INN Í HIÐ ÓÞEKKTA
INTO THE UNKNOWN

Since 2014, Coda Falconry has had the esteemed pleasure of demonstrating their flying team at the ancient and prestigious Hedingham Castle. The Norman Keep, located on the Suffolk / Essex border, is a huge tourist attraction, and every bank holiday, they hold an illustrious medieval show. Knights from Middle England prowl the arena in full armor: seated on horseback, they entertain the crowds with full-contact jousting. The pantomime black knight parades the arena, provoking the audience, marauding his arrogant bravery and skill before he is clobbered from behind with a fully functional mace by our hero, and the crowd cheers in exaltation. It's as entertaining as much as it is dangerous, and the crowd—a mixture of children and adults—revels in the legally sanctioned violence. It seems we haven't progressed from the days of gladiatorial games: a desire to see pain inflicted onto one another lies deep within our genetic makeup.

Part of the day's program includes the falconry display, a much calmer and serene addition to the medieval show. Sarah-Jane, with her knowledgeable yet uniquely comedic commentary, hypes the audience while Emily bears the duty of flying the birds on the huge arena floor.

Among the usual suspects is Poppy the Harris Hawk, Sarah-Jane's "handbag hawk" —a cute and gentle hawk who can really switch it on. Poppy has an esteemed body count: successful trophies include rabbits, ducks, pheasants, and the *pièce de résistance,* an eight-pound greylag goose, which, for comparison, is the same size as a male Golden Eagle. Also on the flying team is Dusk the Barn Owl. Dusk has a real problem with me and most of the other male falconers, to be fair. To say he's cantankerous is somewhat of an understatement. However, with Emily, he melts like chocolate. They are, without doubt, best buds. Blue the Lanner Falcon and Star the Saker Falcon are ever-present at these events and can be seen racing around the castle at exhilarating speeds, roaring over the audience's heads, clocking in at speeds up to one hundred miles per hour. If he's been a good boy and, more importantly, is on a good flying weight, Logan the Eagle Owl will get an outing, as will Otis, our tiny Sunda Scops Owl who loves to be cuddled—he portrays characteristics more like a cat than an owl and manages to steal the hearts of all those get to meet him.

In 2015, Sarah-Jane wanted to freshen up the show and use a few new birds. Loki got his first offsite demo call. We would take his xylophone and his Kong toy to keep him focused, but most importantly, we would take his creance. The showtimes are 11:30 am and 3:00 pm strictly; they have to run like clockwork, which, when you're working with animals, can be, at times, rather stressful.

We arrived around 9:00 am to set up our pitch, get the birds out, fill water baths, and erect gazebos. Woody, the groundsman at Hedingham Castle, came over to say hello and chat about the impending day—the typical topics of "Will there be many people turning up, do you think?" and the classic British conversational piece, "What will the weather be like? Do you think it will rain?" which, being a bank holiday in England, almost certainly guaranteed rain at some point. However, the conversation took a brief pause.

Woody looked down toward our roster of birds, birds he had seen many times before. That tractor beam now had him locked and was pulling him in strong, just like it did to me. "Who is that?"

We turned around, but we knew he could only be talking about one bird.

Woody headed over to Loki's perch and bent down to get a good look at him. "Bloody hell, you are one gorgeous bird!" he said with a thick Suffolk accent.

Loki did what he did best: turning on the charm by showing off his beautiful iridescent crest. He bowed his head and gently cawed in response to Woody, who got out his phone and fired off a bucket load of photos.

"At the end of the day, can I come back and hold him?" He said it with so much determination in his voice that it came across as more of a demand than a question.

Woody hopped onto his quad bike and drove off toward the bridge that connects the castle to the manor house. Within ten minutes, the event organizer, three members of staff, and the owners of the castle with children in tow were all at the front of our pitch, itching to see our new arrival.

"Oh my god, he is so big!"

"Look at the colors!"

"I've never seen a raven so close!"

Loki was already proving to be a show-stopper, winning over the plaudits of the people who owned and ran the castle. Hopefully, all this fresh praise from his new fan club wouldn't go to his head. He still had a show to do.

Sure enough, as the day is long, showtime came around, and we had saved the best, or perhaps the riskiest, bird till last. As Emily put the falcon back in his box, Sarah-Jane requested the thousand-strong crowd to participate in her infamous Hedingham Castle "Mexican wave." The wave rippled around the audience, ending at the foot of the castle with thunderous applause. The crowd was up for it and, so far, been treated to a five-star falconry demonstration. Every bird had performed with aplomb and total discipline. With the falcon boxed, Emily took her cue and departed the arena. Her work here was done: to remain in the arena for the finale would be at her peril. Sarah-Jane took hold of the creance that Emily had left on top of a large black carry box, releasing the springy silver locks that held what was hidden. An eruption of black chaos cannoned out of the box in a rapid flash akin to a warlock casting a spell. *Here we go…*

Loki trotted out into the arena, cocksure of himself, beak up to the sky, and mouth slightly agape, a boasting, cocky air to his stride. He hopped onto the flying perches and followed Sarah-Jane around the arena, trading cooperation for mealworms. I watched from the side, overwhelmed with anxiety, my palms greased with panic as I listened to the throbbing of my heartbeat thumping in my chest. I felt sick.

Sarah-Jane asked the crowd if they had ever seen a musical raven, and as you would expect, the crowd was silent apart from a few childish giggles. Sarah-Jane whipped out the xylophone, and straight away, Loki spotted the toy. With his excitable, child-like state of mind, he bolted a good twenty feet across the arena floor, full steam ahead! He squared up to the keys and played the song of his people. The crowd absolutely loved it, and they gave him a huge round of applause. But before Sarah-Jane could wrap up the show, something rather unexpected happened, which may not be all that surprising.

Loki stopped dead in his tracks, his beady eyes peering into the audience with menacing purpose. Sarah-Jane and I clocked his suspicious behavior: it was all going too well. Loki looked at Sarah-Jane, then back to the audience, then back to her. The showdown had begun. Trouble was brewing, and my nerves were shot to bits. I just wanted to run in there, pick him up like a hamburger, and take him home. But I was rooted to the spot, frozen with panic.

Loki began to pace, his little bum shifting from side to side, making a beeline toward the crowd. Sarah-Jane, over the microphone, playfully asked Loki what he was doing, but he ignored her.

I broke free and started to walk around the back of the arena to intercept him if he decided to dive into the audience. Sarah-Jane was doing a great job of trying to make it seem like part of the act, and the crowd was all humored by his funny walk and scripted disobedience. But I was running out of time as he made up a considerable amount of ground for a creature with such short legs, his pace quickening as he locked onto his target. I could not get there in time as he reached the first line of bodies. He stopped at the foot of the crowd, and sitting in front of him was a very young girl in a pretty white dress who happened to make a fatal error. That error was the audacity to be enjoying a freshly dusted doughnut.

The crowd was silent, curious to discover how the final act in this show would end. Loki looked back at Sarah-Jane, and with that all too familiar glint in his beady little eyes, robbed the little girl of her sugary snack in broad daylight—like a viper, he struck with speed and precision: it was literally stealing candy from a baby. He scurried away with a naughty strut to a safe distance back toward the middle of the arena, putting at least ten feet between himself and the little girl. He was smart enough to know she couldn't get to him and tore into his jammy surprise. The audience gasped as the little girl burst into tears, the crowd suspended in emotional limbo, confused about whether to laugh or be shocked. I, however, wasn't confused. I wanted to be swallowed and consumed forever by the earth, free from accountability for our yobbish raven.

Loki, as per usual, did not care: his Christmas had come early. Sarah-Jane marched toward Loki like an angry headmistress and, with a playful but stern tone, berated him for this shocking behavior over the PA.

"Loki! Look what you've done! You have upset that poor little girl!"

Loki looked at Sarah-Jane and stopped eating, his beak coated white with icing sugar. He dropped his head in shame like a naughty school kid being told off. Mum had spoken. Awash with guilt and shame, Loki picked himself up and waddled back to the little girl. What was he up to? Was he going back for seconds? Was he going to enact revenge on the girl for his being scolded? He was definitely going to bite her, wasn't he?

He arrived back at his victim, the little girl gently sobbing after her terrifying corvid encounter, her parents playfully consoling her, unaware Loki was back for more. He could sense the fear: the audience tensed up with anticipation, and we, the falconers, were completely terrified. *This is it. This is the moment we become a tabloid headline. The new Staffordshire Bull Terrier has been born, and he comes with a glossy black coat and an insatiable hunger for sugary treats and children,* I thought.

He leaned in toward her with that devastating beak and...regurgitated the doughnut onto her lap. The crowd roared with laughter, which cross-faded into a sympathetic "Ah." This apparent act of remorse did very little to prevent the flow of the girl's tears. In fact, I think it made it worse, but Loki's empathetic response was witnessed by thousands. Loki returned to Sarah-Jane's shoulder on command after seeing a chocolate biscuit sneak out of her pocket—his absolute favorite—not that he had deserved it, but our nerves were frayed, and we could no longer style out any more off-piste antics! Sarah-Jane and Loki exited the arena to another round of applause, and the *compère* addressed the audience, waxing lyrical about the spectacular show they had just witnessed with a very special mention to a certain "cheeky corvid." On Loki's first show, he gained notoriety, and yet we acted surprised.

Like security chaperoning our adored rock stars, we slowly strad-dled through the crowds, all craning to see the birds as we escorted them backstage. Most offered words of congratulations, noting they had "never seen such an entertaining falconry show before" —enter-taining for them, perhaps. Eventually, we arrived back at our pitch, where we were completely inundated with people who wanted to get a closer look at our birds. There was one in particular who seemed to warrant more attention than the others: a certain sweet-toothed rogue!

Loki was in his element, basking in the adoration of raised cell phones: crest up, runny beak, and lots of playful vocalizations. He even jumped in his bath and rolled around—the little show-off! My nerves had just about recovered, albeit now shredded and ragged. I held my hands out. They continued to shake as the last remaining drops of adrenaline circulated around my body.

After the crowds had died down, I took a seat next to his lordship's perch. The positive effects of my body's production of epinephrine had finally worn off, leaving me with a most delicious headache—the stress was too much. Immediately, Loki hopped onto my lap and cleaned his beak on my trousers, even though it was spotless. I got the impression that this little behavior trait was a warm, subtle way for him to show me a little bit of affection. I looked into his stress-free eyes, taking a moment to reflect on what had just happened in the arena: the notion that a corvid—a mentally damaged bird at that—just demonstrated in front of thousands of people the humbling, human act of remorse. To be honest, even just writing those words makes me stop and really think about that sentence: to me, that is truly incredible. Loki had added or at least displayed yet another complex human emotion, which I didn't know was possible. It was phenomenal—one more instance added to the list of times this bird had left me gobsmacked.

While still contemplating the success of the show, I did wonder if the little girl was okay; did she get another doughnut, and would she now be afraid of ravens and crows? On this musing, I decided to tuck into my own lunch. My nausea had disappeared, leaving a hole that was to be filled with an immense hunger. I pulled out my sandwich, and guess who wanted to go halves on it?

He bounced back onto my lap, beak bobbing left to right, gingerly cawing, "*Ahhh-ahhhh-ahhh!*"

Like the little girl, I sure did have some audacity! So, of course, I caved in and offered him up some of my chunky homemade ploughmans. He returned to his bow perch and dismantled the sandwich into neat, individual sections: the bread, cheese, and lettuce. The cheese he ate straight away, but the bread, with a thick crust smothered in pickle, he saved for later. Being tethered to his perch gave him around three feet maximum in ground space to work with. He picked up the bread and began to dig a hole. I watched him the whole time as I consumed the remaining part of my sandwich. He knew I was watching, but considering I gave him the food in the first instance, I obviously was not seen as a threat to his secret food cache. He covered the hole up with grass and hopped back on my lap, looking to see what else he could pilfer.

I briefly averted my gaze to an onlooker who reminisced about Loki's cheeky act in the show. I agreed, and just as I did, Loki pulled down on my coffee cup and spilled it all over me, steaming hot coffee burning my groin. *Thanks, Loki!*

The gentleman laughed. Loki laughed. We all laughed.

At times, it does feel like Loki is in tune with what is going on around him, and he plays it up for attention, totally in control of his actions rather than being reactive and instinctive. His newly discovered boldness and confidence allow his true personality to shine through. His actions and decision-making appear completely premeditated, very deliberate, and calculated. It's both amazing and scary in equal measure, as is the range of cognitive abilities and emotions he has.

By the end of the day, the entire Hedingham Castle team came for their photo with Loki, but for Woody, it was love at first sight. "You are definitely bringing him to the next one, aren't you?" He said it with worried anticipation but also with a hint of, "Don't you dare come back here and not bring him!" It was clear a new star had been born.

Indeed, Loki starred in every Hedingham event we attended, and each time, he gained more and more fans. He was mostly a good boy with no repeats of his first outing, but we had to be on our toes, as he's always got something up his feathery sleeve.

Many medieval reenactment folk are really into their folklore and mythology, and one such couple came over to see Loki at the castle. They were dressed in fantastic costumes, and of course, they asked if they could have a photo with the "king of the corvids," to which we were more than happy to agree. He posed on their arms, fluffing himself up. They talked very fondly of ravens, and much like the young lady who visited Loki at our center, they had always wanted to see one close-up.

After doing many of these events, I've slowly learned how very well thought out these birds are with a small portion of the general public—I honestly had no idea. Was it off the back of programs like *Game of Thrones* that have suddenly made them so popular?

In some parts of the world, ravens aren't as popular and are even hated. For example, in Scotland, packs of ravens rain down brutal attacks on sheep who are giving birth, targeting the freshly born offspring, relieving them of their eyes and tongues. In 2018, this led to a petition to the government calling for a percentage of wild ravens to be culled. This fierce loathing is understandable—wild ravens with intelligence are a fierce opposition—but Loki was not a wild bird. Fierce, but not wild.

Back at the farm, the children drifted between the cute bunnies, the adorable baby lambs, and the beautiful horses, escorted by their parents. But amongst the lovers, you have the haters. I would often hear mutterings: *"He's well evil looking…" "Ugh, it will peck your eyes out…" "Stupid looking crow; they freak me out…"*

These remarks are not from kids but from adults. They chatter like a gaggle of bored parents congregating around the school gates, ignorant and petty. But much like those parents, it hurts when strangers call your kid names, especially when they have absolutely no clue about his background and his capability. I've caught people shouting at Loki through the aviary bars, throwing stones at him, and even people trying to poke him with sticks. The mind boggles and sends me into full-on protective dad mode.

On the flip side, I'm always keen to show Loki off to people. A big part of working with the birds in general is to get folks to enjoy seeing these magnificent birds, to inspire kids into thinking nature is cool because, quite frankly, it *is* bloody cool! As a species, most of us are moving away from nature, seeking refuge in binary-based forums, falling victim to believing that life is a popularity contest, yet on their doorsteps, these magical, ancient creatures still exist.

———

The next part of Loki's tale is, for me, perhaps one of the most devastating chapters of his time with us, and it leaves a bitter taste in my mouth to this day. At this point, it's been roughly two and a half years since we met him. He's done demonstrations both offsite and on the farm. He knows the lay of the land and is familiar with the flying arena we operate in: it's an extension of his home, which he feels accustomed to and safe, and this is really important. Like any child, and especially those who didn't have a great start in life, feeling safe in your home surroundings is such a basic and fundamental desire that we worked so hard to provide for Loki.

One Saturday afternoon in the spring, Sarah-Jane was flying Loki, and he was doing what Loki does: a bit of flying, a bit of rummaging, investigating the tree line for some sticks or rocks or things he finds of value, and generally having a good time. He enjoyed these freedoms: the choice to explore, the choice to fly, the choice to interact with his family. He decided to enter the seating area that borders our flying arena—the public sat there to watch the falconry shows. Loki knows the area, and often has a wander around before the public arrives. He has the opportunity to clean up any scraps of food kids have dropped from the previous day. There's an assortment of sandwiches, chips, fruit, and even sweets. As you can imagine, this is a place that Loki is incredibly fond of. He is comfortable and associates it as a good place to be.

On that day, Loki ventured ten feet in, where a middle-aged man was sitting on a bench eating a bag of chips. Loki waddled over to him, fuelled with curiosity, and stood before him, cawing.

Sarah-Jane, carefully watching him from perhaps fifteen feet away, called to the man, "It's okay! Don't worry; he's just being nosey."

And with that, the man got up and kicked Loki like a football square in the chest. He kicked him so hard that he hit the small fence separating the seating area and the flying arena. Loki was hurt, feathers fell from his wings, and in a flustered panic, he tried to clamber back toward Sarah-Jane. It was obvious he was in pain by the yelp he screamed. He found purchase and climbed up onto her chest, wings spread out, hugging her. With his beak, he lightly gripped the back of her neck—he was terrified and wouldn't let go, shaking in fear.

Sarah-Jane was engulfed in rage. She desperately wanted to go after the man, but Loki wouldn't let go of her, begging with short, muted calls for help. She hugged him tight, keeping him close and secure. She made her views perfectly clear as the man scurried off, afraid of what Sarah-Jane might do like the pitiful coward he was and is.

Loki was physically shaken. He remained bound to Sarah-Jane, sobbing into her shoulder, refusing to let go of her neck with his beak. She checked him over thoroughly, looking for any breaks in the wing bones. Thankfully, he was just badly bruised and missing a few feathers. But there was a more worrying issue: how would this cruel and beastly incident affect his mental health?

At the time, I was offsite doing a show, and upon arriving back at the center and learning what had happened, I immediately panicked and rushed over to see him. He looked pleased to see me, but he was not his normal self; he was quiet and withdrawn, opting to sit on the floor in the corner of his aviary rather than high up on his perch. His pride and confidence had taken a fall. He allowed me to check him over, and I stroked his little shiny head. I gave him a little massage on the cere, looking into his warm brown eyes. I was livid and sick with anger, a bubbling rage burning deep inside. I asked Sarah-Jane what the man looked like, and she described him in great detail, which allowed me to construct a clear and identifiable profile of the culprit in my mind. However, the incident happened hours before I had returned, and the likelihood he would still be on site would be incredibly slim. Regardless of the odds, I went off to go and find him. I searched the farm for a good half an hour but with no success. The suspect had successfully escaped the scene.

The rest of the day, and the weekend for that matter, was cruelly tainted by this appalling incident. I just couldn't understand or accept that someone could do that—I still can't. Yes, Loki could be difficult, but that was with us, and we were aware of it. We never had any aggressive behavior with Loki toward another member of the public. If anything, he was always on his best behavior. There was certainly no reason for that man to do what he did, and every time I imagine the scenario, I can't help but shed a tear. It was a completely unwarranted act of violence toward another soul when all he was guilty of was curiosity. It is heart-wrenching—my poor boy.

It really chewed me up inside. I was angry and affronted. I kept wishing that I had been there to prevent it from happening: if only I had stayed at the center and someone else took the offsite demo— maybe if I got back a bit quicker, I could have prevented it.

These episodes of self-questioning didn't matter. What had been done had been done, and there was no changing it, no matter how hard I thought about it. Back to the more serious undercurrent, though: would this single episode of cruelty undo all the hard work we had done with Loki, getting him to trust us and strangers? After all, we were supposed to be his guardians, and we allowed him to be in a situation that compromised his safety. Would he now be aggressive to random members or the public, or would it just be men or just men that fit the profile similar to the assailant? Would he shun and withdraw totally from us? What would I do in his situation? There were many questions stewing in a huge pot of "what ifs," and with a bird so complex, it was hard to tell how to prepare and move forward. Deep down, I couldn't shift the feeling that this was somehow my fault.

To say I was genuinely worried about the repercussions was an understatement. It kept me awake at night on many occasions, recreating and replaying an event I hadn't even witnessed. My mind added more grisly details and prophesied the absolute worst outcomes—imagining the future where Loki became a scorned vessel of retribution and intimidation or my nightmare of him being reduced to a sorrowful husk, finally giving up on mankind.

I delved into my "raven bible"—the book that gave me so much knowledge and ideas in the early days of Loki's training—*Mind of the Raven*. In one chapter, Heinrich talks about the raven's ability to recognize other ravens from up to a mile away. They can determine if they are members of the same pack or are vagrants, possible foes, or even potential friends. For starters, this was mind-blowing. I've been known to walk past people in the street I went to school with and not recognize them. But learning that a raven can differentiate from another raven from such a long distance, wow! Considering that both sexes are jet black with no other (in the light spectrum we can see in) visually distinctive color markings, I totally underestimated their powers of sight and visual recognition. So, I took inspiration and tested out an experiment Heinrich himself once did.

A week after Loki's abusive encounter with *that* man, I arrived at the center as normal: jeans, work boots, and sporting the Coda plum purple polo shirt. As soon as I was in eyeshot, I heard my mate cawing for attention, the standard morning greeting. I went over and gave him a good morning scratch, fed him a few biscuits, then left. With me, I brought a bag containing clothing I had never worn before to the center. I changed into black jeans, Converse trainers, and a bright green hoodie. I borrowed a pair of sunglasses from one of the farm's staff and put on a wooly hat. My face was completely covered by a bandana, and I was geared up and ready to rob the local post office. I even wore thick black gloves to really seal the look.

I headed out of the main farm office, a separate building that overlooks the falconry arena and Coda HQ, and made my way toward the aviaries. As soon as I was in eyeshot, Loki began to call out. How could he possibly recognize me? None of my identifiable features were showing, and he had never seen any of the clothes I was wearing. I went back into the office and asked if a member of the farm's staff could walk up to the center. I looked on from inside the manager's office in secrecy—it felt like I was on an undercover police bust waiting for an exact moment to gain my evidence. The farm worker ghosted through the center without Loki making as much as a peep. Loki had definitely seen the worker because he sees everything, but he consciously chose not to call out. I headed back out, still dressed in my urban bandito outfit, and before I could get ten steps out of the office, he sounded the alarm. There was no getting away from it—he knew it was me! I asked a different staff member to put on all of my clothes— bandana, sunglasses, everything. They, too, walked through the center completely undetected. They even walked past his aviary and stopped to look in, and Loki wasn't interested in the slightest. I smiled. The sense of relief was heartening. Loki has the ability to recognize and differentiate every individual accordingly. Perhaps it was my walk that gave it away or my proportions? It certainly wouldn't be a sense of smell, as ravens are completely devoid of it.

Later that evening, I delved back into my books, learning about facial recognition tests with corvids, which supplemented the above experiment. Ravens are equipped with the ability to store and recognize faces, just like we do, meaning that if that awful man would ever return to the farm, well...he would be remembered, and not just by Sarah-Jane.

I was over the moon, ecstatic to peel away another secret and learn one more of this amazing bird's hidden talents, albeit I'd prefer if it came about in a different, kinder way. The main thing was Loki's health. He was not physically damaged, and it appeared that his mental state was stabilized. We could rest easily knowing he wasn't in the process of metamorphosing into a righteous, revenge-seeking demon. There were to be no vendettas and, hopefully, no random attacks on the public.

The early days of the assault left him shaken and timid, but he soon grew back into his regular boisterous personality, the mischievous little tyke we know and love. On one such occasion, he robbed me of a few coins and a ten-pound note, which he happily ripped up in front of me. I knew he was back, and I couldn't have been happier. I never did get the coins back. They are still, to this day, buried somewhere in our flying arena, and only he knows where.

TWELVE
NÝ-KOMINN
NEWLY ARRIVED

L oki's fame was bubbling away via viral videos—small snippets of some of his more gregarious tendencies were getting likes from all over the world—however, he would now up his game and get the opportunity to be put on the big stage. All the birds at the center are signed up to an animal actor agency: they are all working birds, be it for pest control, Experience Days, or wedding ring deliveries, and they all need to earn their keep as long as it involves doing what they would do in the wild, which generally means sitting still or flying.

We get work from designer fashion labels such as Ted Baker, The White Stuff, and even Arri—the Hollywood-standard film camera manufacturer. I must admit to being jealous of working for Arri, as I longed to be able to own one of their cameras for my own filmmaking projects. We felt now was the right time for Loki to be enlisted into the talent roster, and it didn't take too long for his first inquiry.

We were asked if Loki could appear in a film shooting a few scenes on a warehouse rooftop in Essex. The brief we received was pretty vague but requested that Loki would need to sit on a man's shoulder. There was a call for a few flying shots, but these were not location-specific, and we agreed early on that those shots would be done at our center. I was already a bit nervous about enrolling him as an actor, given his rap sheet, but Sarah-Jane, with her usual cool and calculated instincts, was happy to enroll him. As a fake parent, I have empathy for all those who have paid large sums of money to put their kids through acting school, not to mention the hours sitting through all the rehearsals and terrible plays/recitals (I'm kidding; I'm sure they're great), so I feel slightly fraudulent. All I had to do was provide a few chocolate biscuits and let Loki muck about with a toy xylophone. I guess those are the breaks, as they say. Nevertheless, we accepted the position and headed off to Loki's first film job.

Call time was 8:00 am, which meant I had to leave the warm comfort of bed around 6:00 am. It was November, bitterly cold and dark. I do love autumn, but not at this time of day. As we walked into the center, Sarah-Jane, Emily, and I commiserated over the ridiculous notion of being awake, dressed, and ready for work at such an ungodly hour. Before we got to the office, sure enough, Loki chimed in his good morning chorus, his ears sensitive to our pitch and tone. He's probably been up a while, teasing the owls or working on some supervillain-type project.

"Time for your first film, mate! You going to behave?"

"Bah-Bah!" came the reply, short and sharp.

I guess it could go either way. Loki reluctantly lunged into his travel box. He's not a massive fan of it, and he often calls out to us, knocking on the door if he can sense we are in the vicinity. We breezed down the M25. It was suspiciously quiet, but we didn't complain, instead counting our blessings.

We arrived at the location, desolate and bleak. The surrounding marshland hid the secrets of rare migratory songbirds. We could hear their sweet early morning ballads, but their presence was shielded. There was a multitude of songs mixing melodies and blending choruses—it was a beautiful array of audio delights juxtaposed with the brutalist backdrop of a concrete warehouse.

The producer came over to greet us by our car—a lovely lady whose partner was the camera operator. Shot list in hand, she briskly talked us through the scenes and told us what she wanted Loki to do. I asked her a question, and immediately, there was a loud but muffled crowing.

"Is he in there?" the producer asked. "I can't wait to meet him. I absolutely love ravens."

Another unsuspected fan added to the ever-growing list. I got Loki out so as not to tease him: I didn't want him to feel he was being kept in the box as a punishment while we were all out mingling. Loki always wants to be a part of what's going on—he's all about inclusion and suffers from FOMO (fear of missing out). I warned the producer to stand back a bit from the carry case, as he often explodes out of the box, and true enough, as I opened the lock, out he came like a cannonball. I had a hold of his leash, and he jumped onto my gloveless arm, skin protected by a black Coda-branded hoodie.

"Oh my god, he is so beautiful! Look at those colors!"

While she got to know Loki and comprehended his size and beauty, I gave him plenty of fuss, chest rubs, throat tickles, and head massages, all of which were greatly approved, judging by his soft, passive purrs.

Together, we ascended the wrought steel staircase of the warehouse, our boots making loud clangs that echoed throughout the vast, empty building. We were told we would be filming on the rooftop, so I held Loki close, hugging him with my right arm, his beak resting on my shoulder. He eyed up Sarah-Jane, who followed behind me, gazing at her with curiosity and intrigue; he's always secure knowing his guardians are with him. We reached the summit and exited onto the roof to meet Loki's co-star, a lovely, burly man with a strong Viking-looking face. As soon as he saw Loki, he went gooey-eyed. After a brief introduction, the producer and the team set up for the first shot, which didn't include Loki.

We sat down out of the way, Sarah-Jane worried by the height and the strong winds that licked the roof with ferocity. To my amusement, I watched Emily struggling to hold onto her trademark beanie hat. The conditions were grim, and I placed my right hand under Loki's left wing, resting it on his chest. It served as an excellent hand warmer, and I could feel his little heart beating at a slow and steady pace. Loki thought nothing of it as he played with the toggle on my hoodie. He seemed happy and super chilled, taking it all in his stride, which, in turn, made me feel a little better about the whole affair. We agreed that Loki needed to have a creance, and we fastened it onto his anklet, which he duly allowed us to do with little resistance. So far, so good.

Action!

The actor set off on a long, weighty monologue, and toward the end of this most stoic and deep take, he was interrupted: *"Bah-bah-bah!"*

"Cut!"

We looked at the crew apologetically, but they all burst out laughing, a huge comedic break in what was an austere soliloquy. We offered our apologies and were assured by the producer that it really wasn't a problem. Typical of Loki—always wanting the last word. We took the initiative to move out of earshot from the crew so as not to distract them. I looked at Loki, and there was definitely something in his eye, a little cheeky glint that indicated his outburst was very much deliberate. Did our raven now have an ego?

We spiraled around the rooftop, looking down at the marshland, watching the harriers waver through the blunt green terrain. It was a new viewpoint to watch these birds from, as we are mostly only able to admire them from the ground level. As the sun rose, the array of different songs increased. Sarah-Jane, an expert in various birds—not just raptors—pointed out and educated us on exactly what we were listening to. Loki perched on my arm, completely indifferent to Sarah-Jane's lesson on songbirds. He was waiting for his big moment.

An hour or so had passed, and I was starting to wake up properly and feel more human. A young lad with rosy red cheeks from the cold air came over to collect us. With a spring in his step and abnormal enthusiasm, he declared it was corvid call time!

"Can we have the raven on set, please!" crowed one crew member, possibly the AD (assistant director).

We hurried back to the set and carefully navigated the collection of cables, light stands, and flailing boom poles. With the director, we blocked through what was required. Loki would need to fly into the frame, sit on the man's shoulder, and pause as they both gaze out into the nether. It sounded like a pretty simple task in principle, but it was akin to jacking up a kid full of sweets and fizzy drinks, then asking them to sit still and remain quiet. As people showed Loki interest, he reacted by pushing the extrovert button *on*.

As the camera crew arranged their shot, changed their lenses, and modified the quality of the light—battling the rising sun, we let our actor have a more formal introduction with Loki. We handed him some treats, and the man fed our green performer. Loki took to him like a charm: he was displaying his fluffy crown, and the man was giving him plenty of head scratches without the wrath of his bite. We placed Loki on his shoulder and practiced flying him to and from, gauging his confidence in the wind. He was coping okay, but as soon as he landed on the actor's shoulder, he would immediately look back toward us for safety and reassurance, ready to return on a finger click.

The camera was *in situ*, the lights on, and the sound operator found his mark. I decided to place myself right by the edge of the building's precipice so that when he landed on the actor's shoulder, he could see me, which would provide a more favorable eye-line for the camera. My vertigo was kicking in hard, and instead of adhering to the advice of a "Wet Paint" sign, I made the fatal mistake of looking down, inducing instantaneous nausea. *Loki, please, please, please just get this right!*

"Camera rolling… Sound speeding… Action!"

Out of frame, Sarah-Jane ushered Loki into the air, and he took flight, brushing off the strong side wind, and landed on the actor's shoulder. I looked at him dead in the face, about six feet away, while grasping the frosty-cold steel safety pole. The set was silent apart from the grating wind swirling around the rooftop. I caught Loki's gaze. He was about to crouch and propel himself toward me, but he paused as he read my facial expression. I slowly counted down from five, and he watched me with intent, his eyes blinking rapidly, locked onto mine.

Five, four, three, two, one. And on the beat of one, he took flight like an arrow, landing square on my chest! He scrambled to get a foothold before gaining his composure and standing on my left shoulder. He settled, then wiped his beak clean on my nice, clean hoodie. I picked him up off my shoulder, rearranging his position close to my chest, and made my way inward, away from the balcony and the subsequent drop.

"I'm so sorry—I shouldn't have counted down. I think he under-stands that when I get to 'one,' he can come to me for a treat."

The crew was mute, completely ignoring me as they played back the take. Shot in 120 frames per second, the slow motion gave it a real cinematic look—the actor's long hair and beard subtly riding the wave of the wind. Team Coda looked on with bated breath. They replayed the take, and upon a second review, there was a ghostly silent beat.

The producer conferred with the director, who shouted, "I abso-lutely love it! That's the one!"

Initially, they didn't want Loki to leave the frame, but on review, they decided they did. Team Coda smiled and came over to congratu-late "One-Take Loki." The cast and crew all took time to give him a stroke and take their picture with him on their arm. As normal, Loki was the center of attention and loved every second of it.

On the drive home, I gushed about my boy like a proud parent. I was delighted with how well he had behaved, his performance, his manner—just everything! I could feel the looks Emily and Sarah-Jane gave me. All that was missing was a perfectly scripted sitcom catch-phrase such as, "Here we go again! You and that bloody raven!" Cue canned laughter, and fade to credits.

The feeling of achievement for us both was too much for me to put into words. It wasn't too long ago that we thought he might never be the same again, and now he's a one-take wonder on film sets. The night before, my sleep was disrupted with multiple worst-case scenar-ios: would he be vicious, would he freak out? What if he damaged any equipment... But the problem with worrying is that it never really helps anything, and as with most cases, it was all for nothing. Loki stepped up and reveled in his new line of work, showing us a real flair for the arts. This may be exaggerated—after all, he just flew to someone's shoulder—but it was evidence that he was becoming more comfortable in different, unfamiliar places. I think it was at this point I really took stock and fully appreciated his development and the work we had all put in. What was once an uncontrollable, terrified beast was now a valuable, contributing member of the team—an entity with a soul that was growing and developing, becoming more comfortable with new people and a multitude of surroundings and scenarios. I can only imagine this is close to the same sense of gratification teachers, counselors, and social workers feel when they finally make a breakthrough and succeed with a tough project, a damaged person cast aside because of their differences. With time, effort, patience, and persistence, rehabilitation is the winning ticket for both parties. But Loki was so much more to me than a project now: this was a relationship—one that didn't have a deadline or an expiration date. I was looking forward to spending so much more time with him, and if he kept on progressing and breaking down boundaries, who could say what his potential could be? The sky is the limit, as they say!

It wasn't long before Loki got more acting work. For some actors, getting a call can take weeks, months, or, sadly, never at all. Loki didn't need to do auditions or screeners—he was already a rising star within the community. News quickly got around, and word on the street was that there was a raven who adored the camera.

Loki's next acting role took him to South London to a large, stately home nestled in the city with a lush green public park to its rear. The car park was jammed with various production trucks used for transporting rigging and large lighting equipment. Our call time was midday, but the fortuitous traffic gods for whom we often offer our prayers decided to answer our calls, meaning we arrived an hour early.

I lugged Loki, who was housed inside his large black carry box, into the mansion. I was immediately jumped on by a young lad armed with a walky-talky and a high-vis vest. I was instructed I couldn't go any further and needed to wait outside. I told him I was here for the filming, but alas, he was having none of it. "Please wait outside until you are called for." The fluorescent jacket of power had spoken.

I dutifully complied and did what the lad asked. I left the building, returning back to the car. I dropped the assistant producer a text to let her know we were there but unable to get in. Within two minutes, I looked in my rearview mirror and saw a lady in her mid-thirties, high-vis jacket, clipboard in hand, searching the car park. I got out and introduced myself. She was flustered and hugely apologetic, offering to show us to the makeshift green room. I grabbed Loki's box and hauled him back inside on the way, passing our fastidious doorman with a raised smile.

The AP escorted me through a maze of ornate and grand corridors. The walls were lined with giant portraits going back hundreds of years, documenting various noblemen and women who had once had something to do with the property. There was a lot of gold, and a lot of expensive antiques dotted all over the house, and my mind went straight to the default doomsday thinking. *How much damage could Loki do in here? Some of these ornaments are priceless.*

I shuddered back to reality as I was welcomed into the green room. It was a large square room with at least a six-meter-tall ceiling, but the room itself was fairly bland in comparison to the chintz and gold-dripping walkways of the rest of the house. I spotted the coffee and tea urns and a plethora of food and chocolate biscuits—*mental note made!*

Waiting inside were the director, the producer, the director of photography, and a few production assistants. The atmosphere was heavy, and I could immediately feel the tension grate against my skin, the air dense with frustration and exhaustion. The director pinched the top of his nose and shut his eyes—the look of regret and tiredness a familiar outfit for filmmakers—art is suffering. The producer came over and introduced himself—a lovely, tall chap with a thick RP accent. I asked him how it was all going, and what I got was the equivalent of putting a fifty pence piece in a jukebox and selecting the full, uncut album version of "Free Bird." He gave me the entire low down with all the trimmings. He was quite open about how jaded the entire crew had become, and it was clear to see as dejected crew members skulked around the house.

After I offered an ear to his worries, the crew snapped back into action. They were already massively behind schedule, and frustrated niggles and barbed digs escaped from the mouths of some of the crew members. The environment was saturated in a soup of negativity. I chose to pack Loki back into his box, leave the room, and go outside. I used Loki as an excuse, but the reality was the toxic environment could do with one less worry in the mix.

I stepped out and immediately felt better. The air was fresh and purifying, the rustic smell of autumn twirled amongst the trees, and only the faintest hint of traffic could be heard as Mother Nature took a breath. Loki and I headed to an empty bench under a beautiful tunnel of trees midway through their crimson change. It was quiet—not a soul about—which is strange for a park in London. The odd gray squirrel would scurry across the path, looking for food to cache while fallen leaves scraped against the hard concrete floor on the last leg of their journey to final decay.

I opened up the box, and out he came. He studied his new surroundings and then hopped onto my lap, satisfied with his reconnaissance. He wiped his beak on my trousers and then fluffed up his crest—this meant he was due a head massage. I gave him a good scratch, working the top of the cere right down to where his ear holes are. We chatted to each other back and forth about something inane— probably the teenage security guard—and he would reply as if genuinely interested and committed to the conversation. He started to dribble under the persuasion of a chest rub, and for a while, I totally forgot why we were even there.

There's a lot to be said for living in the moment. These are the special moments often talked about by wise "Life Gurus" and internet motivational memes—snippets in time when you just block everything out. Nothing is relevant apart from sharing that occasion and having a connection with another life. Being able to tune out the noise of the world and the confines of its pressures brings a healthy and euphoric sense of tranquility and comfort: the air smells sweeter, colors appear more vivid, and time is no longer a consideration. But as with all good things, they do come to an end eventually.

Our blissful solace was interrupted by the sound of the producer strolling down the path, coffee in hand. He offered me the drink, and I thankfully accepted—I never say no to a caffeinated beverage. If you can't find peace and harmony in your surroundings, the liquidated offering of a roasted coffee bean is the next best thing! He asked if I wanted a biscuit and reached into his pocket. I sharply stopped him in his tracks.

"Before you bring out your hand, let me just get Loki into his safety position because as soon as he sees the food, he'll grab it off you."

With Loki now safe, the biscuits, like a Smith and Wesson six-shooter, were drawn out of their holster. Loki saw them and barked loudly. His little legs did a mini jig on my hand—he thought they were for him.

"Oh wow, does he like biscuits then?"

I smiled, "Oh yes, he likes pretty much anything—even more so if he knows it's yours!"

I stroked him on the head, and he chilled out but without losing sight of the Bourbons.

"Can he have one?"

How could I not let him have one? He had been so well-behaved—I say well-behaved: all he had to do was just sit on my lap. Maybe I'm just very grateful for this now normalized behavior. I'm not bleeding, so that's good, isn't it? Or perhaps I'm just a soft touch when it comes to rewards!

The producer broke the biscuit in half and offered it to Loki, who gobbled it up and made very childlike noises to show his appreciation. The producer laughed, and I could see that all too familiar look in his eye: he had been metaphorically bitten by the raven bug and was now enchanted by him.

"Can I stroke him?"

I considered Loki's mood and body language and concluded it was safe, so I allowed it and showed him the best way—gently down the back. Loki stood proud with perfect posture, the epitome of elegance.

And then, out of nowhere, the park became instantaneously busy. A cyclist approached, spotted Loki, and stopped to have a chat. Cue the lady with the dog who entered from stage right to see what the fuss was about. Next in joining the gang was a group of half-dozen school kids with their parents. Within minutes, I now had—and no word of a lie—twenty people all gathered in a neat semi-circle wanting to ask questions and have a picture with Loki. I did a mini, off-the-cuff presentation, Loki made a few vocalizations, and people got their picture. The crowd dispersed with happy faces: they had an unexpected treat that afternoon.

I overheard one of the parents say to their child, "How amazing was that? You can show the pictures to all your friends at school!"

I didn't mind the fuss—after all, it wasn't about me. It was all about

Loki, and he deserved his time in the sun, and like the sun, he shone so bright. Being able to make a difference and change peoples' days by giving them the opportunity to be inspired and wowed by these beautiful creatures is partly why we do what we do. I often remind myself how lucky I really am.

The producer's phone vibrated loudly in his pocket, rattling against some loose change. He looked at the message and briskly walked us back to the set. All in all, we had been outside for around two and a half hours. It seemed like only ten minutes, and to be honest, there weren't many other ways I'd like to spend my time, and it was time that really did seem irrelevant.

To save on effort, I carried Loki on my arm through the house. He sat on me as if I was his butler and this was his house. I walked past various crew members who all stopped and did double-takes, scrambling for their phones to grab a photo for their Instagram stories. After meeting a few more of the crew, we were shown to the set where Loki would be required. The lingering, noxious atmosphere was still present, and tired and fed-up faces scampered about the corridors like drones. Loki remained totally silent but observant.

The requirement for this shot was for Loki to fly into the scene and take some meat from a metal tray. The scene depicts a slave from the late 1800s hallucinating and witnessing a raven steal his last piece of food. The room was very large but made incredibly small by the number of crew and lighting; the temperature was uncomfortably stuffy and warm for the same reason. Loki could sense the unease in the room.

We got ready, and I showed Loki the bright red blood-soaked meat, but for once, he wasn't interested. This was very strange behavior, as he hadn't been fed apart from the half biscuit he had in the park. Normally, he would have gone crazy for such a succulent offering. We took our marks, and the director called action. The actor did his piece, acting out starvation and pain, and I was given the cue to release Loki. He didn't go immediately. It took a few persuasive attempts from me, swinging the glove in the direction of the tray, trying to get him to make haste. Eventually, with enough force, he took flight and landed on the metal tray, making a tumultuous racket.

The noise freaked him out, and he flew straight back to me. The take was no good.

I showed Loki the metal tray, and he was instantly nervous about it, turning his back and refusing to look at it. I tapped it a few times and held it up to him with a bit of uncooked steak. His eyes looked at the meat—he wanted it but was too afraid of the tray. The director wanted to go again, but I told him I needed a few minutes to acclimate Loki to the sound of the tray. I could feel his eyes rolling at me, the tension in the room simmering ever higher. It was by far the most stressed-out set I had been on. The assistant director—rather prickly—pushed again to start rolling, and again, I pushed back. I had to remind him that Loki was an animal that needed to be respected: we would shoot when he was ready.

Loki slowly edged to a small chunk of meat and snatched it off the tray.

I praised him and scratched his throat. "Okay, let's try again."

We set up, and the cameras were set to record. I got my nod and released my grip on Loki's straps, gently nudging him off my glove. This time, he landed by the food, avoiding the metal tray, but he took no meat. He casually looked about and then diverted his gaze at me. The crew was transfixed on their monitors, praying this would be the one.

I could hear their inner monologue: *"Just take the meat; just take the damn meat."*

But Loki had frozen.

I knelt and whispered to him, trying not to be picked up by the dangling boom mic overhead. "Go on, mate. It's okay; I'm here."

The burning glare of around twenty crew members all fixated on us, and I could feel the heat.

Loki did an enormous rouse and preened one of his feathers, which was not a good sign.

I turned to the director with a look to suggest it wasn't going to happen. He was just about to shout, *Cut!* but at that exact moment, Loki cheekily stole the meat like a naughty boy and flew back to my shoulder with a slab of flesh hanging out of his gob. The actor finished the scene, and the call was made.

The crew huddled around the monitor for playback. My stomach was in knots, a throwback to being back on the roof. I was concerned, as it felt like the take went on forever, and so did the review. The silence in the room was a killer. I was desperately trying to gauge some kind of reaction from the many faces glued to the playback monitor, but it was like being in a poker tournament—cold, stoic faces that weren't giving me anything. The director looked up from the monitor and caught my eye. He smiled and gave me the thumbs up. That was the first positive piece of energy I felt in that house. He asked if I wanted to see it, so I picked up my mate and took him over to watch his performance.

The authority Loki commanded on the screen was quite impressive. He stood out as bold and imperious as the actor behind him writhed in agony and sadness. Although it wasn't what the director had in mind, he was more than happy with the outcome. In fact, he said, "It was perfect." Loki was beginning to develop a knack for giving directors something they didn't know they wanted: a better alternative to their original vision. Hitchcock would be proud.

A brief swell of reprieve fell on the crew. Loki started to chortle to himself, and his energy was transferable—there was a lightness to the atmosphere now, a much more pleasant environment to be in. People started to smile, and it was because of the chuckling corvid.

I love people-watching—the way we connect and interact with each other is fascinating. We give off so many subtle, subconscious signals that tell a much bigger story of what is happening in our daily lives. This film set felt like a giant petri dish, an elaborate experiment into psychological behaviors: how we perceive and allow hierarchy to affect us; how we portray signs of discomfort, unease, and fear; and how we skillfully show dissidence in facial expression and simple body language traits. Then, we add a new variable to the experiment, a game changer for which the control is not prepared. Loki made the whole set a better, more friendly place to be, and all he had to do was be himself. It was that simple. I could feel it in the air—the looks on people's faces, even people's postures, changed from hunched, tightly folded arms to a relaxed, more animated freedom of expression. I wonder if Loki knew the full extent of his impact on his environment.

Was he like his mythological counterpart? Was he able to cast spells and manipulate people? If he could, then Loki the Mischievous, Loki the Sorcerer of Trickery, now needed to be rebranded: "Ravens: the new therapy bird, perfect for mindfulness and inner peace." Can you even imagine!

The filmmaking machine began to crank into gear. The brief mental refreshment was over, and it was back to work. There was one more shot to do, and it was with Loki alone *and* would conclude six highly strung shoot dates. I could tell the crew started to feel the warmth of a definitive end.

The crew set up for the last shot. It was incredibly simple in practice: Loki would need to sit on a pedestal and pose like a victim of a Victorian taxidermist, pausing for a brief moment before flying out of shot. Easy.

The lighting rig had been set in place, and a set of Arri T5 lights shone onto the mark, transfusion provided by a bedsheet on a scaffolding rig. The crew was in position and called for the raven to take his mark. I shimmied Loki onto the pedestal and gave him a stroke on the chest. I turned and began walking off, but I now had a raven on my shoulder. The crew all laughed. I walked him back and put him back on his mark, turned, and made my way off-set. But before I could, there he was on me again, my shadow nuzzled up against my ear. The set floor laughed again but not as hearty—a tinge of "it was funny the first time; let's hurry up and get this done."

In the interest of moving the story along, this happened another four times. I could not get Loki to stay on the perch. It was only twelve feet away, hardly an excuse for him to be worried. So, like before, we went back and tried again. I slowly backed out of frame, keeping eye contact the whole time, and as I was walking backward, I was trying to be conscious not to trip and break my neck. The AD told me I was out of shot, the cameras were rolling, and we all held our breath. The director signaled for me to call him back. I took a cat biscuit out of my pocket and pointed to my shoulder, and…nothing happened. Loki was doing what Loki does best: whatever he damn well wants!

The director was looking over at me, wanting Loki to fly. I felt around in my pocket and pulled out some of the leftover meat from the previous scene. Nothing. Not even a hint of interest. This was not the time to be yourself, Loki; this was the time to fly! Like before, I started to feel the stress of the crew rise, and I began to panic. How much film stock did they have left?! I rummaged deeper in my jacket pockets, desperately trying to find a miracle…*ah!* A whole day-old chick! I was saving this for his final reward, but now it seemed like a better time. I lifted it into the air like a trophy, gazing at its glory. He would surely come to me to claim the nugget of champions. Nope. Nothing.

The daggers were being sharpened, and it wasn't just the director. I could sense the sound recordist's arm aching as he held the boom pole, the camera department worrying about eating up film roll… Everyone was getting fed up. I thought, *okay, there is another solution. I remember seeing the corvid's weakness back in the green room—chocolate biscuits! I'll go and get them.* I made my way to the door, and one of the runners opened it; all the while, the camera was still rolling—he could fly at any second! Loki kept a firm lock on me but was fixed to the plush mahogany post. I was twenty feet away in the corridor and got to the green room while all the time still in eye shot. I grabbed the biscuit and turned around, holding it up like the holy grail. Loki did another rouse. He was more than comfortable where he was.

I stood in another room, separated by a corridor, trying to coach a normally glutenous raven back with every possible treat known, but it was futile. I sighed and looked down in defeat, and in my head, I spoke the words: *"Come on, Loki; don't do this anymore. Let's just go home."*

I raised my head, and I heard it—the clattering of thick, glossy black feathers hurtling toward me—and saw a raven ripping through a stately home, a clumsy black mess of wings and feet scrambling down the corridor, landing square on my chest. He climbed to my shoulder and poked his head down and forward so I could see his eyes. He cawed a soft set of buttery sounds.

"Good boy; you done good. Let's go home."

It was good to get out and off-set. All the crew came and thanked us and were incredibly impressed by Loki. I thought they would have hated it, but to their credit, they praised Loki's good behavior and were smitten with the eventual results. Maybe it was the energy of the room that hindered another one-take wonder, or perhaps he just wanted to be himself, and that was fine with me. At the end of the day, this was filmmaking; no one was dying, and my most important priority was Loki—and not to push him to do something he didn't want to do.

With the birds of prey, it's a much simpler affair. As long as their weight is correct, generally, they will fly on command if they have been cared for and trained properly. But they lack the intellectual depth of a corvid—they aren't stimulated by inanimate objects in the way corvids are, nor do they play up for praise and treats. It was a gentle reminder that Loki comes with a lot more baggage than the other birds, and he needs to be dealt with carefully and with respect.

THIRTEEN
GRAFINN FJÁRSJÓÐUR
BURIED TREASURE

B ack at the ranch, I talked to Sarah-Jane about Loki. Upon hearing his name, and with a fluttering of propelling wing beats, he glided over the flying arena, landing on my shoulder. He craned his neck, locking his little peepers on mine. It was an intense gaze, yet playful and curious at the same time.

It was fascinating to watch him analyze us, scanning over our faces, reading every lip twitch, eye blink, and muscle movement. It got us wondering if there was a deeper level of intelligence at work. Ravens are well known in myths and legends for their violent, unscrupulous ways, often directing their pinpoint attacks at their victim's most vulnerable spot—the eye—regardless of whether it is human or animal. When Loki is on my shoulder and sharking for snacks, I can immediately see that worried look on people's faces. Folks always ask if I'm ever worried that he will peck my eyes out while perching on my shoulder, and with utter honesty, I always say no. Ravens instinctively know this is an extremely sensitive area for their foes and gives them a purposeful target, but it's an extreme course of action. Ravens are known to fight with one another in the wild—sometimes playful, sometimes to defend their territory or food, and to win potential mates —yet they rarely attack each other in the eye. This area is taboo and off-limits, as they innately know the significance and the consequences of launching an attack in that region. Therefore, it is only reserved for their true enemies.

Loki commands the center with his all-seeing eyes: like Sauron, he sees everything, and I really mean everything. If I sit in the office with the door slightly open and attempt to eat my lunch, that damn raven can see me from a good thirty yards away and always demands that he have a piece of whatever I have. It's no surprise that eyes are so very important: a raven will dilate their pupils when they feel threatened and contract when not.

I decided to try another experiment, one that had been originally tested on Jackdaws at the University of Oxford. Out in the flying arena, I asked a member of staff to stare at a piece of food I had put on the fence. The human participant was roughly four feet away. I brought Loki into the makeshift testing zone, and sure enough, he was aware of the food. I placed him directly opposite the food and asked the volunteer to remain fixed on the food. Loki shuffled a few inches toward the food, keeping a watchful eye on our human test subject. Loki was utterly unaware that he was being tested. He looked around and nervously edged closer—I could tell he really wanted the food. He stopped to preen—it was like someone who was lost, pretending *not* to be lost—using his body language as a distraction to hide his true intentions. He gained a bit of confidence and crept ever so closer: he was almost in reach.

I remained at the same point where I had left him, my eyes studying his every move. All I needed was a white lab coat and a clipboard to make it official. He turned his gaze upon me and cawed as if saying, "Is this a trap?" He could definitely sense something was not quite right—perhaps he thought taking the food would result in something bad happening to him. I kept silent, and my human volunteer was doing a great job keeping their gaze locked on the food. Loki did a rouse and continued to look back and forth between the food and our human, locked in a thousand-mile stare. He shuffled his tiny little feet a few steps closer, then slowly craned his neck and swept in, gobbled the food, and rapidly darted back toward me for safety.

We repeated the experiment again, but this time, our human subject looked ninety degrees to the left, eyes well away from the post. I offered up a newly replenished food gift and brought Loki back to the same spot on the fence. He had seen the food well before I even put him down; he was excited at the prospect of getting some more food, and he very much reminded me of myself. He looked at our volunteer and calmly, in one swift motion, strutted over to the food, picked it up, and walked back to me.

Best of three. We repeated the test again, and I asked the volunteer to stare back at the food. The result was the same as the first test. Loki was very cautious; he took his time and made sure the threat percentages were low enough to take the risk. The overall conclusion was that he was completely aware that we were monitoring the food scenario. He was analyzing the potential risk and progressing cautiously in his plan. It was astute, calculated thinking.

I've witnessed this kind of behavior in him before and have heard about wild ravens being canny concerning surveillance from other birds, humans, and predators in the wild. It's worth noting that I tried the exact same experiment again a few weeks later on my own and was surprised to discover that the results were different. Whenever I looked at the food or looked away, Loki would zap over and take the food instantaneously. I was part of his pack, I wasn't a threat anymore, and he felt at total ease with me and his food. I also imagine my being the main food benefactor also had something to do with it. The volunteer in the previous tests was a farm worker who had never worked with Loki or had any social interaction with him, and therefore, he was a complete unknown. What we don't know, we tend to fear or, at the very least, show caution. He is more than capable of filing different people into specific categories depending on his trust in them. This I found quite remarkable and also privileged: it was warming to know he was completely at ease with me, and I got the impression he thought of me like I was part of his family. The feeling was mutual. I saw him as very much a part of mine.

When I fly Loki, we do structured flights to and from perches with activities to stimulate his curiosity and his natural, unique desire for play. After which, he gets some free time where he can wander about the flying arena and have a general mooch about, all under my supervision.

I will sit on the bench, tucked in the furthest corner of the arena, so as not to cramp his style. Loki mills about picking up sticks and stones, flitting about keeping himself occupied and entertained. He will now and again venture over to me, interested in what I'm doing or to show me a stick or a rock. If I fail to pay him any attention, he will tug at my laces or jump on my lap, ready to investigate my pockets for contraband. I will give him a few little treats, which he takes and scuttles away.

Unlike most raptors, or chickens for that matter, corvids do not have a crop. A crop is a pouch that exists in the throat of a bird where they can store food. When a bird is ready and feels safe and comfortable, they will then pass the food over into their stomachs for digestion. So even though Loki doesn't possess the ability to store food in a crop, he does have a throat pouch called a "gular." I feed him treats, but he doesn't eat it in the sense of passing it down into his stomach. Instead, he lurks around me, eyeing up my treat pouch, which he knows is kept in the right-hand pocket of the flying jacket. Any sign or indication of my hand edging toward *that* pocket, and Loki stops in his tracks. His eyes widen with full attention to my movements, and he stands still, waiting for the next move like a showdown. As the hand goes in the pocket, he comes running over, beak open in excitement. He has such a playful, childlike smile, and I can't help but beam from ear to ear every time I see it. From the floor, he gazes up at me: like a dog, he's waiting for his invitation. I slap my knees and call him up to my lap, he bursts with glee and launches up onto me. I tell him he's a good boy—the standard issue of praise from me—I give him a nice scratch on the head and offer him some fresh plump blueberries, which he adores. He's got to have one of those five-a-day!

Loki loves his fruit: we alternate between berries, grapes, apples, and mango. However, Loki can be very much like a child in that he will take whatever is in front of him as long as he is unaware of what else is in the pocket. When he realizes that inside my pocket, I have fruit *and* cat biscuits, the game somewhat changes. I offer him a few biscuits in my cupped hand, which he vacuums up like an anteater, and then I will offer him some fruit. He takes it from me and throws it on the floor with contempt. The fruit no longer cuts it when he knows there is something better available. But don't be mistaken; the discarded food is not wasted—he really does take after me! When Loki knows the good stuff has run out, he will go back to every piece of discarded food and scoop it all up, storing it in his gular, and together, we wander the arena and cache the second-rate snacks for a later date.

The gaggle of magpies, starlings, and jackdaws spy on us from the trees as the king of the corvids stores his perishable bounty. Will they know to leave it be, or do they seize upon it, an easy taking?

The truth is sometimes they do, and sometimes they don't. If Loki buries a sizable quantity of food, the other corvids tend only to recover some of the cache—ones they have actually seen Loki store. They do not search the area in the hope of finding others, of which there are plenty.

The next day, I'll walk around the arena; Loki will fly to me, pushing for fresh food, but as long as I resist the urge to reward him, he will eventually take the hint and get bored of hounding me. He will drop to the ground, walking alongside me, and we will jointly redis-cover his hidden goods from the previous day. Once we've found all of his treasure, we can begin to play some games, and his attention is focused back on me because now I have all the leverage, which of course he wants.

However, in the early days, he was incredibly sneaky when storing food. He would watch everyone's movements as he carried out his reconnaissance mission, and once he had a suitable hiding spot, Loki would keenly keep one eye trained on us as he buried his food. If he saw us watching him, he would do a fake bury, pretend he had stored his loot, and then when he felt the heat was off, he would dig another hole away from prying eyes. I had counted on one occasion Loki deploying five fake buries before ultimately settling on an appropriate place to store his food. To help gain his trust, I used to help him bury food. I thought this would be a good way of bonding and establishing good relations. The allocation and sharing of food is a concept that I believe transcends across all species—it's such a basic instinct, one which can potentially forge iron-like bonds. In the beginning, Loki was very cautious and understandably wary of my intentions. Was I trying to steal his food, or on a deeper level, was I helping him bury the food, knowing that I could ransack the stash on a later occasion? Were cache location points a source of intelligence that Loki could comprehend?

As he dug holes with his strong, stout beak, I could see glimpses of food peeping out from within his mouth—a delightful concoction of cat food, apples, grapes, and raw chicken. I would go and source materials to help cover up the hole: I brought him sticks, leaves, and wads of grass. I would hold one end of the stick, and he would work his way down from the other end, cutting them up into smaller bits. I'd then pass him leaves to finish off his secret stash. It was really fun, and I felt like we were part of a team, working together to contribute toward a common goal. Only he and I knew the location of this secret location, and as I returned him to the comforts of his aviary, he would watch what I would do next with extreme interest. I was very conscious of what I was about to do: Loki had put a lot of faith in me, and as I walked away from the aviary, Loki stood tall and silent, watching with anticipation how the scenario would unfold. I could tell by his posture, and his little agitated hip throws that he was anxious that I might betray him. Would I go back to the location and pillage his food? I looked back at him bolt upright and hawk-eyed: this was a test and one which could possibly undo and potentially hinder our future relationship.

I walked toward the stash and I could sense him nervously twitching behind me, bobbing up and down on his perch, attempting to gather data. I looked down at the location and breezed past it all under the watchful surveillance of our dark lord. Later on in the day, I would get him out and walk him directly to the location. I sat next to him on the grassy mound as he unraveled our previous work, watching him as he rediscovered his food. I resisted the overwhelming urge to interfere, as trying to help him could be conceived as a snatch-and-grab attempt, and that would be the cardinal sin of betrayals! I would then be punished accordingly, and to be honest, I was quite happy with all my digits on each hand. He let out a pleasant cawing call. I think I had passed the test.

The flying arena soon became a corvid's treasure trove: the land had become peppered from Loki burying various items of worth ranging from money—both gifted and stolen—magnets, again both gifted and stolen, to plastic novelty keepsakes, and much to our annoyance, padlocks.

Another anthropomorphic quality Loki demonstrated was how he could read and understand human reactions. For instance, when we entered his aviary to clean his various pieces of makeshift furniture, he had decided one day to escalate his curiosity to a class three felony in the form of burglary. He jumped up onto our large yellow cleaning bucket and peered into the water. His initial confusion was at seeing the frothy white bubbles—he carefully took little bites of the foam, tasting the soapy solution. It wasn't to his liking, but then something caught his beady little eye—the cleaning sponge! Like a kingfisher, he plunged his beak into the sponge, submerging his face into the water.

I shouted, "Loki, no!" and went to grab him, but he was too quick. Off he went out the aviary door into the arena. I chased him, trying to catch him, but as soon as I got near him, he would make a sharp turn, evading my efforts. To the other staff members who came to see what the commotion was about, it must have looked rather comical. A fully grown adult chasing a raven around the flying arena with a soapy sponge in his mouth—the fact he chose not to fly made it even funnier. It was a game to Loki, and he was having immense fun teasing me. I continued to chase him, but I wasn't having any luck, so I thought about it another way. I stopped and sat on the ground, and to tell you the truth, I needed the respite! Loki stopped, too, staring at me roughly ten feet away. I talked to him like an adult, using the art of negotiating to broker a deal whereby we enter a win-win scenario.

"Okay, I'll tell you what. You give me back the sponge so I can clean up the mess you have made in your aviary, and I'll give you...some grapes?"

Loki cocked his head and stumped two short calls, slightly muffled by a beak full of soggy sponge: *Bok, Bok!*"—which I think was raven for, "Show me the money!"

Fair enough. I put my hand into my pocket, and instantly, he reacted, his body shape changing from defense to excitement. He slightly opened up and shook his wings, but he didn't come over just yet. But I reckon I'm on the right track, so I pull out a single grape. He slowly bowled over to me, clutching his stolen sponge; he got within inches of touching distance. I could make a grab for it, but if I missed it, I could burn the deal. Instead, I offered the grape to him, and he inched closer before cawing.

"One not enough, eh?" I pulled out another grape, and in the palm of my hand, I introduced the new, improved offer to the table. He paused briefly, his mind working out the math, pontificating on whether he could max out his gains. Another soft caw. I reached in and grabbed a third grape. "This is the last offer; I'm not going to give you any more," I said firmly. The truth be known, I had no more grapes left anyway. Would he buy into my poker face, or would he call my bluff?

He crept closer to my outstretched palm. He dropped the sponge and gobbled up all three grapes before bouncing off back to his aviary, incredibly pleased with himself. I picked up the sponge and returned to cleaning duties, and I was also slightly pleased with myself. When I arrived back at the aviary, Loki was already sitting on his supervillain perch, looking at me as if to say, "I've been expecting you." So, now we have a raven who can barter, but more worryingly, he knows that he can steal items from us in order to be rewarded. Loki was fast becoming a criminal mastermind!

His journey into the murky crime underworld didn't stop there: he would expand on his new resourceful methods of acquiring food. But the take-home point is that my reaction to him stealing the item would ultimately introduce to him the value of items. What we determine an item to be worth is a very personal decision. What I think has value may seem inconsequential to someone else; one man's biscuit is another raven's feast. Loki understood the sponge was of high value, but what would he do if he could get his beak on something with even more worth?

When we clean out Loki's home, we don't use a sponge. Instead, we use a big, thick scrubbing brush and only one—which has to be on your person at all times. Honestly, it's like dealing with an inmate! Every time we entered with the bucket, he would jump straight onto the rim and poke his beak in, looking for the sponge and the opportunity for leverage. He had gotten used to patterns and our repeat behaviors and had learned our habitual nuances. After we decided that we didn't want to spend all morning chasing him around, Loki sought out new entrepreneurial avenues.

I ushered him off the bucket, telling him it's no good, we've clocked on to your ways—and this said with an air of smugness—so he decided to waddle out of his aviary, which is absolutely fine by me. Suddenly, I heard him flapping about outside his door. He was jumping up and down, trying to get something. I went to investigate, and the little git had managed to free his padlock from the loop by the bolt lock. As he unhooked it like a duck at the fair, I once again screamed, "No, Loki, not the lock!" He then made off with the lock raised high in his mouth, and I'm pretty sure I can remember him making laughing noises as I began my pursuit. This was a little bit more serious than the sponge: we didn't have any spare locks, which would render his aviary completely vulnerable. Sarah-Jane, Emily, and I all circled him in the arena, trying to narrow down his options. However, with guile and finesse, he ducked and dived, avoiding our attempt of capture, shaking us off with ease. We changed tact and offered up grapes in a plea bargain, but it was a deal he was not interested in. My shriek was the indicator that this was a serious piece of loot, one which couldn't be haggled for with mere grapes.

I headed into the office and scavenged the cupboards and fridges to see what I could use as a bartering device. I opened a shelf door, and there it was, illuminating in a golden glory—it was like discovering exactly what was hidden in Marsellus Wallace's briefcase—a fresh pack of chocolate hobnobs. I ripped open the pack with the vigor of a child tearing into a cereal packet, eager to fish out the tiny plastic chokeable toy. To this day, I can still hear the sounds of Emily and Sarah-Jane bumbling around the arena, trying to apprehend our crook. The tables had turned, and for once, it wasn't me being teased and humiliated.

I breezed into the arena and composed myself: it was time for another impromptu experiment. Everyone was calm, even Loki, although a little worn out. He was getting tired but still had the lock firmly gripped in his mouth. I slowly approached him with my hand deep in the right side pocket. He slightly turned his body in case this was a trap, but he was also keen to see what I may produce. I edged to about six feet in proximity, which triggered a strong three-note warning: *"Boh, Boh, Boh!"*

I froze, knowing I had come close enough. I pulled out my hand and showed him three grapes. He rasped at me, a series of caws indicating his displeasure at my pitiful offer. I put the grapes back and slowly pulled out the golden ticket. As he saw the circular disc of chocolatey wonder, he all of a sudden became super interested: the deal was back on! He strode over with that all too familiar cocky swagger. I offered an empty palm ready to catch the trade, and he caws with a purposeful demand. I gave him a cookie, and he released the lock into my hand—we've achieved another win-win situation. His evolution into higher-priced items meant that we would have to be extra careful now: if it wasn't chained down, we knew Loki would attempt to take it.

After removing sponges and making sure his lock was actually locked and theft-proof, Loki did what any good businessman would do: adapt and hustle. This came in the form of going around to each of the closed aviaries and trying every single lock. Of course, it made the birds inside the aviaries throw a fit of hysteria as this giant glossy corvid was trying to—in their eyes—break into their home. He was successful on one occasion and managed to steal a lock belonging to a Barn Owl aviary. I heard the commotion, and my first thought was he was attacking the owl, but it became clear he had been caught stealing, and the occupant was pissed. I hurried over to defuse the situation. Becoming agitated, he furiously attacked the lock, desperately trying to pry it off the door: knowing I was coming meant it was a race against time! Just as I got there, he freed the lock and flew off to safety. I closed my eyes and took a huge breath. I was never going to get anything done if I was constantly trying to retrieve stolen items from an unlawful raven. I searched my pockets for possible trade items, but I had nothing. I looked up to the highest perch where our thief sat, backlit by the morning sun, a blend of beauty and trickery. I told him to stay put as I headed into the office to search for a worthy exchange.

I started to panic: we were out of grapes, and there were no more blueberries. I rushed to the cupboard, eager to acquire my secret weapon, and what did I find? An empty pack of hobnobs! Not only are there none left, but someone left the bloody empty packet in the fridge —something which irritates me immensely. Why do people do that? I had no choice but to try the humble cat biscuit—the staple of his diet and the cuisine responsible for his immaculate sheen and glossy feathering. Maybe that's how I would sell it to him? I trotted outside. He had obeyed and remained perfectly still and proud on top of his perch —king of the hill! I headed over and explained the situation: "...that's all we have; either take it or leave it!" He didn't buy it, and with a shrug of indifference, he flew off toward the bench at the far end of the arena.

Well, that was that. I thought I'd just let him play with it for a bit, and when it was time to bring him home, I'd then go and retrieve it, no big deal, and maybe it was his turn to learn about the efficacy of business and his particular pricing plan.

I finished cleaning up the remains of quail feathers, broken plastic toys, and other innocuous materials from his aviary. It was sparkling clean and equipped with fresh drinking and bathing water. I even provided a few welcome home cat biscuits neatly stacked on his log, like chocolates on a hotel pillow. I called him back, and, to my surprise, he obeyed the first time. He landed in front of me and coolly strutted past me back into his newly cleaned home. Something wasn't quite right: he seemed...*too* cool. He didn't look at me with an air of confidence and self-righteousness, which made me think that something was up. I closed him inside and left him to his complimentary biscuits while I went to find the lock. I searched for a good forty-five minutes, but could I find it? It was nowhere to be seen, bearing in mind the arena is a finite space about thirty feet long by twenty feet wide. I enlisted the help of some of the team who also were unable to find anything. His lordship gazed on from his perch brimming with smugness. He was up to something, and it all felt like we were falling right into his master plan.

Later that evening, Loki was let out for his last meander of the day. The park was empty, which allowed him a complete free reign of the site. He wandered around as he normally does, investigating various items, catching insects, and chasing the odd butterfly or daddy longlegs. I watched as he removed a chip packet from a fresh burial site. He poked his beak in and pulled out the missing lock. *That little…!* He began to walk over to me and then hopped onto my lap, purring at me. Was he taunting me, or was this a second attempt to do a deal?

I had a rummage in my pocket, and all I had was a banana that I had forgotten to eat at lunch. I thought, *What have I got to lose?* So I pulled it out and peeled the skin halfway down. Loki looked at it and seemed utterly confused. He barked, warning me that he was unsure of this weird yellow object—I guess this was the first time he had seen one. I took a bite and ate some in front of him, and he turned his head from side to side.

"Look, it's pretty good. Do you want to try it?" I offered it to him, and he dropped the padlock onto my lap.

He softly took delicate little nibbles, giving it a good taste with his blackened tongue. He seemed to like the sweetness and took a chunk off to examine further on the floor. He mushed it about and slowly ate what he had taken. He returned to my lap, wanting a bit more, but first, he wiped his filthy beak on my legs. Cheers, mate! To be fair, he had learned this particular human behavior from me: I had taught this gesture of sanitation and cleanliness indirectly. When I gave him messy food in the past, I would wipe my fingers on the astroturf perches. Loki watched me do this and began copying me—strange habit, but it's nice to know he takes pride in his appearance!

I stood up, and he scrambled to my shoulder. We walked back together, and all the time, he was taking random nibbles out of the rest of the banana. I set him down and offered him the rest of it. Surprisingly, he politely declined and sat on his log. He had his fill, rendering this particular transaction complete.

———

Loki is a master at reading people, blessed with high-functioning parts of the brain dedicated to facial recognition, higher thought, and problem-solving capabilities. It allows Loki the shrewd ability to read the subtle, almost invisible signs people involuntarily put on show. This was demonstrated perfectly one afternoon, much to the displeasure of one bratty child.

I had just finished an Experience Day with a group of four guests. They spent the afternoon flying a mixture of raptors in our arena, finishing off the afternoon with the fan favorite, taking Dizzy the Barn Owl out into the woodlands, where she flew effortlessly to their gloved hand with ethereal elegance. I offered to show them around the center, and they were all keen to meet one bird in particular after hearing stories of naughtiness. All afternoon, Loki had been mimicking my laugh and doing his utmost to get my attention. The guests found him incredibly endearing and likened him to a jealous child, and that's exactly how he was acting. They asked many questions and couldn't believe most of what I was telling them—not because they thought I was lying, but because the thought of a bird being able to act out human characteristics seemed so far-fetched. I happily offered to show them as a little "Brucie Bonus."

I opened his door, and he sauntered out like the coolest badass you've ever seen—all that was missing was a pair of shades, a cigar, and some funky Nile Rodgers guitar licks. The guests, at this point, are with the general public, standing on the other side of the flying arena. Loki hopped back and forth from the fence, coolly standing next to them as he caught food after a count of three, then returned with a nod of the head back to me to play his piano. He was in full show-off mode: he had been calling out for attention all day, and now he was getting what he wanted.

However, there is always one bad apple that has to spoil the bunch. Now, maybe I'm being a little harsh because, in my eyes, the kid could be no older than eleven, which for me, makes him fair game: at that age, you should know the difference between right and wrong, in my humble opinion.

"Oi, I wanna feed it?" he bellowed in a thick Essex drawl, lunch stains splattered all down his shirt.

Immediately, I formed a dislike. I politely rejected his request with a good reason, not that I needed to justify it. I carried on talking to the guests who loved this little extra, ad-libbed show.

"But I want to have a go!" The child rudely stopped me mid-sentence, which I wasn't best pleased about—the insolence and persistence confirmed my initial disliking—but deep breaths and happy thoughts can often help save the day.

Once again, with a perfect smile and professional tone, I kindly offered a *bonafide* reason why it would be a bad idea for me to let him feed Loki because he may bite.

The kid retorted with impotence. "I'm not scared; it's just a stupid crow."

The boy naively continued to act the fool, relentless in his ignorance. He kept on and on, and even the guests shot him looks of disdain. I tried to ignore him, but it was hard. I looked at Loki, and he read the frustration on my face. In my mind I apologize to him: *You are not a stupid crow*!

Loki looked at the kid and back at me. With that, he jumped on the fence by the guests, walked five paces over to the bothersome child, and nipped him on the forearm. He immediately flew back to my shoulder, grinning like a jester. The guests covered their mouths with shock. They were seconds away from bursting out with laughter, which they quickly suppressed as it was not the right thing to do. Apparently, you can't laugh at a kid being pecked by a raven with impeccable comedic timing, or can you? The kid started to cry and ran off. I walked over to the guests—they couldn't believe it. They were baffled that Loki could tell I was getting pissed off with this kid and that he took it upon himself to resolve the matter for me.

I was secretly appreciative and gave him a little wink. For those parents out there, I did go and check if the little boy was okay. He didn't have as much as a scratch on him; it was more the shock of it that sent him packing. I think we all learned something here.

FOURTEEN
SORG
MOURNING

Affection, warmth, and a desire for company are not common words that are used to describe a raven. We are so used to demonizing, assuming, and buying into the lore of doom and sorrow that the true and more complex, human-like traits are never given a chance to be celebrated.

In September 2014, I returned from my annual jaunt to Norfolk to the news that my mum had been diagnosed with terminal cancer. The doctor's prognosis was three months. Many of us have had the misfortune to deal with the anguish which precedes this most terrible and merciless of diseases. The sense of helplessness, the numbing of all emotional sensations, which, as bizarre as it sounds, is very common. Introverts like myself tend to recoil into ourselves, bottling up thoughts and feelings into a dark cloud of self-despair. Generally, as a species, we are awful at talking things through: there's a tendency to let the mind play havoc and cook up some pretty dark and emotional thoughts. The result eventually leads to the emotional dam bursting. Being away from people and having to talk about the news is a formidable task for me, one which, in the early stages, I totally opted out of. I didn't want to share feelings, and I didn't want human contact. I wanted to wallow and be left alone.

The long, warm September nights began to hand over ownership to the imminent arrival of autumn; biological decay is approaching and is inevitable. One night after work, I decided to swing by the center, sit outside, and bask in the peace and emptiness. It was the ideal chance to contemplate the future and anticipate various macabre scenarios, all of which swirled in a self-deprecating cauldron of misery and pity. The farm was desolate, void of the happiness brought by children and families. Nature called "time," prompting the sun to set and giving the cue for the birds to roost. It was a swift handover as the nocturnal crew readied themselves for the night shift. As I walked into the center, a happy, bouncy raven called out. He wasn't used to me being here this late at night—an unexpected but pleasant surprise. I rudely ignored him and made my way over to a bench near the flying arena.

I'd been keeping emotions on lockdown, pretending to immerse myself in society as if nothing was wrong or changing. It was fraudulent, but so far, people bought it. They were none the wiser to my situation. It's extremely hard and emotionally exhausting to wear the mask of illusion; hence, escaping to the valley to let me be whatever I need to be at that time, away from others in the safety of my own solitude. Loki was at the front of his aviary, just looking over at me, head cocking side to side, trying to attract my gaze and attention. He bounced along his perch like an excited kid. However, he didn't call out, which was very unlike him.

I had a break in my thoughts of worry and sorrow and reawakened back to the present. I headed over and let him out of his aviary—I don't know why I did. I had no food on me. It felt like a subconscious decision and that I wasn't fully in control. I turned and headed back to the bench. Loki walked by my side and chaperoned me to the bench, his little bum waggling with ignorant joy. We sat together in silence, admiring the variety of hues that shifted in the turning sky. He preened his beautiful, pearlescent feathers—purples and greens all shimmer in the dim glow of the burning sunset. He hopped off the bench to have a wander, every now and again turning back to check if I was still there watching him, like a child learning to ride a bike in front of their parents.

I watched him with distance, contemplating what would loom in the foreboding months. It was the first time I had given myself a chance to fully comprehend the news. My mum had told me at our family home, the place I had grown up in. She sat me down; my younger sister Sophie and my dad were both present. They had a weary look drawn across their faces, for they already knew.

"Look, it's not good news, and we didn't want to tell you when you were on holiday, but I have lung cancer. It's already at stage three, and they have found it in my lymph nodes."

There was a pause, and I looked at my dad, whose head was sunken, eyes on the floor, trying to hold back his pain. My sister had gone from weary to heavy streams of tears, both doing their best to keep the silence.

My initial reaction was of immediate acceptance. "Okay, so how do we deal with this? What's the plan?" There was no plan; it was too early for a plan, and they were all internalizing the news. This kind of thing happens to other people, not to us. I remained stone-cold and began to draw up plans to get treatment sorted, but their feeling of defeat was hanging in all of their hearts.

It's a known fact that ravens mourn their loved ones just like we do. I wonder if Loki would mourn me if I were to leave and never return. *Did he love me? Can corvids love?*

After a while, the light began to fade. I had never let him out for this long with such limited light, but Loki seemed happy enough, not wanting to drift too far from my side. He stood proudly on top of his perch, looking down at me. I looked up and smiled, grateful for the tranquil time we had spent together, enjoying being outside and breathing fresh, sympathetic air without a crowd to fool. He dropped to the floor, waddled over to me, and stared deeply into my eyes. I sighed and asked if he wanted to come up.

"Come on then, mate; up you get!" And just like a dog, he jumped at the chance. He stood on my lap, gently stretched out, and grabbed the red tassel that tightened my hoodie. He waggled his head, holding the tassel in his beak, making a dainty collection of calls, noises I'd never heard before. I smiled, my eyes beginning to well up. I tugged on the tassel, Loki tugged back, and we began to play. Eventually, he let go. I looked toward the almost-set sun and was whipped back into the present. A huge wave of sadness washed over me, and the numbness began to wear off: I began to feel again, and it hurt. A rogue tear escaped down my cheek, which turned into a steady, flowing stream.

What happened next wanted me to break out into a full-blown cryfest: my impenetrable dam was about to burst. Loki saw and recognized my sadness. He crouched down on my lap and rolled onto his back, legs stretched out to the sky. I instinctively rubbed his belly like a cat, and he rolled from side to side, making more of those cute noises, his little legs paddling in the air. This was such bizarre behavior. I'd never witnessed anything like this, especially with Loki. I burst out laughing, and the tears' escape plan ramped up. This was the first and last time Loki had ever exhibited this behavior. It's as if Loki knew no one else would ever believe me if I told them, that way keeping up his hard-earned street cred and bad boy persona intact. However, you now know. We can share this little secret together, and that way, we all win. Loki, none the wiser, and the rest of us can love these creatures just a little bit more.

Twilight had set in, and darkness was well on his way. The creatures of the night were beginning to stir, and I could just about make out bats darting overhead. Unfortunately for me, the belly rubs would need to end, and Loki would be returned home. Loki sat up and did a huge rouse—he knew it was home time. I jumped up and began to walk toward his aviary. I turned to see if he was following, and a black cloud of feathers landed on my shoulder: this black cloud wasn't the normal metaphor for sadness but rather a vessel for joy and temporary relief. He sat on my shoulder, reached down to grab my red tassel, and softly tugged on it until we arrived at his place. I walked in, and before he hopped onto his branch, he dropped the tassel and gently wiped a very clean beak across my neck. I gave him a good head scratch and thanked him for being my support and my friend. I offered him a tidbit and left for the evening.

The drive home allowed my autopilot to kick in, and subsequently, my subconscious took complete control. Like my car, my mind sent me twisting down a lane of uncontrollable thoughts—some pertinent to my family's situation, others completely mundane and inconsequential. However, my train of thought—as it always does—eventually arrived back at Loki. Suddenly, my grip on reality took hold of the wheel, and conscious decision-making was once again activated. The question I pondered was: how was Loki able to tell I wasn't myself? And even more perplexing was that, by using this information, he was able to change his behavior and act upon it—why? Was it to make me feel better? *What exactly was I to him?*

I've had dogs and cats all my life, and I'm well accustomed to dogs picking up on subtle subconscious vibes and energies that we humans give off, but a bird? Some experts claim that dogs simply mirror our energy, which portrays an empathetic response, but this is something different. I know some people have very close connections with parrots and cockatoos, but with ravens, the so-called harbinger of doom, responsible for all of the world's evil? Was that even possible? Okay, that might be an overstatement playing on the cliché, but the zeitgeist is that these birds come with a dark past. If ravens could comprehend the law and work the judicial system, they would be suing mankind for damages due to libel and character defamation.

I often think back to that evening spent with Loki, and it still gives me goosebumps, a deep feeling of warmth and inter-species connection. I often tell visitors to the center this story, and they all have the same reaction: they can't believe a raven could possess such an ability. But I wholeheartedly believe it's true: it's an experience I'll never forget. This is one of the main reasons for writing this book, and when given a chance, I will gush about Loki, often bombarding anyone who will give me the time of day to share all of my Loki stories because this bird has so much to show us and there undoubtedly, more like him. I want people to know and be aware of this beautiful, unknown side of his story.

———

Growing up was an amazing time for me. I always felt loved and safe at home, and for that, I am truly grateful to my family. My sister is eight years younger than me, and like most older brothers, even though I cared for her, I gave her a really tough time growing up. We never really got along, and I think most of that friction was my fault. She wanted me to like her so much, but I would never reciprocate. I guess that's what being a teenager is all about—rebelling and going against the grain—or I was just a bit of a dick. We are very similar and very different, and I think on a bizarre level, I pushed her away because she reminded me of myself—the parts I didn't necessarily like. Looking back, the relationship was very similar to when I first got Loki. I wanted him to like me. I wanted it so badly, and all I got was aggression and push-backs. I know how that felt, and I now understand how Sophie must have felt. It took an unwanted corvid for me to understand this cruel, harsh lesson, and for that, I'm eternally grateful to him. It's helped to mend our relationship. Both my sister and I are very different—dare I say it, she's actually pretty cool.

My mum and I are also very similar and incredibly different. This juxtaposition of opposing characteristic dichotomies meant we clashed on many occasions. We are both stubborn and would have quite spectacular rows, opting to save face and not buckle. We could draw out an argument or silence for weeks. A fiery red-haired Scot living in England, she always saw herself as the underdog and always played the part expertly well. She had a soft spot for Loki—something about his rebellious and rascal nature was endearing to her. She would always ask when I went to visit her in the hospital how he was getting on, and she found much amusement in his villainous acts of defiance. I would show her video clips and pictures of him playing, feeding, and enjoying his life.

She would always say, "When I get a bit better, I want to come and meet him!"

Even from afar, he was able to endear himself to people.

Unfortunately, she never did get the chance to meet him and lost her fight to cancer on November 13, 2017. She made good on her promise to last more than the initial three months—she even managed to be at my wedding—but she couldn't make it to witness Loki in the flesh. It's a shame because I know she would have loved him even more, and like birds of a feather, I reckon he would have liked her too.

In the initial days of the aftermath, I experienced a variety of emotions available on the spectrum: overwhelming sadness, immense pain, anger, frustration, and then nothing. For weeks, I drifted through life like a ghost, void of emotion and mute to the world. There is one place I would always go to, though. Being me and unable to properly express emotions meant talking to people was a skill I never properly learned—a problem most men of my generation and older are plagued by, which is only now starting to be addressed. For most, the inability to properly deal with the noise of every emotional state slamming together in your head and heart can lead people to dark and difficult places. Fortunately, I did have a release, a valve that not just anyone could open.

It's at these times I feel really blessed to have the opportunity to spend my time with such amazing people and animals. The staff were incredibly warm to my situation, and as usual, I brushed off any sign of pain and suffering. To them, it looked like it was just another day for me. I wore the mask well. After all, I had spent my entire life perfecting it.

Loki, on the other hand, could sense otherwise. Maybe the staff did, too, but as Brits do, they didn't press or extend any further questions; they just let me be. Loki wasn't so "British" in that respect. He spoke his mind, and there was never any subtlety.

The first time I saw him after my mum had passed, he knew where I was emotionally, like the time when I learned of the news. His actions and energy toward me were different; they were affectionate, warm, and full of knowing what it's like to be alone. This cast-off, a sometimes malevolent creature who scared and wounded many but also captivated others from afar, was able to offer so much only so few could. Despite the physical trauma, the emotional stress, and the differences in species, love is love. We all have souls, and we must ensure that the animals we share this planet with are seen as more than just animals. They are sentient beings with capabilities far beyond the credit we give them. For us to progress as a species, we would do well to look to the animal kingdom for wisdom—but look hard beyond the superficial. I believe that Gandhi was right: the way we treat animals will, in the end, reflect what we are as a species. In the future, I hope we can look back and realize that how we see and treat animals is not how we want to be remembered. I've learned so much compassion from a "horrible-looking crow." I've learned about forgiveness, and I've learned that with time and love, you can fix most emotional problems. I've learned that trust comes in various forms, but ultimately, it's how we build strong, solid bonds. I wish my mum were here today to see what Loki has become. I know she would be proud of us both.

FIFTEEN
VIÐFANGSEFNIÐ OG FRÆÐIMAÐURINN
THE SUBJECT AND THE SCHOLAR

n January of 2017, Sarah-Jane's mum, Julie, read an article in *The Telegraph* written by Senior Feature Writer Joe Shute. The article mentioned he was writing a book on ravens. Julie saved the article and passed it over to us, as he was looking to learn more about ravens, and in particular, captive-bred ones. We contacted Joe on Twitter. I let him know about our Loki and offered him an open invite should he ever want to come and visit and see him. To our surprise, Joe responded very quickly; he was very keen to come see our boy.

Joe and his wife, Elizabeth, an extremely talented artist and illustrator, made the journey up to us on a fresh and crisp January morning. The farm had closed for the winter: the tranquil, cobbled pathways were silent, the children at home wrapped up and warm. It was just the custodians of the farm who inhabited our calm and serene spot in the Lee Valley.

Sarah-Jane, Emily, and I met our two guests and showed them around our center, introducing them to our raptors. Joe, a very keen and very knowledgeable bird enthusiast, settled down in our office with a warm tea and began to delve into Loki's story. Joe was very interested in Loki's backstory, and I was more than happy to regale.

The scratching sound of pen etching on pulp helped to bridge the silence as I paused for air. Joe detailed all of my musings in a small black leather notebook—it was good to know the art of good old-fashioned journalism still exists—he scribbled at a great tempo, asking plenty of probing questions and keeping up with my excitement to document all of Loki's colorful mannerisms. I have a lot to tell him but even more to show.

As I talked to Joe, Loki called out. He couldn't see us, but he knew I was close. Joe was acute to Loki's vocalization, confessing to not having heard this kind of call before. He was very keen to learn more and asked me what I thought it meant. I told him that Loki was getting impatient and wanted attention! After a thorough and lengthy portrayal of Loki's past and his personality, Joe was eager to go and meet him. I led them both through the barn past the owls, who each called out with their own unique and distinct calls—from siren-like, ear-piercing cries of Freya, the snowy owl, to the deep-bellowing hoot of Logan, the eagle owl. We reached the end of the line. Loki glided from the back up to his perch by the front of the door. Joe's eyes beamed. I could tell he loved these birds, which was a mutual feeling. Loki poked his long, scythe-like beak through the gaps in the enclosure. I stroked him on the cere and asked if he was going to behave today. It was more of a "soft demand" rather than an optional request.

I walked into the aviary carrying his wooden box peppered with dings and chips, the pen-inscribed "Loki's Box" starting to fade. He bounced around with excitement, like a little boy who has been told to wait until he can play with his new toy. I rigged the box up and let Loki show off to his observing audience. He was in a very sprightly mood, making lots of playful sounds and performing many a rouse. It's like a rehearsed act. He followed me around his aviary, sticking tight and constantly watching my every move. Joe continued to ask questions while Elizabeth, with guile and speed, sketched Loki in poetic action.

I didn't give him too much food, as he needed to be weighed. I invited him onto my arm and walked him to the scales. As the space between us and these strangers is constricted due to the narrow barn corridor, I sensed Loki's anxiety kick in. He watched Joe and Elizabeth closely as they followed behind. His slight movements in his legs suggested he wasn't quite sure of our guests yet, so I kept him pressed against my chest, one hand hugging his back, my finger softly stroking his nape.

We arrived at the weighing station, and I hit the *on* button. Loki knew the drill and immediately hopped on, but the scales didn't have time to register. I politely asked him to step back off and back onto my hand with a courteous "please" at the end. He responded with a delicate affirmation and gently stepped back onto my ungloved arm.

Joe and Elizabeth commented on how it was like he understood what I was saying and verbally communicated back. They also inquired if his talons hurt on my skin.

Thankfully, unlike the raptors, Loki's weapon isn't his feet. Birds of prey have tremendous crushing power, which defines them: their ratchet-locking-foot system binds onto their unsuspecting victims, rendering them powerless to escape. The scratches on my arm were superficial, no more damaging than a gentle scratch from a dog. I explained how he is so much calmer and at ease without the presence of a leather gauntlet, so we have this relationship that conforms with his established comfort zone.

Two pounds and seven ounces. We are still old money when it comes to metric and imperial, which roughly translates to just over one kilo, or for you *Bakeoff* fans, a bag of granulated sugar. He was slightly more abundant than usual, and that was due to the cold weather. We like to keep the birds slightly heavier as the cold temperatures accelerate their metabolic process, which in some cases can mean the difference between surviving a frost or not. Joe immediately asked if Loki's heavier weight was indeed for this reason. It was refreshing to know he was knowledgeable and to be able to affirm his assumption.

This small piece of the puzzle sat amongst all the other loose but connecting bits in the box, concluding the reasoning as to why having a bird in captivity is not a cruel practice. Folks struggle to comprehend how merciless and unforgiving nature is. Some people can't, and sometimes, they outright refuse to believe us when we say it's not fun being "free" in the wild. We explain that our bird's menu is richly rotated between chicken, rabbit, mice, rats, goose, and duck, providing them with only the best food—the kind of food wild birds could only dream of having, not just now and again as a rare treat, but for every single meal.

We inform our guests that every other day, all the birds receive aloe vera and propolis treatments massaged into their feet to keep them nice and supple. We even treat grazes and cuts with manuka honey due to the fact that it is a great natural antiseptic, but it all serves a dual purpose: its high viscosity helps to provide a protective barrier to prevent infection. However, as you may or may not know, manuka honey is far from cheap!

We often explain how these birds never need to worry about finding a nest or defending themselves from bigger, more aggressive predators. We highlight that their homes are fully protected, allowing them to sleep easily without fear of their offspring being hunted in the dead of night and blissfully heated by special heat lamps. And even then, after watching with their own eyes the birds flying free and returning to us willingly, some people still question the ethics of what we do. Sometimes, we feel it's a losing battle, a further indicator of how detached we as a species have become from nature—the ignorance plunged deeper, making the public defensive with borderline-aggressive questioning as we struggle to educate and undo this anthropomorphizing theology.

But for every disgruntled "I'm not having any of it; they should be free" member of the public, we unearth a gem—those people willing to see it from another side, people willing to use science, logic, and rationale. More importantly, we strive to be a catalyst, the spark you can ignite in kids who learn to understand and respect wildlife, who can grow up to help try to conserve what many of us are unknowingly destroying. That is the hope, and that is why we persevere.

I explained to Joe we were going to take Loki into a room he had never been in before—one used for kids' birthday parties. The thought of enduring one of those fills me with dread. Alas, it was empty and peaceful. I told Joe because Loki's behavior would potentially be somewhat different. In his home, he is rebellious and confident, but how would he react to a small group of strangers in an unfamiliar surrounding?

We walked down to the room named "Dobby's Tack Room"—ironically, there wasn't one single piece of equine paraphernalia in the entire room. All of the time, I was holding Loki close to my chest, a slight reluctance to let him go. I placated his worries by scratching his head with two fingers, gently swirling in a clockwise rotation. He looked up at me with sweet vulnerability in his eyes. We huddled into the cold, brassy room, our voices pinging off the hard walls, the lack of soft furnishing reverberating every sound, however slight. Loki's acute senses dashed from side to side as he experienced this new echo effect shimmering in the long rectangular room.

I set him down, and we took up a position at the opposite end of the room. Loki swaggered around, keeping a constant eye on us as he headed to the back wall—it had a meadow scene painted all along it. Loki investigated the painted grass, lightly probing. I put my hand in my pocket, and immediately, he noticed and came bounding over, shaking his booty with his beak open and smiling. Everyone laughed at his comical waddle. I gave him a few dried mealworms: these are definitely on par with cat biscuits in the food hierarchy. He headed off back to the far end of the room and investigated a bank of brown metal lockers. He began evaluating its food storage capabilities and whether or not there were any shiny collectibles for him to loot. With his beak, he cautiously opened all the unlocked doors and pulled out any materials inside that could possibly be of use at a later date.

I called him back by name, to which he duly agreed. Elizabeth was to the side of me, accurately sketching down his playful mannerisms. Out of my back jacket compartment, I revealed a rather crass, homemade Kerplunk knockoff that I made a few months back, comprising of a liter Coke bottle and a whole bunch of wooden kebab skewers pierced into the fuselage-shaped toy. Joe and Elizabeth smiled: they appreciated its function over its style. It was ready-loaded with a day-old chick in the top. Loki hopped up onto my lap, and Joe instinctively pulled out his phone. Loki, with ease and supreme dexterity, removed all the sticks individually, claiming his reward, which he then took and scuttled off with his back toward the lockers.

"Thirty-nine seconds," Joe timed it and made a note in his book.

We chatted for a bit longer while we watched Loki explore the room and tend to himself. I elaborated more on how our relationship developed in the early days. The conversation eventually made a turn toward Emily. Joe asked how Loki behaves with her, intrigued to get perhaps a less biased appraisal.

Emily explained in detail about their one-sided relationship and jokingly remarked, "I just want to be his friend, but he's always so mean to me. I've never done anything to hurt him."

I jolted, reminded of my relationship with my sister Sophie. Emily demonstrated to Joe by calling out Loki's name. He took little notice, more interested in storing food in the vertex of the room, using materials from the locker to place on top of the food. She then approached him, and he barked a burst of direct warning shots—it was aggressive and suggestive that he would escalate the matter further if she persisted in her course.

She turned back to us: "See!"

Emily began to walk back to us, at which point Loki's dark side was activated. He sensed an opportunity as Emily's guard was down, her back toward him. He locked onto her and made a beeline straight toward her. He petulantly dropped a *blitzkrieg* of pecks at the back of her ankles, which made her jump. He switched it up, grabbing her shoelace, tugging with a sibling-like bitterness, and spewing grunting sounds expressing his want to annoy and hurt her.

Loki sees Emily as a sister—older or younger, I'm not too sure—but what is apparent is their individual position within a social hierarchy. Through tribalistic dominance and violent acts, Loki has established his own idea of where he sits within the chain. What is strange is his stubbornness to change his ways and let Emily into his circle of friendship. Emily is right: she hasn't done anything to deserve the constant abuse and intimidation Loki sees fit to bestow on her. Does he see her as some kind of threat? I can't see how. She plies him with food, and she sees him on a much more regular basis than I do. He was beastly to me in the beginning—he's put me in the hospital; he's torn my arms, legs, and ears to shreds; he even pretty much destroyed a pair of tough and rugged walking boots while I was wearing them so he could find a weakness and inflict as much pain as possible. But eventually, he let me in. Why wouldn't he accommodate Emily? Maybe because I was able to suck up his reign of terror, push through his painful, torturous outbursts? I do feel sorry for her, as she tried so hard, but his will is strong as iron, and he is determined to uphold the elevated status he has carved out for himself.

Emily laughed off Loki's barrage of abuse, proving her point, but deep down, I know how painful those beak blows to the ankle really are. She's a tough cookie, our Emily.

Joe asked if Loki would play with his pen. I nervously called him to my lap. I sensed he may now be in one of *those* moods—the confidence had grown in him. I was very mindful that the aura I put out into the room needed to be one of confidence and control. Loki took a treat from my outstretched hand, and Joe, who was sitting next to me, offered his pen to Loki. Removing the lid would carve a route to another treat. Loki immediately tried and failed: it was on pretty tight. His response was cranky as he nipped Joe on the hand. It was a warning shot—an indicator of his frustration at not being able to win and get what he wanted. *Little brat.* I told him off with a stern tonal put-down, a reflection of Loki's impatient, childlike mindset. Joe loosened the lid and prompted a rematch. This time, Loki was able to pry the lid off. He gained a gentle applause and was compensated for his part in the game.

Joe and Elizabeth began to wind up their visit with us, and I managed to catch a glimpse of some of Elizabeth's drawings—one of Loki on my lap, taking a biscuit from my hand. It captured him and the moment beautifully. I found the whole day incredibly invigorating, being able to share Loki's story with other corvid fans.

Joe noticed that, over the course of the morning, Loki's vocal communications varied between who they were directed at. For me, they were playful, tactful, and attention seeking; for Sarah-Jane, soft, warm, and lower in volume; for Emily, dark and factitious. I mentioned that on the occasions when we are forced to pull a late one in the office, we hear Loki trying to join in our conversations by mimicking human-like sounds—it's incredible as it is eerie. At times, he produces sounds that have convinced us there are two adult males in the center having a conversation with each other, and as always, never wanting to be left out, he even mimics lambs being born on Easter!

Joe was particularly interested in raven vocalizations which was one of the main reasons why he came to meet Loki. I offered to set up some recording equipment and send him the results. It never occurred to me to do this before, probably because I hear him all the time calling out for food, playtime, or just to be part of the conversation.

Being a filmmaker, I have a plethora of recording equipment, so I took a portable field recorder and set up an X-Y mic configuration outside of his aviary and set the device to record overnight. The next day, I came in to rip the recording from the SD card and load up the audio. I imported the file and played the first couple of seconds, which included me talking to Loki (the sound of my voice, ouch!). More disturbing than the pitch I resonated at was that the waveform on my editing timeline—the audio signal captured—looked completely flat. The batteries must have run out. I zoomed into the timeline and boosted the decibel output, and to my relief, there was a recording. The recording was ten hours long, and there was something incredible. It was completely silent. The chatterbox only talks when he is endowed with an audience that is in earshot.

I spoke to Joe and sent him the results. He, too, was equally surprised. If you think about it logically, it makes perfect sense. Loki will only vocalize when his friends and family are near him, just like most humans. There really is no real benefit to being vocal if you don't have a fanbase that will listen.

A few months after Joe and Elizabeth's visit, Joe got in contact to thank us for our time and to ask if we would grant permission to let him write a chapter on Loki in his book. We were more than happy to do so, and a year later, when the book was due for release, *The Telegraph,* planning on writing a piece on Joe's book, asked if they, too, could come down and meet Loki and take the opportunity to get some editorial photos. We were told that they found Loki's story the most compelling from Joe's account and wanted to publicize Joe's book by doing a piece on Loki. We set up a date, and almost a year to the day when Joe visited, a crack team of journalists and photographers descended onto our little shack in the valley to come and see what all the fuss was about.

"I hear he plays the piano?" said the chief editor over her glasses, a very elegant, powerful, and professional lady who I imagined had worked in the industry for a number of years and didn't take any nonsense from anybody.

"He certainly does; would you like to see?"

She warmed up instantly and suggested we set up his rig for the photoshoot.

I escorted the photography team, who brought in flight case after flight case of equipment. I was quite surprised at how much equipment they intended to use. We set up in the same room where Joe and Elizabeth witnessed Loki in action: this would be only his second time in there, and it was still without horse equipment. Once they were ready, I bounced off to collect Loki and bring him to the set.

A matte, royal blue paper background was erected, a camera and a 32-inch monitoring screen were rigged so they could instantly see the images being taken. As I walked into the room, all I could hear was the sound of jaws hitting the floor. The photographer was a well-respected wildlife photographer who boasted many awards and credits to his name and was utterly blown away by everything about Loki.

"Wow, he is incredible!"

He armed his camera and fired off a few rounds of images, which flashed on the screen behind him. Loki was totally taken aback by everything and looked a little off-color. His silence was a dead giveaway that he was unsure of the environment. Was it the people, the equipment, or the fact the room he knew had been completely transformed into a makeshift photography studio?

I walked over to the table on which lay the blue paper roll. The photographer fired away a few test shots and asked his assistant to modify the flash settings to a more favorable light. Loki wasn't entirely sure or confident of the situation. He kept his eyes on me, and his body suggested he was about to fly back to me any second. *Snap!* The flash fired, and he made up his mind. Nope! He didn't like that. He leaped into my chest and scurried to safety on my shoulder, panting.

I suggested we just give him a few minutes to calm down and relax. I put him back on the table and gave him a few words of encouragement followed by a little throat tickle. After a few minutes, they began to snap away. He stayed on the roll but still wasn't a hundred percent at ease. I stopped the shot briefly and headed over to him. He eagerly met me halfway and landed on my forearm.

I spent a few minutes talking to the crew and the editor, telling them all about him. It was a way I could get Loki used to all the new faces and let him see all the new equipment. I suggested we get out his party piece, the Fisher-Price xylophone! Like kids, the crew all beamed with anticipation. I put it on the table, and Loki completely ignored it. In fact, he went one better and dropped a large, acrid shit on the table. Everyone laughed, but I was horrified. Like an embarrassed parent, I offered to clean up my child's inappropriate accident. The crew was fine about it, but Loki could sense my flustered faffing and let out a huge belly laugh: *"Ho ho ho ho!"*

My god, did that send the whole room into hysterics. Once again, everyone got a kick out of my embarrassment caused by Loki. He found it immensely amusing, and so did everyone else. He then started to play his piano without command. Photos were fired left, right, and center. Loki bashed out his tune with aplomb, and he even started to show off a little, blooming his beautiful crest, drawing *"ahhs"* from the audience. He played right into the camera, showing every possible angle.

The flash stopped firing, and I asked if they had got some nice shots. They signaled over to us both to come and see for ourselves— they had!

They were smitten with Loki and the shots. They couldn't have asked for a better model and were surprised at how much like a human he was—how he needed time to warm up, but when he was warm, he was cooking!

A few months later, I got a phone call from Julie, who was excited to tell me that Loki was in the paper. I asked if she could save me a copy so I could have a look. A few days later, Julie came up to the center to help clean out the place. She always does such a good job, even painting the whole office for us, so it's always a treat to have her at HQ. In her hand, she was carrying a large frame, roughly A1 in size. She handed me the frame, and I was totally blown away. There he was, my little golden boy. The newspaper had done a huge spread on him, using extracts from Joe's book and the wonderful photos taken weeks before. It further immortalized him in both a book and in the national press. The cost to have that amount of real estate in a national broadsheet would have cost a fortune, but there he was, the cheeky boy!

A week later, I returned to the center and saw the team had put the frame containing the article up on the wall by the weighing scales. Only the staff could really see it, and I wasn't having that, so I surreptitiously moved it into the main room, where all the Experience Day guests were greeted. I was milling about, and I heard a voice: "Look who has already moved the Loki article!" I walked into the guest room to see Emily and Sarah-Jane staring at the frame on the wall. They, with jest, turned their knowing look to me, but *I don't care* was written all across my face. I wanted everyone to see it because I was super proud.

———

One thing that bothered me was that, due to work commitments, some weeks I could only be at the center on the weekend, and there were definitely times when I yearned to not be at my computer but instead be playing with a xylophone in the field with a corvid. In March 2017, I was commissioned to film a documentary in Las Vegas and Los Angeles. After being out for a few weeks, I returned to the UK for a grand total of twelve hours before I got in my car and drove to Belgium, which started a ten-day-long tour of Europe with my band. It was a mentally and physically exhausting month. I longed for some downtime, some peace and tranquility. I often thought about sitting on the bench in the flying arena, watching the sun go down. The last day of the tour finally came. We finished off by playing in Gothenburg's legendary venue, "Sticky Fingers," and we ended the tour on a massive high, playing to a packed crowd. However, I was more than ready to swap hotels for home. What faced us was a grueling sixteen-hour drive home from Sweden. We did it in one hit. Nervous about missing our scheduled ferry time to cross the English Channel, we consumed all kinds of stimulants to make sure we made it back home on schedule. I walked in the front door at 9:30 am. After all the driving, you would think I would be tired, but I somehow induced a second wind, probably from the excessive intake of various caffeine-based products.

Sarah-Jane and Emily were back at Hedingham Castle, the first one of the year, which is always a big and eagerly anticipated event. Over the bank holiday, the castle admits thousands of revelers who come to jeer the pantomime-esque Black Knight while cheering when he is displaced from his horse. It's a great event, with storytelling, artisan food stalls, and our now-famous falconry show.

With my eyes wide open and my brain in full thought mode, I knew that sleep would never be an option, so I got back in the car and drove to Suffolk. It's just over an hour's journey, and I fondly recollected my recent travels, existing in a partially conscious state. Playing a sold-out show in Sweden only hours ago to being shot at in the Nevada desert while filming a documentary on murder—it was a whirlwind of multiple lives being crammed into a short and intense experience, and for a while, I didn't really know who I was. That's the good thing about long, silent drives: it gave me the perfect opportunity, even with a slightly weary head, to realign my focus to the here and now and to my current reality.

Normally, the bank holidays are a shoo-in for rain, and yet the plucky British public continues to head out into it nonetheless. "It's a designated holiday! We *will* overcome the weather. There's no such thing as bad weather, only unsuitable clothing." However, on this rare and welcome occasion, it was warm and dry. The distinct smell of spring churned around the castle grounds, the grass a fertile green, hot pokers in bloom smiles all around. I made my way up the long, narrow drive to the castle, passing kids flailing replica swords, dueling with their siblings, and being told off by their parents—I don't envy them.

The large Norman Keep imposing over me, riddled with secrets and bloodshed but now a family tourist attraction, grew larger as I approached. I heard Sarah-Jane's voice from afar—the afternoon flying show had started. I trundled over to catch the end. Emily was flying the Lanner Falcon, Blue. He whipped around the keep, driving over the audience. Emily passed the lure, which he missed by inches. He bolted straight for the audience and, at the last second, climbed vertically over their heads. Sounds of excitement and awe rippled through the thousand-strong crowd, all seated in a gigantic box configuration. Sarah-Jane gave the cue for Emily to wrap up the show.

Emily loudly shouted out the command, "Ho!"

Blue stopped his ascent and circled back toward the arena. Emily flung the lure pad high into the sky, which Blue expertly caught. The ratchet system in his feet locked, and he brought the leather pad to the ground, followed by a huge round of applause.

Emily and Sarah-Jane left the flying arena carrying all the birds inside their carry boxes. I met them halfway to help out, and they were very surprised to see me. "I thought you were in Sweden?" Emily said.

"Well, I was a few hours ago." I quickly moved on to more pressing issues and asked if they used Loki, and before they could respond, from inside one of the boxes, an almighty racket went off. He heard my voice and began thrashing about inside his box, which I presumed was with excitement. I smiled and took *that* specific box off of Emily. We got back to the falconry camp, and already a huge line of people had formed. Folk who had watched the show wanted to come and see the birds up close.

I set the box containing the over-excited raven down, and I grabbed his bright yellow leash protruding from a small hole in the front of the box's door. I took a deep breath and unlocked the door. The clicking sound of the switch lock signaled to Loki the door was free, and before I could open the door, he burst out, landing on my lap. He knocked me off balance, and I stumbled onto my arse. My absolute main prerogative right now was to keep my grip on that leash: that was all that I could think of.

If I had let go of the leash, it wouldn't have been the end of the world because Loki smothered me with hugs. It's very bizarre to witness, I imagine. You get hugged by people, dogs, and even some cats, but a raven? He clung to my t-shirt with his little feet, his wings spread across my chest. All of a sudden, I see the queue of people all watching, phones out, filming the omen of death, cuddling his human. I put my arm under his legs, and he relinquished his grip on my t-shirt, transferring it onto my hand. However, he grabbed my collar with his beak and shook his head playfully with a mouthful of cotton, making cute little noises and expressing his happiness to see me. I used my other arm to cuddle him back, reciprocating my happiness to see him. He let go and wiped his beak sideways across my shoulder. It had only been a few weeks, but it was clear for all to see he had missed me. Have you ever heard of a bird missing someone?

I turned to our newly formed, spontaneous audience, and I picked out one face from the crowd—a lady who had a tear running down her face. I headed over to her with Loki on my arm. I asked if she was okay. My initial and perhaps paranoid defense mechanism was ready to reel off the "he's okay; no, he's not trying to escape" spiel. But it wasn't a tear of anger or distress but of pure happiness and joy.

The lady introduced herself as Jane and said she had heard about Loki from her granddaughter, who had previously had an Experience Day at the center. She was in her mid to late sixties, immaculately dressed in a lovely elegant burgundy wool coat: it screamed class and elegance. She went to speak but was caught, unable to get her words out, choking on raw emotion. Jane put her hand to her mouth, breathed, and composed herself.

She explained that her daughter had done one of Coda's Experience Days and was briefly introduced to a raven there. Jane went on to explain how it was one of her lifelong dreams to see one up close—she was obsessed with them and often painted and made abstract pottery sculptures of ravens and other corvids in her studio.

For years, they had tried to find a place that had one that the public could see, barring the ravens at the Tower of London. They eventually came to the conclusion that animal attractions didn't use ravens. After hearing from her daughter that Coda had one in residence—one with a "cheeky personality"—she followed Coda on social media and discovered that they were attending Hedingham Castle.

On the off chance, Jane decided to try her luck and turn up, hoping the cheeky raven would be in tow. Jane went on to say that as she sat and watched the flying demo, she had butterflies in her stomach. There was no raven at the falconry camp, so she was hoping he was in one of the carry boxes that sat beside the flying arena. She sat holding her husband's hand so tightly that he complained about his wedding ring crushing his fingers! He proudly showed me his hand, and sure enough, there was a red indent!

The moment Sarah-Jane announced on the mic that Loki would be coming out, well, it was like being a teenager again, she had said with a sparkle in her eye. She watched as he strutted out of his box toward Emily.

"When I saw him play that piano, I just wanted to cry!"

Jane had learned a little about his backstory from her granddaughter and had completely fallen in love with him or the thought of him anyway. "I must be one of the very few people who does not see these birds as demonic," she giggled.

I was quick to concur.

We stood and chatted about ravens in general, and I filled her in on some of Loki's backstory. She knew about his poor upbringing but was totally blown away by his ability to trust again. Her husband joked that he was going to walk around the castle and pick Jane up when the event closed. She took the hint and began to wrap things up. But before we parted, I asked if she wanted to hold Loki. She looked at her husband like a child asking for permission, and he smiled.

I shouted over to Emily to pass me an eagle glove—the last thing I wanted was a raven fan to be bitten by her idol. (They say, never meet your heroes...) Emily scurried over and fitted the glove onto Jane's hand. It covered all of her arm, right up to the elbow. I invited Loki onto the glove, and he gleefully hopped up. Jane stared at him in pure adoration, and he stared back at her, cocking his head and reading every subtle facial movement, decoding and analyzing. Jane looked like she might start crying again. I felt a little bit like the third wheel, so I struck up a general conversation with Jane's husband. He wasn't in any way, shape, or form interested in ravens or birds. Vintage cars are his thing, he explained, American muscle cars in particular.

It seemed like an age that these two had locked eyes. One of them was to break the silence: three knocks and a *"Gwah."*

Jane started to laugh. Loki immediately recognized that this new human also found him funny, so he did it again. She asked me what this meant. He fluffed up his crest and looked at me, making sure I said the right thing. I told her it was a playful call—he was showing off.

It was all going so well until my nightmare spawned into reality.

Without thinking, Jane raised her hand to stroke Loki on the head. My heart jumped into my mouth, and I began to signal battle stations internally—it all happened so fast. Her hand landed on his soft, fluffy head, and she stroked him half a dozen times. Loki remained perfectly still: no aggression, no anxiety, or defense mechanisms activated. I tried to play it cool with a nonchalant poise, with deep but silent breaths, but to Emily, I would have looked uneasy and on edge.

I asked Jane if she wanted me to take a picture of her and her new best friend, but with regret, she informed me her camera was in the car. I whipped out my phone and snapped away. Her husband gave me his email address, as Jane didn't have one, and I reluctantly had to separate Jane and Loki from their newly kindled friendship.

As Jane and her husband melted into the crowd, my initial reaction was just how exhausted I felt. A mixture of driving back from Sweden the previous night and hoping—no, *praying*—Loki didn't bite someone, the cacophony of emotions with fatigue washed over my entire body.

Once again, Loki, unbeknown to him, captured someone's heart and made their day. His powerful story draws people from all walks of life to meet him. I genuinely experience a sense of euphoria on his behalf, just knowing someone's wish had been granted that day. Such simple deeds can be incredibly powerful. Jane had made a real connection with Loki that day, an encounter she will never forget.

I often remind the human team at Coda just how lucky we are to work with these souls. If we take the time to stop and really listen, we as a species can learn how to better ourselves to be more forgiving, empathetic, and tolerant. Agents of fear and manipulation propagate agendas, forcing us away from the natural world, hell-bent on reducing the value of life.

Now that I was just as happy as Jane, the feel-good endorphins were spreading, and much like smiling, it can be infectious. I taxied Loki back to his perch and tethered him. From behind, I heard a little girl say, "Look, Mummy, there's that crow that played the piano!"

The mum replied, "Oh yeah, evil-looking thing, ain't he!"

In life, you win some, and you lose some. It's all about balance and is a firm reminder our work is never done.

Throughout the rest of the afternoon, revelers came to see the birds, and by far the most popular was the "piano-playing crow." After his comedic demonstration, his stock had certainly increased. Even the knights and the jousters came over to have their picture with Loki. And, of course, he lapped it up. You could tell he was in his element as he drooled salty happiness from his beak. As disgusting as this sounds, it's a sign he is having a ball.

I took a moment to stand back and observe the people taking so much interest in him, asking questions, and confessing their secret love for ravens and corvids. Equally, I watched Loki, remembering his old ways, looking down at my scarred hands. This would have never been possible—overwhelming fear and anxiety would have conquered him, and the rage button smashed repeatedly. He deserved this, to be fawned over and for people to really see how affectionate and delicate ravens are. Most people confess to only recently liking ravens after jumping on the *Game of Thrones* bandwagon, but in all honesty, I'm glad they did. People are becoming more aware, even if they still believe what they see in fiction programs. It's a good sign. Awareness is happening, and this is the beginning. Next comes the education and unlearning of harmful myths.

SIXTEEN
ENN VATN
STILL WATERS

arah-Jane is one of those incredibly rare gifts. She is completely selfless and always looking to see the good in people and scenarios. Above all, she always puts the birds' welfare at the forefront. I've never known anyone to instill more love and care into animals than her. This huge heart of hers is the essence of Coda's mantra: kindness—something we are all capable of giving but, as a species, so rarely do. Fortunately, it's this belief in kindness that galvanizes the team to be the best they can be, providing platinum-level welfare for the birds they have chosen to care for and work for.

Regarding the human factor, the Coda ethos adheres to allowing people a chance to experience the often misunderstood and most ancient of sports. Those who traditionally work with birds of prey do not care for the likes of me—commoners diluting their quaint and regal sport. For some, women (especially those who are good at it) aren't tolerated and often bullied out of the sport. It's staggering that in this day and age, this childish behavior still very much exists. Sarah-Jane works to change that. Her journey in developing not just a center but a sanctuary allows people who would have never had the chance to work with raptors the opportunity to contribute to something positive.

When people fly birds free for the first time, there is a common emotion, a driven sense that induces an instantaneous love affair—being outside walking in the open fields and lush woods accompanied by a creature who, at any time, could fly off into the magical, liberating wilderness but who instead chooses to come back to you with elegance, grace, and power. So, after being inundated with constant requests, Sarah-Jane was more than happy to let people volunteer at the center. It was a perfect opportunity for folk to get close to nature and learn an ancient sport. Unfortunately, the writing is on the wall, as falconry is more than likely destined to be lost to the gods of technology and the dwindling attention spans of their worshippers. But we can always hope and strive to inspire, keeping the torch burning for those seeking an alternative way to spend their time. It's about providing access and a nurturing environment.

People who had been to Experience Days and wanted a more active involvement in the sport could now do so. This now comes without the burden of having to build housing and buy a bird. This way, people could learn the art of falconry by first working with fully trained birds, gaining confidence, and developing their skills under Sarah-Jane's supervision and mentorship.

Luke, a young lad obsessed with reptiles and dinosaurs, once saw a falconry show in Ireland, and from that moment on, he was hooked. He found it fascinating, and being so closely related to dinosaurs, he imagined that this would be something he'd very much like to get into. Already boasting an impressive menagerie of various reptiles, Luke wanted to experience warm-blooded relatives of the dinosaurs and found himself doing one of Coda's Experience Days. According to him, it was everything he thought it would be and more. In fact, he liked it so much that, at the end of the experience, he asked Sarah-Jane if there were any volunteering opportunities: such was his newly discovered passion for birds. It was refreshing to see so much enthusiasm from a young lad, so we took a chance and offered him a slot. Emily, Sarah-Jane, and I pitched in and trained Luke, who came up to the center when he could. He absolutely loved the birds, and he was progressing well, getting to know each of the various birds' personalities.

Unfortunately, circumstances led to Luke not being able to be around as much, and his visits soon became few and far between. It was such a shame because he showed a real passion for the birds, and he was making excellent strides in his training. A year later, Luke appeared back on the scene with even greater enthusiasm. His willingness and more regular visits got him reaccustomed to the birds, and his efforts were duly rewarded. Sarah-Jane offered him a part-time role at the center, which he happily took.

The great thing about people like Luke is that when they find something that fascinates them, they want to explore it as much as possible. Luke and I would often chat about Loki—the magnetism of this creature had snared another victim into his field. Luke would often watch us play around in the arena, which was a totally different kind of relationship compared to the ones we were able to have with the raptors. Luke wanted to get to know Loki better but was rightly cautious of him. Luke was present when Loki almost severed one of our staff members' ears in half; as you can imagine, he has since been wary of our shadowy rogue.

I didn't have to tell Luke that this air of caution/borderline fear would be something Loki would prey on and exploit. Emily had already vouched for that, so Luke would always watch us from afar. I could sense his hankering to have a go with Loki, each time trying to build up enough confidence to join in, but it was just a little too much out of his comfort zone.

In the spring of 2017, we came to the center and found a little brown cardboard box on our doorstep. Hoping this wasn't a remake of the film *Seven,* we carefully opened the lid to see what was in the box. What greeted us were two tiny silver eyes piercing at us. It had this look of pure anger on its face, for what was in the box was a young jackdaw. When the hedges at the farm had been trimmed, this little fella had fallen out of the nest, and one of the workers picked him up and took him home. After three or four weeks of living under the care of the landscaper, the bird was getting a bit much, so he was left on our doorstep, literally. He was a spunky little fella, and like most corvids, he was into everything. He played with Emily's ear stretcher, picked at my teeth, and got excited when humans were around. He would shake and vibrate every time we walked into the room. The juvenile Jackdaw had been successfully imprinted, which, for both us and him, wasn't necessarily a good thing.

We—well, I—didn't want another corvid at the center for a few reasons, but the main contention was that it was a wild animal and, therefore, illegal for us to keep it at the center under zoo licensing regulations. The options were to have him put to sleep by a vet or let him go free. We chose the obvious option and allowed him to go and find his original flock. But we had a bit of a problem. He simply didn't want to leave and, like a boomerang, flew straight back into the barn, which had been his makeshift home. We made another attempt to release him, this time locking the barn to avoid another squatter's rights situation. We set him free, cheering him off into the wilderness. He buzzed around the flying arena, landing on each of our shoulders. This was a significant problem. Throughout the day, we encouraged him to fledge, and he eventually went up into the giant oak tree that stands tall over our center. It protects us from the elements but also provides perfect refuge to local squirrels and an array of corvids and other passerine birds, including an influx of noisy but beautiful parakeets.

When we arrived the next morning, guess who was there, ready and waiting? It dawned on us that being free was no longer an option for this young Jackdaw. He wouldn't be able to survive, and by the look of it, he didn't want to live in the wild. By being picked up at such a young and impressionable age, he had imprinted totally onto humans: setting him free would be a death sentence. We all knew and thought the same heart-wrenching idea. It looked like we would have to give the vet a visit. After all, it would be kinder for the poor thing, but Luke took it upon himself to intervene. He built a huge aviary in his garden at home and offered to adopt him. Our mini corvid orphan would be able to have a second chance and live on. We named him Merlin.

Luke said that watching Loki and I inspired him to move into the world of corvids, and it was lucky they both found themselves in a rather serendipitous position. Inspiration comes in many guises, and opportunity fortunes the brave.

At this point, Coda was a growing enterprise. Year after year, more people were visiting, and the need to fortify headquarters and provide vital upgrades was a welcomed headache. All the birds located inside the barn were to have brand new aviaries built outside, and Loki would be one of those who would get new accommodation. As you can imagine, I was particularly pleased about this—nothing but the best for my boy!

And that wasn't the only growth happening. The human team at Coda was expanding, too, and best of all, it was developing in a truly organic fashion. Emily and Luke, both homegrown talents, had been acquired at a young age. This provided us with the opportunity to carefully mold and instill our core values, uploading a positive ethos that was putting the bird's welfare at the forefront. However, youth, as enthusiastic and great as it is, has its limitations, and in my opinion, always benefits from an experienced head to help nurture their development. Not only that but from a customer viewpoint (rightly or wrongly), there is an expectation to see a person of a certain age, someone with wisdom and maturity at the helm. I think it reassures folks.

Sarah-Jane was contacted by a man who wanted to volunteer at the center. He had previously worked with animals at another zoo-turned-farm based in the east of Essex. His professional background was in computer networking, and he had a wealth of experience working in London and abroad in Europe and America. Basically, a chap with a lot of life experience and a very different set of skills.

These kinds of inquiries are always very welcome. It suggests off the bat that someone is willing to help out for authentic reasons, a love for the natural world placing the needs of the animals first. That's the kind of base-level requirements we look for.

Paul, a fellow Arsenal fan, was brought into the circle and began volunteering during the week. His knowledge of British birds was impressive. We often talked about different RSPB reservations we had visited and which rare species we had seen or were keen to see in the wild. Like Luke, Paul was also a keen reptile and spider enthusiast, owning a variety of species, which to this day completely baffles me. I still can't completely understand why people keep such nightmarish creatures! It was abundantly clear how passionate he was for his animals, reinforcing our decision to bring him on board. Upon his induction, he talked fondly of the birds he managed to bond with at the zoo where he previously volunteered and showed us good competency. For example, he was already familiar with the falconer's knot. This is Falconry 101—if you can't tie the knot, you can't pick up or put birds down safely. His attention to husbandry and cleanliness was also very much in line with our expectations.

We pride ourselves on the condition of our birds and their living quarters. Being a public-facing center requires fastidious attention to cleanliness: the last thing we want is people crying about welfare, especially those completely ignorant of animal husbandry. Another key element that I believe is crucial for any business to succeed is the relationship between the people who make it happen. What is great about the people at Coda is that they all respect and like each other. It's very rare, but I believe this is one of the key ingredients to a successful and effective business.

In the early days of working with Paul, it was clear he had taken a shine to our Loki. Whenever I was in, he'd be keen to see Loki at play and was eager to be involved. Naturally, I was delighted to show Loki off—I don't need an excuse. Paul would absorb all the information I had to offer, and I could see him making mental notes, observing diligently, and asking all the right questions.

One thing Paul took note of was the act of gift-giving. We walked up to Loki's enclosure, and in my hand was a go-karting trophy I had won at a bachelor party. It stood about five inches tall and was a tacky faux gold and black. Paul was puzzled as to why I had it, but all became clear. We arrived at his lordship's palace to hear him cawing in anticipation. Loki had seen the trophy and contorted his head in all manner of ways, even upside down, to get a good look at what was in my hand. He had never seen an object like this before.

I opened the door and walked in. Loki stood to attention—bolt upright, his beak almost touching my nose. He was quiet as an exam hall, but you could tell by his inquisitive personality—this student was being tested. Demonstrating jerky head movements, he was excited to know more about the object in my hand. I saw his pupils constantly changing aperture, a sign he was very much working things out. Paul hung in the doorway, respecting Loki's space—he had been fore-warned of Loki's darker side, and we agreed prevention was much better than rectifying an incident.

I held up the trophy, rotating it before Loki's eyes like a magician. His approval was needed to move on. He cawed, confirming the trophy was, in fact, a real trophy. I offered it to him, and he softly grasped the plastic prize, nibbling around the edges to form an opinion of its consistency. Once Loki had gathered the data required, he gently tugged it out of my hand and stood with it hanging in his mouth, looking back and forth at me and Paul. His tail began to vibrate rapidly up and down, the sound of his feathers slapping like a mini round of applause. To me, this was an overt gesture of pride and elation. Paul laughed and reached into his pocket to grab his phone. He, too, was grinning from ear to ear after never seeing such a reaction from a bird.

For the rest of the day, Loki would parade up and down in his enclosure with the trophy in his beak. He wouldn't let it go—first-place go-kart champion! He had no idea what it was or its intended significance. He, however, identified my giving it to him as a gesture of huge importance. I was higher in the chain of command, and I had bestowed upon him honor with such a prize. The thing is, we are a family, and this plastic token of temporary greatness had immense value to him, but it wasn't the materialistic value—it was the gesture. Another anthropomorphic gesture that crossed species. I think I have been taught another very important lesson about my own humanity.

Later on that day, I took Paul back up to the aviary. I could tell all day he was keen to go back and see Loki, as we had been discussing this strange body language in great detail. But as we walked up, he wasn't visible, nor could we hear him. I called his name, and he quickly appeared. Guess what was in his beak? He hopped to a branch close to the door, spritely still buoyant from his present. I asked Paul to open the aviary door and check the inside ledge. He did and found a dirty 50-pence piece. I told him I had given that to Loki a few days ago as a gift. I was keen to see if he had returned the favor after my golden-black offering that morning. And sure enough, he had.

I first established this rapport well before Paul had joined. Loki and

I had signed a mutually beneficial trade deal, one that saw both parties win. I had explained that one day, Loki had taken a shine to a badge I wore on my hoodie. It was the logo of my band, a colorful moth pressed on a white background. Loki would inquisitively pick at it, and knowing that certain corvids like Jackdaws and Magpies are well-known kleptomaniacs of various metallic items, I unpinned it and offered it up. Loki, apparently, was no different from his corvid cousins.

Paul did a lot of work with Loki, and I can't express how huge a sense of relief this gave me. It used to niggle me that if I weren't there, Loki wouldn't get the attention he wanted because of his brutish ways. Don't get me wrong, he was attended to and flown every single day, but not in a way I necessarily wanted. I wanted him spoiled. Paul worked hard to build a relationship with Loki and did as I did. He gave the raven his treasure and, in turn, was himself rewarded with trust and friendship. We would get regular updates on the WhatsApp group chat of Paul working with Loki: he would be my eyes and ears when I wasn't there. Paul loved Loki, and they worked brilliantly together. This is what I wanted. I also didn't want Loki to be solely reliant on me, and as much as it is nice to boast that I was the only one who could work with him, it is egotistical and counterproductive. It's not healthy for Loki to close his circle; he needs to be able to work with others. However, it wasn't through the will of trying. Emily and Luke both tried and still do try hard to work with him, but it's generally on his terms. Paul had managed to establish himself in Loki's pecking order. Was it because he was an older male? Was it because he had learned the secret of placating him? Truth be told, it's probably a bit of both in conjunction with regular playtime and rewards. It's funny how the power of food and shiny objects of perceived value transcends across species.

So, we've learned Loki is fond of *things*, and after all, he had his very own toy box. Now, his collection was expanding into trinkets and keepsakes and a handful of British Stirling. To further cement this concept of Loki's desire to own precious items, we found out in a rather peculiar way. One which could have been quite disastrous.

SEVENTEEN
HINN MIKLI FLÓTTI
THE GREAT ESCAPE

When the new bank of weatherings had been built outside, the birds in the barn were transferred from inside to outside. These were all native species who would be able to deal with whatever was thrown at them in terms of weather. This gave us ample time to renovate the barn, converting the main space into a large traditional museum while also making other amendments, like putting in internal doors and sealing it off from the elements.

Now, our flashy new enclosures had permanent occupants. We put brand-new padlocks on all the doors for protection. These were for safety and not to be removed unless you were putting a bird away or getting one out!

At the end of a rather busy day, the team was beginning to make haste and leave for the evening. All of the birds had been flown, fed, and cleaned. The last task we do is prepare food for the following day, and if there is spare food, we either include it in the next day's allowance or give it to a lucky raptor. On this particular occasion, there were a few spare quail wings leftovers. There really isn't much nutritional value in the wings—it's mainly bone and feather—but Loki likes them. He takes great pleasure in making a mess of his aviary by pulling out the feathers one at a time. One of the team members went and deposited the wings but, for whatever reason, made a paramount error.

The next morning, we arrived ready to tackle the day, but all was not well. The office was a complete mess. Sarah-Jane began to panic immediately: it looked as though we had been burgled. Important documents were all over the floor, containers emptied—it was utter carnage. If we had been burgled, the thieves would only be after one thing: our birds. The office contained all official documents relating to the legal ownership and registration of all the birds. I rushed back outside and checked the falcons. All were present, sitting on their perches, confused as to why we were all panicking. The owls were all tucked up and safe. Frosty the Tawny Owl looked at me with one eye slightly opened, disgruntled at being awoken. I looked up to the new bank of aviaries on the hill. One of the doors was wide open. My heart sank—that awful, abominable churning in the stomach made me instantly nauseated. I jumped the fence and shouted out for my friend.

I ran toward Loki's gaping aviary, the door gently swinging in the wind. I arrived at the entrance and froze as though gazing into Medusa's eyes. Marred with panic and fear, my eyes searched all over his aviary. I couldn't see any sign of him! I could hear Sarah-Jane shouting up in the background, asking if Loki was okay. I was rooted firmly to the spot, eyes still frantically crisscrossing the aviary. I could hear my heart beating, an *allegretto* tempo merging with a manic *vivace*. Then, all of a sudden, I experienced the "Oz effect."

The Oz effect, or factor, is often associated with paranormal experiences, particularly when people have claimed to encounter UFOs or just before being confronted by a spectral being or cryptid. Experiencers have described that it feels like they are transported to another realm—like Dorothy in *The Wizard of Oz*, hence the name—where time feels slow and viscous. Sounds of the world disperse, and the overwhelming feeling of dread and emptiness engulfs the body.

"Is he okay?" Sarah-Jane came from behind and put her hand on my shoulder so she could peep into the aviary.

I recoiled back into the present, like a shot of adrenaline to the heart. There he was. And there he was, standing on his log, four feet directly in front of me, silent and glossy.

We both took the biggest sigh of relief. The sodden veil of hysteria and fear dissolved like salt on snow, revealing to us something remarkable. Loki was standing on his log which was about a foot and a half tall and roughly the same dimensions wide, smack bang in the middle of the aviary. Now, the metaphorical snow had melted, revealing quite the scene. Scattered all around him on the floor were pens, Coda merchandise, magnets, nails, screwdrivers, and other miscellaneous tools, a packet of biscuits, and a tin lid that once housed said biscuits. Loki had a vast array of loot he had acquired for himself, and he couldn't look happier or more pleased with himself. He looked at us with amusement—he was immensely satisfied with his achievement. The only conceivable thought we could process was how lucky we were that he hadn't literally flown the nest. But there was this intuitive, empath-like voice that yelled at me.

"Why would I leave? This is my home!"

It was at this exact point in our relationship I truly grasped that our bond went far beyond "You give me food, and I won't bite." He really was like a human, and we were really like family. All this being said, the outcome could have been much different—a thought that I dwelled on for too long and still makes me shudder even to this day. Recounting this memory brings out goosebumps.

After double-checking all the birds and the office, we confirmed we hadn't been burgled; well, not by a human anyway. The only missing items were quickly located as raven bounty. We convened around the table, all sipping from our choice of hot beverage. Mine was a strong black coffee, sweet (could have done with a shot of liquor to steady the nerves). At most centers, this is where the blame game would begin. The person responsible for forgetting to lock the door was present, and it didn't need to be said. The elephant in the room could remain among us without being poached in the open. The one thing I did offer up for discussion was: exactly how did he get out? All the doors have a sliding bolt that closes the doors, and the padlock is then added for further security. It was confirmed that the bolt was definitely in its proper place. So, how did Loki make it out? There are two important questions to ponder. Firstly, how did he know the lock wasn't on, and secondly, how did he go about sliding the lock open from inside the aviary?

Before dealing with the two aforementioned riddles, we considered the incredible possibility that Loki knows exactly what a lock is and its function. For me, that already is pretty damn mind-blowing. If indeed he does, then he would have established this by watching us use the lock, leading him to test the effects of the lock. He already knows it's precious to us, so is it really that much of a stretch of the imagination? This would suggest an almost scientist-like mindset. Armed with this knowledge, he would then have to exit the aviary. The design of the doors inadvertently makes it impossible to open from inside, even by a human. The only logical conclusion would be that he had help from a tool.

The corvid community is known for being astonishingly resourceful in the wild. Utilizing Mother Nature to glean what they desire, be it harnessing the power of gravity by dropping snails onto rocks, cracking shells revealing a jellied delight, or using twigs to scoop out bugs from inside logs, crows and ravens are the "Mac-Gyvers" of the animal kingdom. When you consider they are more than capable in the art of trading, the concept of a raven exchanging an attractive tool for food implies an incredible level of intelligence.

It was the only logical reason for how Loki managed to pry open the door. I went into his enclosure and had a root about. He stood on his branch, peering down over me, curious as to exactly what it was I was doing. On my haunches, I turned over the shingle, trying to find evidence of a tool. All the time, Loki was silent, studying my actions and trying to determine the nature of my intentions. As I got close to his bath, he shot over to his log and cawed at me: it wasn't aggressive, but it was like a soft warning. I knew I was warm.

As my hand hovered over the bath, he barked at me. I turned over the bath, sending water gushing over the sides, and there it was, Loki's secret stash. Hidden under his bath was a multitude of items: a few padlocks we had presumed missing, some grapes from the day before, and none other than our prime suspect, a six-inch tent peg.

Like the glutton he is, Loki quickly assessed his priorities, grabbed the food, and scampered, leaving me free to take the evidence for test-ing. I asked one of the team to close the aviary door and slide the bolt over. I was now locked in with Loki, which was an interesting situation to be in.

I headed to the door, Loki watching over my shoulder from his branch, almost goading me. "I bet you can't unlock it."

I took his tent peg and fumbled it around in between the gap in the door and the aviary support. After a few minutes, I had succeeded and felt quite proud of myself. I looked back over my shoulder and gave Loki a little knowing smile, a bit like when a dad scores a better goal against his kid in the backyard. Although, in the end, it was fairly straightforward to do, I have the advantage of two arms, opposable thumbs, and being five-foot-eleven. My biological design vastly outweighed Loki's. All he had was a strong beak—one not to be under-estimated, mind. However, though it was a devastating weapon, it came with dexterity, tenacity, and desire.

It's unclear how long it took Loki to break out of his aviary, but the fact remains: he managed it, which led me never to underestimate his potential to utilize tools in the future.

And with that very sentence, I ultimately underestimated his potential to utilize tools!

As already mentioned, every bird needs to be weighed every morning to ascertain how heavy they are. This data is imperative for training and flying birds of prey. Every bird has a "flying weight"— this is what we refer to as a kind of prime, athletic weight for the birds. It sits in between a bird being starving and a bird being fat. The bird is keen enough to see food and respond to it but with enough energy to be still able to fly. These creatures are bound to a pure protein-based diet. It's like being on a rubbish Atkins, but without the luxury of having nice cheese, so energy comes at a premium and cannot be wasted.

Most of the birds are more than happy to be weighed. Thankfully, they never get upset if they put on a few ounces. Loki, in fact, is one of the easiest to weigh these days, but this wasn't always the case! We bring up a portable digital scale set, put it on the floor, and open his aviary. His lordship comes shuffling out, sees the white plastic and rubber scales, and happily hops onto it without fuss. Of course, for him to sit still long enough, he needs to be compensated for his time, so a few cat biscuits are generally a handy way to placate him while we can take an accurate reading. What also doesn't help is he often decides to be very vocal. This sends the reading into pandemonium. I think he knows this and does it on purpose. However, his next-door neighbor, Freya, is a bit more of a handful to weigh—well, for me, anyway.

The protocol for weighing Freya, a colossal female Snowy Owl—the adjective used is one of endearment—is to take the scales into her aviary and do the reading in there. The problem is sometimes she can be reluctant to be weighed. I, too, know that feeling. So what tends to happen is she makes a bit of a fuss and flaps about her aviary—a little like a game of chase, a game whereby she actually doesn't want to be caught. To the layman, it could be perceived that she is being aggressive and attacking me, which is exactly how Loki perceives it.

On one such occasion, I got close to Freya and took hold of her flying straps, and she flared up. In doing so, she smacked me in the head with her three-foot wing. A mass cluster of feathery white engulfed me, and I held on tightly like some kind of bizarre avian rodeo, waiting for her to calm down. Next door, also erupting with a furious rage, was Loki. He scaled the aviary wire, screaming incessantly at Freya. He was tearing at the metal wire mesh, desperate to break it open. He was hell-bent on trying to stop her from attacking me. He was livid!

I managed to weigh Freya eventually and vacated her aviary unharmed, but Loki was still locked onto the mesh, scowling at Freya. His beady little eyes were permanently transfixed on her—it was like watching the birth of a supervillain. Freya, being an owl, had no idea her neighbor was glaring from up high. She went about her business, plopping herself onto her large gray-blue rock and preening her immaculate feathers.

My first immediate thought was of surprise. I'd never seen him really turn from playful to full-on *blitzkrieg* mode, especially that quickly. He obviously hated the green glove, but he had never shown this kind of aggression to a member of the flying team before. He stared at her with a burning hatred, silent and calculated. A part of me felt honored that my mate had my back, and I could count on him if I ever got into a ruckus. It was further proof to me how Loki considered our relationship. He was not only a pal, but now he had turned protector.

I think many people out there believe animals are incapable of having feelings. I'm sure those who have pets will rightly disagree, but for the majority, it's either not possible, or we choose to ignore the possibility. After all, the way mankind treats animals on this planet is, at times, pretty barbaric and downright torturous. From the cruelty of mass-farmed animals to the cliche "fish don't feel," we believe the lie to propagate the fact that it's okay to spear them for sport and pose for pictures as they gasp for breath; it's different if it's hunting for food—let's just be humane about it. As a species, we are right to be feared. The systematic extermination of the animal kingdom for food, trophies, or just for fun could be construed as sociopathic. Do we tell ourselves animals can't feel emotion so we can continue to persecute them without guilt?

Now, I don't want to turn this into a "meat is murder" rant, but I do think we need to see animals as more than just food, pests, or dumb, ambivalent creatures. New Zealand made huge steps in 2015 by legally identifying animals as sentient beings. Such a simple and basic action can have such a huge influence and effect on the animals we are fortunate to share this beautiful planet with. Giving them the right to proper welfare should be a given, but why did it take this long, and why isn't the rest of the world following?

Loki showed me that he could express a range of emotions. We've seen fear, frustration, empathy, panic, and, now, anger. Was it an instinctual "my human is in trouble," or was it deeper? Did he think Freya was attacking me because she didn't like me? I believe one requires a deeper level of consciousness and awareness. Does Loki see himself as higher than Freya in the chain? Like humans, did he assume her intelligence and categorize her as just another dumb animal, one who was now causing a threat?

His eyes continued to shoot daggers, body locked in position for what seemed like an age, suggesting that he was still furious with

Freya. This wasn't a "fight or flight" type of instinct; this was something else brooding and complex.

After "Freya-gate," Loki and I had a little mooch around the farm. We practiced his long-range catching skills with grapes, and we even got him flying and catching food in mid-air. After food supplies had been depleted, Loki took himself off into a small patch of trees. It was a breeding ground for magpies, a particular location where a family often used it to roost and plan coordinated pincer attacks on starlings. It is quite marvelous and, at the same time, an astonishing sight to watch as the corvids execute their perfect tactics with subtle tail wags and minimal but clear vocalizations.

Loki emerged with his feathers slightly ruffled from where he'd been truffling in the undergrowth. He had in his beak a nice long stick, perhaps a meter long. He tottled about the arena proudly, punching with his big stick, and like a puppy, he came over to show me. I went to take it, and he flicked his head slightly, so I missed my grab. I went in for another attempt, and again, with a slight snap of the neck, he moved it out of my reach. I tried again, and this time, I successfully grabbed one end of the stick: the game was on! Back and forth, we played tug of war with Loki doing his utmost to win, grunting with determination. In the end, I conceded. The victor glowed with glory, showcasing his prize stick. Tiny drops of dribble drip from the tip of his beak: now that was one happy raven!

He headed back over to me, still holding his trophy stick, and just like before, he let me get just in range before pulling the stick away. He was actually teasing me—the cheek of it! He waddled off, looking over his shoulder to check that I was still keeping pace. I made another desperate lunge, but he was too quick. I picked up the pace, which he easily matched. I was now chasing him all over the flying arena; the irony wasn't lost on me. We have played this game before, and I could see the general public filming my feeble attempts to reclaim the precious stick! I swiped down and finally got a grip on the stick. We had another game of "My Stick!" and like before, Loki reigned victorious. He swanned around the battle arena, once again parading his stick, showing anyone and everyone. After soaking in his rapturous applause, he took himself home to revel in his spoils. I slipped him a few apple slices and commended him on his triumph.

Over the course of the day, I'd check on our newly crowned champ. Surprisingly, his stick was still in one piece. Normally, most items taken into Loki's lair are meticulously taken apart. I find it wonderful that Loki continuously showed us new emotions and secret areas of his ability to communicate. It's a bit like a computer game. As we progressed through the various levels and completed certain tasks, new achievements would be unlocked. Like any keen gamer, once I had finished school—or work, in my case—I would rush back to play the next level, keen to see what other secrets I could unlock.

When I got home from work, Sarah-Jane and I chatted about the day's events. We talked about the birds, how well they flew, how our guests were on the various Experience Days, and who was the favorite bird of the day, and then I'd steer the conversation to my boys. Firstly, how did Logan get on, and secondly, what antics did Loki get up to? Was he okay; did he get plenty of playtime?

All that week, I was getting the same response regarding Loki. He was a good boy but generally pretty quiet all day; in fact, every day that week, he had been unusually quiet. I didn't want to read too much into it, but that sounded odd. *Loki, quiet?*

I asked if he still had his stick, and Sarah-Jane remembered seeing it a few days ago. She recalled that it was nestled in a well-constructed trench but couldn't recall seeing it today. Maybe he was hiding it, or perhaps it went the way of all the other items that ended up in his aviary—disassembled.

The next day, while I was at work, I got a call from Sarah-Jane. I never get calls from her at work, so this meant something was wrong.

"You will never guess what *your* raven has done!"

No "Hello, how are you doing?" just straight to the point.

I also picked up on a subtle piece of deliberate language. The fact that it was my raven and that he wasn't mentioned by name meant that something terrible had happened. I took a deep breath, ready for the charges.

"So, the stick you were asking about? Well, he hadn't destroyed it."

"Okay...that's cool. I wasn't that concerned if he had."

"He was hiding it," Sarah-Jane said.

"Ha, clever boy."

But though he was clever, he certainly hadn't been a good boy. I was then told the rest of the story.

Sarah-Jane had been fixing information signs for the aviaries. They give a brief description of each bird along with where they're from and their Latin names. Just as she was getting to putting up the sign for *Corvus Corax*, she heard rustling from inside the aviary. She hung back to see what was going on. After a few silent minutes, Loki appeared. He popped up onto his main branch, holding *the* stick in question tightly in his beak. In the aviary next door, Freya was right up against Loki's divider with her back to him. For Freya, that was a mistake. Loki sneaked up behind her and maneuvered his stick in just a way that his game plan was ready to be executed. Loki jabbed Freya three or four times through the mesh before she flew away to safety.

Sarah-Jane was in total shock. She ran over and berated *my* raven, giving him a harshly-toned telling-off. Loki showed no remorse—in fact, by all accounts, he looked rather proud of himself. Sarah-Jane went in and retrieved the offending article.

This part of the story is the real zinger. As Sarah-Jane went to retrieve the stick, Loki put up a defense. The two danced off, Sarah-Jane trying to loose-foot him by shimmying her shoulders from left to right, Loki mirroring her movements. He would not let her take his prize, and he grunted and barked at her to stay away.

Emergency maneuver: hand in the pocket, and like a grenade, toss the weapon—a quarter piece of corn on the cob—to the back of the aviary. Loki conceded the stick and chose the golden yellow vegetable block. Sarah-Jane seized the moment, scooped up the stick, and swiftly exited the aviary. She slid the bolt across the door and checked on Loki: he was happily eating his treat. She headed over to the wooded area where the offending article came from and was about to throw it in the bushes before something rather intriguing caught her eye. The stick at the business end had been whittled down into a sharp point, perfect for stabbing. *He made a homemade shiv ideal for shanking unsuspecting owls!*

Loki had embarked on a project—he had been working on it all week in complete secrecy. This was a premeditated, well-thought-out process that required skill, dexterity, planning, and, above all, patience. When all the ingredients were in place, he seized the moment to strike, acting on an event that happened nearly a week ago to me! He hadn't forgotten Freya's treachery, nor was he willing to forget. That is what I found truly remarkable on so many levels. Our journey together started tempestuous, to say the least. He damaged me, tried to intimidate and sow the seed of fear into me, but those days are only remembered by the scars on my hands and distant memories. Now, he was my ally, my friend, and my protector. Weapon-making skills: achievement unlocked! If Loki had the faculties to act out revenge, then I sincerely hope the man who kicked him never returns to the farm for his own sake.

From here on, Loki was no longer allowed to have sticks or other sharp implements in his aviary. The "thug life" he may have chosen, but under "The Coda Falconry Convention," we could not be his arms dealer for the continued safety of both raptors and people.

––––––

I'm going to jump back to the winter of 2017. It was mid-December, and by now, like every year, the sickly saturation of Christmas music had ground me down. I'm one of those people—everyone knows one —who is triggered by any mention, any advertisement, or any piece of music that endorses the Christmas spirit before December 1st. Call me a humbug; I don't care! It seems we are being bombarded by these torturous and manipulating commercials earlier each year. As soon as Halloween ends, the Christmas hamper adverts appear—furniture manufacturers slop their USP of buy now and guarantee delivery before Christmas, that one big day consisting of twenty-four hours, which the country seems to go absolutely nuts for. Stocking up on food that can feed a small country and the social aspect of forcing people to expunge money they don't necessarily have to have the "perfect Christmas." It happens every year.

Part of this idyllic, utopian Christmas scenario is propagated with the wish for a white Christmas, the sound of crunching snow, and

Victorian backdrops. 2017 gifted the people of Britain with a huge snow dump—what a lovely early Christmas present—maybe this would be the perfect Christmas we are made to believe we need.

For Loki, this was an unexpected situation, for when the snow came, he was a confused contradiction of excitement and suspicion. It was quite a hefty snowfall for England. The valley became a homogenous blanket of silky white; the topography was indistinguishable. Navigating the icy virgin snow was as treacherous as it was thrilling.

That morning, the center was eerily calm, as if we had been literally blasted into an ice age, nature frozen and locked in time. That visage was quickly scuppered by the rowdy call of a certain corvid. As soon as he had visual confirmation of us, he rattled around his aviary like a pinball. I raced up the mound to his door so I could greet him—he had his head upside down, cawing. I granted him access to the arena and turned my back, expecting him to come waddling out and join me by the highest perch in the arena, but as I arrived, there was no Loki. I looked back and saw him right on the edge of his aviary, still and cautious, like a sufferer of vertigo standing at the edge of a platform before leaping into a bungee. I playfully asked him to come out, surprised as to why all of a sudden he had lost his appetite for exploration, and then it had occurred to me—this was probably the first time he had ever seen snow.

To be honest, I struggle to remember the first time I ever encountered snow. My earliest, most vivid memories put me at around nine or ten. I remember with untainted cynicism the excitement of hearing the weatherman preach the forthcoming arrival of biblical snow, like a sermon. I rejoiced; my landscaping father, not so much. I now understand my parents' grumblings. For kids, snow is the gift that keeps on giving: no school, sledding, snowball fights, and an excuse for hot chocolate. It now means insufferable traffic jams, frosted car windows, snow burn on the hands, and falling over on icy pavements while being filmed by teenagers on phones.

Loki was a confused combination of adult and child mindstate. He wanted to come out, but something innate was telling him to be cautious. Ravens in the wild are shown by their elders what to fear—they teach each other what friend or foe is—but in Loki's case, he'd never been in this scenario. I walked back over to him, chuckling. The big bad raven was scared of a little snow—what would his Scandinavian kin think of this? I crouched down at the entrance to his aviary and tried to talk him out. He stood firm and silent, beak pointed upward. His body language and energy were exactly the same as the very first night we met. I sensed that very same vulnerability in him: it's still very much there, and only when presented with extreme circumstances does he lock up. He was trying to use whatever decision-making skills he had learned, in conjunction with past experiences, to determine whether setting foot on this mystical white froth would be a positive move. His confidence was being tested.

I reached over and grabbed a clump of snow, and I cramped it in my palms. The pitter-patter of my gloved hands molding the snow intrigued Loki. He cocked his head back and forth, investigating my actions. I wondered what he was thinking of all this. I molded a snowball and offered it to him, and as fast as lighting, he sprung to the back of his aviary with a series of warning caws alluding to me the fact that it wasn't a cool move: he was mad at me. I held the ball and rotated it, and like an illusionist, I was demonstrating to him that it was completely real and, more importantly, safe. Loki was still not sure: he remained planted at the back of his palace, his caws turning to light barks, a sign to me that he was feeling uneasy. I didn't want to scare him or make him feel anxious, but I did want to show him that this was nothing to be afraid of, just like a parent raven would do in the wild. Two thoughts crossed my mind: the first was to go into his space and bring the object of concern closer to him. I quickly dismissed this. It would be just like us pressuring him with the green glove, and I didn't want to create another trigger for Loki to enter fight-or-flight mode. The poor lad had enough traumas in his time to have an elemental one added to his list. So I thought, how do parents get their kids to eat food when the kid doesn't want it or know what it is? I decided to tap into one of Loki's most accessible methods of communication: food!

I looked at the snowball, looked back at Loki, and took a bite out of it. Yes, I know it's ridiculous, but anyone who says they haven't done this as a kid is a filthy liar! I pretended it tasted nice and went in for a second bite.

"Hmm, this is really good," I said out loud, even though my sensitive teeth were screaming for me to stop—(those of you who bite into ice cream are simply built differently!). I stood up and went to take another bite, and suddenly, we had movement. I took a smaller bite this time—any bigger, and I'd have no snowball left.

Loki slowly moved from the floor to the log and finally to his perch.

I held the remaining snow apple in my hand as the dark mass of anxiety edged closer. His head hovered over my hand, and he went to bite the snow. As he did, he jumped back too soon before he could make contact. He was slowly drumming up the courage. He walked back over and had another stab at the snow; this time, he got some. He leaped back to safety and tasted the snow, the sound of a gently clicking beak resembling the licking of lips. I asked him if he wanted some more, and he silently headed back to my opened hand. This time, there was no recoil. He lapped up the snow as if eating cat biscuits, and his little tail waggled from excitement—not because of its taste, but because he knew it didn't pose a threat. He wiped his beak on my hand and then, like the big boy he is, waddled out of his aviary all by himself.

It was definitely an unconventional way of doing things, but it was the only thing I could think of that he could associate with without driving him further into the fear zone. Loki has been described as "a toddler with a machete," so sometimes unconventional methods are the only way forward. As long as we get the best outcome, I don't mind looking silly.

He edged closer to the thick blanket of snow, which had now taken the green grass as its hostage. He gingerly raised one leg and placed it on the ice. He did the same with the other leg, and now he was walking—or should I say waddling because of the thickness of snow he has to hurdle his way through, much to my amusement.

Within seconds, all jittery signs of unease and trepidation had vanished. Loki was now pecking the snow, barking at it, and incredibly, he began to roll around in it. The apprehensive adult state of mind had given way to the playful and spunky child-like frame of mind, and he was having a ball. I rolled a tiny snowball, half the size of a satsuma, and when he wasn't looking, I gingerly threw it at him. It splashed against his back and disintegrated. He quickly turned around and started to run toward me. While chuckling, I made and threw another one at him, which he caught in his mouth. We played for a good hour, chasing each other, making snowballs, and Loki catching them. He flew up to my shoulder, and I took him toward the wooded area, where he collected his materials for his next weapon-building project and showed him the trees. He reached up and grabbed a branch, and he yanked on it with all his might. A huge fall of snow covered us. Loki got scared and flew to a nearby perch, sugar-coated in snow. I let out a laugh, and his face was a picture—a real look of "Don't laugh at me!" He flew back to me, and I gave him a grape as a pseudo-apology. He went to grab a different branch, but this time, he didn't tug so hard. Instead, he repeatedly pulled it, but gently, as if ringing a church bell to a moderate *andante* tempo. The downpour of snow was slow and steady as if he was trying to recreate an authentic snow pour. This time, he knew what was to happen and, instead, was happy to cover us both in the snow, *sans surprise*.

The morning flew by, and to be honest, it was the most fun I'd had in the snow as an adult. His innocent attitude and approach coerced me into forgetting my age and letting me enjoy myself like a kid. It was joyful, pure, and carefree. Loki had new experience points. In a single morning, he, like many children, was allowed to play and revel in the elements. The phases of anticipation, fear, anxiety, caution, and glee all rolled into one morning's outing. It was the kind of stimulation I wanted him to have, and for me, it was uplifting to see him overcome his obstacles and enjoy himself. I felt a huge sense of pride and happiness watching him, and in doing so, he allowed me to return to a child-like state. Nothing was important anymore. We were like two young lads messing about, having a great time together; my grumpy, introverted demeanor melted by the playfulness of a corvid. But he wasn't just any bird: he was my friend.

EIGHTEEN
HEIMSFARALDUR
PANDEMIC

As a species, there aren't too many occasions where we are all universally united, brought together via one common event. Sure, we have the Olympics, various world cups for football, rugby, and sometimes the odd global crisis meeting, but nothing in my lifetime will ever compare to the subsequent events of 2019.

I sat down in my seat, fastened the buckle, and gazed out of the window. I usually opt for an aisle seat, but I was happy enough to take the window. Our plane was currently sitting on a runway at Geneva airport, and the deicer truck was hosing down the plane, ready to ferry us back to the UK. I had just spent ten days snowboarding in the French Alps with a group of friends, and it was time to return.

As we were waiting, the echoing murmurs of rumor propagated through the narrow walkway of the plane. Apparently, people back home were fighting each other in shops over pasta, flour, and, of all things, toilet paper. I chortled to myself over this bizarre reason for fellow humans to squabble. Ravens in the wild will often bully each other if there is an equitable sharing of scarce resources, but the real reason only became apparent as we landed.

The plane touched down back in Stansted, London (which is not actually in London), and one of my friends showed me an article on his phone. Posted hours after we departed, it proceeded to detail how the entire French Alps had been closed down. All those happy people who departed on the very same plane we boarded to go home were now heading toward closed mountains.

It had started.

Before this point, not many people were familiar with the term *coronavirus*, but it would soon be a household term in every part of the world.

The UK, like most countries, went through a myriad of chaos and confusion, propaganda, and misinformation over the next two years. This was a unique time in our modern history, and the result would be catastrophic. There's no need to refresh our memories of this particular period of time, but like a lot of people, our lives would never quite be the same.

As the government's attempts to mitigate damages from the pandemic increased, we became bound to our homes. Fortunately for me, I had a gig producing animations with a team in the US. This meant that I was able to work at home. For six months, it was doable, but the novelty wore off, as did my mental grip on reality. I descended into an uncontrollable spiral of dark depression. I suffered numerous mental breakdowns of quite spectacular proportions, which today I'm still actively working on and trying to address. I managed to destroy all my relationships, I alienated my friends, and I withdrew from society to fester in a pit of despair and hopelessness. My marriage was perhaps the biggest casualty. Thirty years of repressed emotions and frustrations were released from the shackles of a dark, forgotten part of my mind to wreak havoc on my perception and state of wellness. I moved out of my home to take refuge with my dad. For him, it was a welcome return, as I could help him as he nervously battled leukemia and the virus that was plaguing the globe, but I became a husk of misery.

We were under a mandate where we couldn't travel unless for "essential workers." The team at Coda needed written permission from local authorities to travel to look after the birds—a document that needed to be presented if stopped by law enforcement. It was surreal. Only minimum numbers were allowed, which meant that my involvement became redacted.

As we all acclimated to the "new normal," the planet's wildlife made a powerful resurgence. Migratory birds, for example, flourished, as did the seas. While the roads were closed and the skies became bare of planes, Mother Nature took her opportunity to rejuvenate with limited human interference.

For the birds at the center, it was almost business as usual, except the farm was quiet, void of the sound of children playing, the routine of public shows, and the interaction with Experience Day guests. They were totally oblivious and seemingly without care—for them, the world just kept turning.

The team battled to keep themselves safe so that they, in turn, could maintain the welfare of the birds in their custody. In some respects, it was a prime time for the birds to rest and for additional training to be ramped up. But to do this, the birds needed food, as did the staff, which cost money. However, without a source of income due to the lockdowns, Coda faced a very troubling time.

We applied for every possible grant: some were successful, and some were not. There were moments when the company was on the brink of folding, sometimes with only a month of money and resources left. The stress was compounded further. The new owners of the farm wanted to turn it into a cheap, tacky attraction where they could exploit the animals. We battled hard but were under no illusions that our time was up. In order to have any chance of survival and not jeopardize the morality of what we do and the safety of the birds, we needed to find a new home.

While all this was happening, I didn't visit Loki much, perhaps a handful of times over the year. I had abandoned him. I knew he was being looked after as the videos continued to surface in the Whatsapp group chat, but I was deeply ashamed of my neglect. I would sometimes contemplate if our relationship would be the same again. I needed to do better and break the circuit—this insidious feedback loop that stained my creativity and love for life. I needed this—I needed him—perhaps more than ever.

I'd been pretty secure, very rarely fazed by anything. At this point, however, I was experiencing a plethora of emotions that I only thought happened to others. I would have daily panic attacks and thoughts of suicide; forcing myself to return to the center was definitely one such trigger.

Because of my deterioration, I felt nervous and embarrassed when I returned, sheepish to be around those who were now seeing a new, vulnerable, and broken embodiment. To their credit, the whole team was incredibly warm and supportive, which made the process of getting back to the center a little easier. But there was someone else I needed to win over.

I took a big gulp of air and made my way to see my abandoned friend. There wasn't a sound emitting from his aviary—so far, it wasn't looking good. As I got to the door, fumbling around with the padlock combination, I looked up to see two beady eyes staring me down. Loki, in full analysis mode, scanned my face, piercing his gaze directly into my eyes.

"I'm sorry, LoLos. It's good to see you again, buddy," I uttered, struggling to maintain eye contact.

The lock pinged open, and the door creaked open. I stepped in and gave my friend a stroke on the head. His eyes still firmly fixed on mine, he allowed me to stroke him. I rubbed the sensitive rictal bristles on his upper mandible, but he didn't move: just stared, no noises, no purrs. It almost felt like a standoff. I considered that, at the moment, he was evaluating whether I was to be trusted—whether I should be allowed back into his domain. I didn't want to push it, so I quickly affixed his telemetry and left, pushing the door open wide so he could go about his business.

I got down to cleaning his aviary, on my hands and knees scrubbing his logs, discovering hidden treasures—some I didn't recognize. I checked over my shoulder, and up on high, he was there. Just watching. I took a brief pause in my cleaning to offer him a grape. His beak was firmly closed. I gently rubbed the grape on the tip of his beak, trying to encourage him to take my token, but there was zero interest.

Fair enough. I'd just let him be, but he showed no interest in leaving his aviary, choosing to preen instead. Well, that was good news, I thought. I finished up by filling his giant bath with fresh water and headed out. I sat on the bench opposite his pad, and eventually, he came waddling out. Throwing his bum from side to side like a catwalk model, he sauntered to the perch nearest to me, hopping up and having a good scan of the area.

I chose just to watch and pay attention to his mannerisms. He was still very much mute. As the other falconers went about their business, he resumed his personal grooming duties. I pulled out my phone to check what was happening in the world, only to see in the corner of my eye that someone else was also curious.

"Caw, caw, caw!"

"I haven't got any games on here, mate," I joked. Then the tugging started. I felt a beak in my pocket, pulling at the fabric. I looked down to see Loki with a mouthful of my jacket clasped in his beak, then a muffled *"Caw, caw, caw,"* followed by a few more tugs.

The ice was thawing, so I seized the moment and scooped him up onto my shoulder. We marched toward the flying perch where he alighted, awaiting further instruction. I turned and set off to the next perch. As I got half to the post, Loki zipped past me, turned about, and patiently waited for me to arrive. I petted his paws and gave him a grape, which he silently accepted.

Over the course of the day, I took it slow, but it seemed like I had somewhat been forgiven for my prolonged absence. It's funny to think that a bird would hold such a human, grudge-like trait, but by now, I should have realized how sensitive he was.

———

March, 2022. This was the time. Over the course of the pandemic, we had this uncertain period hanging over our heads; we needed to be gone. It was simple: all the birds, equipment, and some of the aviary materials had to be dismantled and off the premises in one day. That's over twenty-five birds and a colossal amount of falconry-related para-phernalia that needed to be shipped all the way to our new home, located right next to Heathrow Airport. We enlisted some volunteers to help ferry our precious cargo, but it would take multiple trips courting the notorious M25 that acts as a ring road around London.

As the sun rose, we cracked on with our task. The outdoor weathering birds, which consisted of falcons and owls, would be first to make the voyage, each bird boxed up and loaded into a vehicle. We only had so many carry cases and so many cars, so the excess voluntary help would remain at the base to begin aviary deconstruction.

It was a monumental effort by everyone who clubbed together to get our feathered army into their swanky new accommodation, and by gosh, were they swanky.

I stood back and took it all in. These aviaries were like palaces, a significant upgrade from their previous abode. I remember visiting the site before they were built; it was just scrubland, and it was very difficult to imagine the wondrous new center that now stood before me. The birds and the team deserved this. Years of hard work were rewarded. The reputation of the business, the professionalism, and the care of duty to the birds were key factors in why Hobbledown, in my opinion, chose Coda to be a part of their setup. Although still a separate trading entity, the prospective site would be leagues above the farm, and although the rest of the park was still a giant construction sight, there was a fresh new adventure on the horizon.

But such a move can be quite stressful, not just for the birds but for humans too. Instead of a ten-minute drive, the journey would take at least an hour and a half, mostly determined by how the traffic gods felt on that particular day; sometimes, it would take up to three hours. We couldn't just nip down there. The distance was a challenge to deal with. The birds would also need time to acclimate. Because of the pandemic, they had a full year of tranquility and peace in their slice of an open valley. Now, they woke up to the sound of heavy cranes, construction, and giant jumbo jets flying directly overhead. The noise was, at times, quite intense. Some of the birds took a long time to adapt: Misty, the Great Grey Owl, for example, was so nervous that we had to make sure she was located in an aviary where she couldn't see any heavy machinery.

I returned to the old site to pick up some railway sleepers and trees.

It was really quite sad. What was once our home was now a dilapi-dated crunch of raw materials and emptiness. The barn was a shell, and the utter silence was eerie. No Barn Owl shriek, no deep Eagle Owl hoots, no *"Gwahs."* I had spent a long time traipsing this land—training, entertaining, and being taught the intricacies of raptor and corvid mentalities. I had been footed, bitten, had crawled through shrubs, and climbed up trees to find and help birds, and now that was all a memory. This was the site where I managed to connect on a deep level with another creature who, at one time, wanted to inflict much pain on me. However, like the rings on a tree, I have scars on my hands. I would take them to our new home. We were all moving together, and we were all on the same page. How would Loki find his new London home? Would he try to fly home? How would the move affect his mental health? We were certainly going to find out.

After a few months, we were deep into spring. The wild birds were making the finishing touches to their homes, ready to bring new life into the world. Daffodils emerged, and the bees snapped into harvest-ing. The smell in the air was of promise and hope, as was a dapple of dust and industrial debris from the whirling cogs of construction. Flight preparations had started with the more confident birds, like the Harris Hawks, who spearheaded the aerial program. We were still keeping birds on creance and only flying them at the weekend while the construction machines slept.

I had taken Loki out a few times, utilizing his harness. I would walk him around the new, currently unconstructed flying arena, which was uneven crude scrubland, allowing him to map out the new surroundings extensively.

My phone vibrated in my pocket. There was no tone; my phones haven't made a sound since 1998, and I intend to keep it that way. I don't even have notifications turned on, and this is my battle to keep myself untethered from my device. An email came through to Loki's personal inbox. I had been contacted by a major wildlife TV show based in Central Europe. The show went all over the world, looking at some of the amazing talents of captive animals and those in rehabilita-tion. They contacted me because they had seen Loki and heard about his story, and wanted to feature us for an episode.

I did my due diligence and checked the show and the production company out, and they were, as they said, a very popular animal show. *Great!* So, I had a Zoom meeting with the producers about what they wanted to see. After a productive meeting, they ended with a real desire to see him play games, demonstrate his vocalizations, and fly free.

Okay…

Oh, and they want to come in a few weeks.

Oh…

I wasn't quite sure if Loki was ready for free flight. He was still a bit anxious about the construction work going on, and those massive plans were still thought for concern among a few of our more timid birds. But, I knew with telemetry and our various mapping sessions that I would be confident of a successful return home. Also, a pocketful of high-value snacks would see me right.

One Sunday afternoon in May, the film crew arrived. Because of the nature of the park, it was still very much a construction site. Therefore, we had to do a health and safety induction: fit the whole crew out with steel toe-capped boots, a fetching high visibility jacket, and the icing on the cake, a construction company-branded hard hat, very dapper.

We chatted about questions they wanted me to answer as the sound guy wired me up. I suggested that they get some B-roll first. This is general footage of Loki they can use to cut away in the edit. It also served as a way for Loki to get used to all these new faces invading his home. I set out some games, and the cameras rolled on and off for about an hour. Loki seemed a little uneasy at first, very quiet and watchful. But he thawed out, and I was there interacting with him the whole time. I cleaned and moisturised his feet and weighed him—the normal things we would do together so the cameras could get a good insight into how we became friends.

We approached the time when I was to do my on-screen *vox pop* (an interview derived from the Latin *Vox Populi*—voice of the people). The presenter wanted Loki to be in shot while we did the interview, which would have been fine if it was a set of quick-fire questions. When Loki isn't the main focus, and he's made to sit still for too long, he'll decide to act out like he's the main character in need of some serious attention (which we all know he is), but this diva-ish behavior can come in the form of random bursts of vocalizations or acts of mild violence. Neither of which, in this scenario, I particularly wanted. Because I knew roughly the questions being asked, I gauged the interview would likely take about forty-five minutes to allow for longer explanations, anecdotes, and slip-ups. I'm not a great speaker and can often get tongue-tied or mangle words together. I made the call to wear a glove and have Loki sit on the fist. Now, I can't remember the last time I used a glove to handle Loki, and it really didn't cross my mind how this change of behavior would affect him.

I slipped a large black gauntlet onto my left hand, grabbed a leash, and made an attempt to scoop him up. He turned his back slightly, a worried look in his eye. The feathers on his head lay flat against his head: this showed me that he was confused, perhaps concerned that I was coming at him with his old nemesis.

I edged closer, and he croaked at me. He wasn't pleased. I assured him everything was cool and there was no need to worry. The presenter was watching and remarked how you could see a totally different bird—his energy, body language, his whole aura were different. I managed to corner him and usher him up. He wasn't interested in treats, so I had to be proactive with regard to coming to me. I started to think that he was now in the wrong mood for the interview. He probably thought something bad was going to happen, but this didn't make much sense. He was totally fine with the glove when it came to Experience Day guests: he would happily fly and sit on their glove with no issues. Why was he being so off with me?

I snapped the leash onto his jesses, and as soon as I closed the clip leash, he bit me on the thumb. It bloody hurt and took me by complete surprise—no warning, no vocalization, just a petulant peck.

I thought nothing of it, and we went out into the courtyard, where the crew and presenter were set and ready. The interview started well: I managed to complete full, fairly coherent answers, and I felt confident. Loki was sitting pretty, even preening himself, seeming not to be bothered one bit by what was going on around him. I was starting to feel quite confident, and I grew more and more into the interview, but there could only be one star. He waited for his moment, and as the presenter asked about Loki's unique calls, he stepped up to the mic.

"Hubba bubba bub."

The presenter chuckled. I began to talk about the aforementioned call, and it was as if someone put a coin in the *Gwah* Machine. Could we get him to stop? No chance. I could see the camera operator chuckling to himself as Loki, with great importance, seemed hell-bent on trying to put me off, and he succeeded. The more I stumbled over his cutely timed chuckles and gwahs, the more he did it. He looked me square in the eye; when I began an answer, he would start. I found it quite funny, to tell you the truth, and it exemplified my answers with regard to his unique personality. God help the editor who had to sort that mess out!

We wrapped the interview, and Loki and I gave the crew time to set up for their last shot—the one that had the potential for an upset.

The croaking of the zip closed the loop. I snipped the excess and checked for the flickering blue light. It was on: all systems go.

I ferried the glossy boy out of the courtyard and into the free world.

"Rolling."

I opened up my hand and hoped for the best.

…

"Still rolling," cried the camera operator.

…

Wait a second, something was happening. Loki looked like he was about to fly. Here we go.

…

"LoLos, you going to fly, mate?"

But nothing. He shimmied on the glove to get better balance and then did a rouse and began preening.

"Okay, cut there," the camera operator called.

Loki looked at me, checked back over his shoulder at the disarmed camera, then took to the skies.

I heard some fumbling behind me in the camera department, but my gaze was firmly fixed skyward as I watched the silky, pearlescent comedian cut the skies like a ribbon. He soared overhead, looping the center with effortless guile. Loki kronked like a wild raven, a call the local wildlife had most likely never heard. An eruption of starlings, magpies, and crows emitted from every tree as our king approached.

Just over seven and a half minutes later, this swooping sheen of feathers came to a halt just outside of his aviary. Loki took a second, his beak open as he caught his breath. I think that we were both surprised by just how long and how fast his first free flight in months went. He swaggered his way with sass back home and hopped to his new log.

I approached the camera crew, who were playing back the footage.

"Did you get enough footage?" I cautiously asked, looking to see what they had captured. I looked at the director and the camera op. I don't think they heard me as they played back some epic slow-motion footage of Loki gliding and twisting on the wing. They spoke in their mother tongue, and both seemed ecstatic with the results.

"Oh yes, this is very perfect," the director said. He shook my hand and thanked me. I felt a bit guilty as Loki did all the work.

Oh shit, Loki's aviary was still open! I completely forgot to close it in anticipation of seeing the shots. I rushed back, and there he was, slurping big gulps of water from his bath. What a good chap! I snipped the GPS tracker and closed him up so he could drink, bathe, and chill in private.

This little bundle of trickery and mischief certainly kept my heart pumping. Just watching him overcome and thrive was a beacon of hope and light. The more time passed, the more the birds became accustomed to their new home, and within six months, we had seen a scrubland turn into a fully-fledged and now-operational zoo and children's activity world.

But that also came with its challenges. People were now allowed out: a genuine concern was that all that time being locked up came with some serious pent-up energy, and I really worried that some members of the public wouldn't, let us say, return to civility as well as some others. And I was right.

For a bird who has, let's be frank, a quite devastating amount of bite power, we needed to make sure that his aviary mesh, which looked out onto the public, was secure. We went for some tough, almost military-style material. Strong like steel but flexible like a spider's web, with big gaps so people could see what he gets up to.

This worked well for perhaps two weeks before we had to make some drastic changes. You're probably thinking that our dark prince had bitten through the mesh. Well, I wish that was the case.

We have an L-shaped center, which has public-facing aviaries and a bank behind them with a large space in between. One afternoon, while Emily was attending to her duties, she heard loud, slamming thuds. Then it went quiet, then a whole barrage of them. She said it sounded like gunshots. Then she heard a loud shriek from Loki's aviary. So she ran out to the front aviaries to find a load of adults throwing rocks at Loki: the ones that missed smashed into his inner aviary walls.

Suffice it to say, Emily gave them the absolute bollocking of their life and requested the management of the park to remove the people, which they dutifully did.

She went back to check on Loki. He was very jittery with his beak open, darting about very unpredictably. Once he calmed and Emily managed to get close, she could see on his back there were marks: he had been hit with rocks. She checked him over, and he seemed okay; no serious physical damage. She turned to leave the aviary and saw that the back wall of the aviary had huge dents from the rock impacts. My poor boy.

We've already seen just how callous and inconsiderate people can be toward animals: never assume, because sadly, there is always a batch who think animals, especially ones in captivity, are there for the sole reason of their entertainment. They think because they are paying to be there, this gives them *carte blanche* to do stupid things, and they are ignorant of how badly these petulant acts can seriously damage the mental well-being of animals.

Friends, if there's anything you want to take from reading my words, we need to look out for the animals we are fortunate to share this world with. I know many of you reading will already be on this page, but as a collective, let's make sure we can give them a voice. Stopping abuse and cruelty should be a base-level commitment. Pass it on to the next generation. Children are compassionate, I believe, at birth, before they are imprinted with bad habits. We can instill in them loving curiosity and vigilance, the need to always speak up, and the desire to be an ally.

We reinforced Loki's aviary by adding another thinner level of mesh over the existing one. No stones would be able to pass through now. It does mean visibility into his aviary from outside is now limited, but that's the cost of making sure our family can be protected in their homes.

We have to learn and adapt to what scenarios are thrown at us: that's all we can do. When I could muster up the courage to get to the center, I tried desperately to channel some positivity. It gave my mind a break from the reality I conceived for myself. I wanted to spend more time with LoLos and wanted to share his personality. I started to post more on social media, and it was very comforting to see how much joy he brought to so many people: many who were really suffering and saw his mischief as a break from their dark times.

But as we know, social media, a razor-sharp tool, has another edge. I continued to get harassment from people, public condemnations, and people hunting me down on social media—even on LinkedIn, the odd death threat would also make its way to my inbox, and over time, I just couldn't deal with it anymore.

I came away from socials, and I stopped seeing Loki again. I pretty much gave up on photography and music.

"*Nolite te bastardes carborundorum.*" The way my English teacher spoke these words as we studied the horrors of World War I through the disturbing and evocative works of Wilfred Owen—rang in my ears. "Don't let the bastards get you down." It was a fine example of gallows humor in the face of one of the bloodiest and most brutal acts of violence committed in modern history. Why let them win? They are a minority.

Now, let's be one hundred percent clear. I am in no way comparing my reality to what the men of 1914 suffered. But I was going to keep that sentiment in my mind. Loki brought so much light, and rightly or wrongly, I was the gatekeeper. I don't mean that arrogantly.

I wanted to push through and continue the socials, not for fame, likes, shares, or financial gain, but for education and awareness. Don't get me wrong: the social media followers of which you, my dear friend, might be one, perhaps one from the early days or a recent addition to Team Peck and Wreck, have been so very generous with supporting our various merch items and funding requests. It has helped keep the business alive, food in their crops, and vet bills paid. I'll freely admit that when it comes to money, I'm terrible. I'm very conscious that all merch and TV work goes directly to the birds, their charities, and the upkeep.

The hateful remarks and threats may continue, but so will we.

NINETEEN
HAF BREYTINGA
SEAS OF CHANGE

As life unfolds, you can be lured into a dangerously false sense of security. After a while, you think, "Yeah, I got this; I'm in control." That's when you slam into a gaping pothole, things start to shake, and you are plunged into a whirlwind of panic and the unknown. It was 2023, and the sun was still browning the skin and grass alike, but for me, I'll remember that summer not for the raging heat waves but for that massively hidden pothole.

Loki's natural black gloss would be a magnet for the heat during the day, so flying was kept to a minimum. He would still come out for a mooch, but he wasn't up for any strenuous activities. Our raven, therefore, put on a few extra ounces because of this, so we decided to cut back on his treats and exchange them for something a bit different.

Emily had a great idea: she took one of the plastic pots we use to keep food in while flying—these pots are around four inches long by three inches high. She filled the pots with berries, vegetables, meat, and, of course, a few of Loki's favorite cat biscuits. She then filled the pots with water and put them into the freezer to set overnight. What we were left with was a block of ice riddled with various tasty morsels —perfect for keeping Loki cool and stimulated. This had a three-fold use: one, it kept him cool; two, it was a new and stimulating delivery medium for food; and the third point, the act of chipping away to get the food would help keep his beak from growing too much.

Being a member of the esteemed corvid family, Loki has a pretty strong constitution when it comes to what his stomach can handle. After all, these birds are specialists at dining on dead carcasses for mains while selecting the best berries nature has to offer for dessert. With this in mind, he is unlikely to get sick. Being a native, he can also deal with even our coldest winters: they are hardy birds, to say the least.

When birds get sick, they remind me of my parents' generation; they pretend everything is okay. Part of that stiff upper lip, "I don't want to burden anyone" mentality.

A sickly bird in the wild will do its utmost to hide any ailment, as any sign of weakness paints a plump target for other predators who will be more than happy to take advantage of the situation. This in itself poses a huge problem with captive-bred birds. Their cunning ability to shroud the truth is counterproductive—their stubbornness, much like my parents, can conceal continual suffering. The unpleasant truth is that by the time you can see the cause of a sickly bird, it's usually too late. This further highlights why constant health checks are paramount. Knowing what to look for is half the battle.

I was eventually forced to come face to face with this truth. I turned up to the center on a usual Saturday morning. The calendar was thickly packed with a half-day experience, plus the two public demonstrations, so it was a standard busy day at the center. I got in late, and to make up for the time, I jumped straight into helping the rest of the team clean the inside mews. We raced around weighing, cleaning, and preparing birds for the first public show. Once the food was prepped and the birds were ready for action, we had a moment to spare and relax. I remember standing outside, sipping from my coffee cup, and noticing the only sounds were from families in the distance. I couldn't see them, but the repetitive instructions from parents telling their kids not to run off painted a pretty clear image. It was then I realized that I was outside in clear sight of Loki, and he hadn't called out. In fact, my tardiness meant I hadn't said hello to him all morning. Was he perhaps returning the gesture and ignoring me?

I mentioned as a passing comment to one of the staff that he was very quiet, suspiciously quiet, and I hoped that he wasn't making another shiv! They agreed and mentioned he had been fairly quiet all week. Normally, that response wouldn't have bothered me. If none of Loki's favorites were in, then this would have been fairly normal behavior. But I had a horrid feeling in my gut—something wasn't quite right—so I put my coffee down and marched over to him.

As I approach his lair, I always call out to him: this usually warrants a response with him bolting about the aviary in mad bursts of excitement, but this time, there was nothing as if he wasn't even there. This only added more fuel to my already nervous fire. I picked up the pace and got to his front door. He was on the floor, which for him is most uncommon: as mentioned, as soon as I'm near that aviary, he always scampers up to the perch to greet me. He looked up and rotated his head from left to right, muted.

Something was definitely wrong.

I unlocked his door and sat on his log. "What's wrong, mate? Why are you so quiet today?"

He vocally ignored me and slowly paced the floor with no real purpose, as if lost or mentally distant, keeping his back to me. I felt myself burning with panic. I had to keep measuring and assessing the situation objectively, keeping emotions in line, and checking all the physical facts. His body language was unwelcoming but not aggressive, vocally dampened. I offered an outstretched arm, biscuits nestled in the palm of my hand. For the first time since I've known him, Loki did not take any of the food. I insisted and moved closer to him—again, total passive behavior. With most animals, being disinterested in food is an alarm bell. I crawled over to him and gently picked up his jesses, encouraging him to step up onto my arm, which he did while uttering a most gentle, high-pitched sob. *What was wrong with him?*

I looked over his eyes—both perfectly responsive—and his beak was also in pristine condition. I felt around his keel and under his wings, but nothing seemed damaged or irritable to the touch. I slowly worked my way down, and the problem shone like a Maglite in the face. Three scales that serve as armor on his foot had been ripped off, exposing the flesh on his middle toe. It was covered in a soft, gooey puss and blood concoction. It looked aggressive and painful. I was annoyed that I didn't see it immediately, but Loki did well to hide it.

I scooped him under my shoulder and quickly took him to the office. The team was due to start the public show, packed with around 80 excited people waiting patiently. Normally, I do the commentary, but on this occasion, I told them that this was urgent and needed immediate attention. I ferried him, one arm wrapped around him tightly, hugging for protection, toward the office, his little head shifting frantically. He knew where he was heading, and he was working up a panic. His legs were squirming, and I could feel his heart rate increasing.

With him under my left arm, I gathered all the various medical equipment I could: swabs, bandages, antiseptic, tea tree oil, and the special ingredient: manuka honey.

Most people use the costly and sweet viscous treat in their porridge or as a remedy in their tea, but we smear it on our birds. When they pick up little cuts and grazes, the antibacterial properties laden within the honey serve as a brilliant natural way to combat infection and, at the same time, help to stimulate the healing process. When we tell our guests how we use the gloopy nectar, they think we are mad!

With antiseptic solutions, I dabbed away the congealing gunk on his toe. It must have been painful, and Loki sucked it up. He didn't bite, nor did he resist, but his eyes painted a different picture. When the wound was clean, I inspected it further: it was very swollen and raw. I lightly gripped the bulbous wound with my fingers—it was solid and hot. This wasn't a good sign. I cleaned the wound a bit more with an iodine solution before applying the honey, and within seconds, Loki saw fit to peck at his toe. The sweet taste was good enough for him to eat, but he didn't understand its true purpose.

I would need to create a wrap to prevent him from pecking at the wound, thus making it worse and more inflamed. I had to call in extra help to administer a wrap, as this requires the use of both hands. This is quite tricky, especially as birds, in general, don't like their feet being handled in this way. After some cunning distractions, we got Loki's poor little toe wrapped with gauze and bandaged tightly. I'm not sure if it was just me, but he looked a bit more spritely. He gladly took my latest offering of biscuits, and he happily flew back to his locked aviary. I tried to fly him into the arena, but he wasn't interested—he just waited patiently by his door for me to open it up. I exhaled sighs of sadness: it was awful to see him like this. I knew he was in pain, and to see him disinterested in life was heartbreaking. Loki, for all his faults, loved to play, loved to interact, and enjoyed being a part of everything. Loki's demeanor was lackluster and miserable.

Throughout the day, I kept a constant eye on him, and he was nowhere to be seen. I had to go up to his aviary and peek in. I caught him having a peck at his bandage, so I asked him not to, and he stopped. As soon as I turned away, I knew he would be back at it. I was proved right. By the end of the day, the bandage had been completely removed, as had any trace of honey. I picked him up and brought him back to the bad place, the office. We cleaned the wound and made a new wrap. Hopefully, this would last the night. I wasn't in the next day, but I made it abundantly clear to everyone that Loki needed to be heavily monitored. It was reported back that the re-wrapped bandage had been a success and had just about survived the night—there were attempts of removal, but all in all, it held. We left it on for a few days to make sure the antiseptic mixture had been given a sufficient period to be effective. The bandage was taken off, and the wound was re-cleaned. Sarah-Jane let me know when she came home that the wound didn't look septic, which was good, but that the swelling hadn't gone down: this was not so good. We agreed that we would continue this course for a few more days and wait to see any improvement.

As sure as the sun rises and sets, the weekend came along. I was keen to get to the center to evaluate Loki's little foot. On the journey, Sarah-Jane and I discussed the possible reasons for the swelling and, more importantly, how it occurred in the first place.

We arrived, and I was pleasantly surprised to see Loki leap onto his perch. He was alert to our presence and sang his usual morning greeting. This was a much better sign, and I was already feeling much better about his condition. I trotted over to him to say a proper good morning. His whole aura was different. He greeted me with his familiar chorus of chattering and buzzed his tail in excitement—that was my boy! I went in and checked his dressing—the bandage coincidentally Coda purple—was nice and tight and had held well. The team did a brilliant job looking after him. I was slightly concerned he might be a bit of a handful, but credit to the team, he was expertly taken care of every day.

I really shouldn't have worried. The staff are always extremely conscientious when it comes to the welfare of our birds. They really are a credit to the company and to themselves, and I'm extremely proud of them all. Even though Loki is a handful, they made sure he was given the best care every single day, and for that, I'll always be grateful.

I picked up my mate, and we headed to the office. I could feel his anxiety begin to kick in. I held him close to my chest and gave him a few kisses on the head. We went inside, and Sarah-Jane began to unravel the bandage. He was behaving extremely well—he didn't look fazed at all—the everyday routine may have settled his nerves. The last remnants of the bandage were coming loose. Sarah-Jane inspected the toe.

The oppressive silence irked my patience, and I prodded her for an answer, "What is it? What can you see? Has it healed?"

She didn't answer and began to feel around the swelling. "I think it might be cancerous."

As you can imagine, this is the very last thing I wanted to hear.

I was devastated. I locked up and couldn't speak; that huge, sinking, all-consuming sensation of dread soaked my entire being. I went to speak, but I couldn't. Of course, it might not be cancer, but Sarah-Jane is incredibly gifted with birds and is usually spot-on with assessments, which is why I was so worried and crushed.

It didn't look good for Loki. We agreed to strap it back up and get him to the vet. The resources we had were not potent enough to remedy this ghastly infliction. I held him and stared into his eyes. I was struck with anguish and expecting the worst. He, on the other hand, had no idea the predicament he was in. If it was cancer, then amputation of the toe or foot may be the only remedy. That would be the best case. Cancer could have spread meaning...well, I'm sure you can work it out for yourself.

I fought the sadness hard, but my eyes welled up involuntarily.

Sarah-Jane was quick to offer comfort and bring the situation back to reality. She realized that her harsh and damning assessment had upset me, so she changed tact and offered comfort in the form of suggesting that perhaps the swelling could be something else entirely, something less extreme. The one thing we agreed on is that we would try our hardest to make him well, regardless of cost.

He had come so far, and I was heartbroken—my poor Loki was staring down a barrel he couldn't even see. Animals are such a precious gift to this planet, and we are so privileged to have them in our lives. The thought of Loki—or any of our animals—suffering hits everyone at the center hard. They are our extended family, our friends, and our colleagues. The harmony of working together day in and day out creates a bond that, in the end, puts them and their rights in alignment with our own: the way it should be.

We got an emergency appointment at our vet, boxed Loki, and headed straight there. The drive was a mixture of us continuing to speculate on the cause and potential treatments. I felt sick and dominated with worry, but my worrying wouldn't change anything. I knew that.

I hauled Loki's large black carry box into the vet's waiting room. A mixture of dogs on leads, cats in boxes, and a small girl clutching her hamster—all very textbook stuff. My first thought was that the hamster could probably feed most of the hawks, maybe both eagles—such a weird thing to think, admittedly, but it distracted me from the reason why we were there. The room was quiet, too quiet for Loki's liking, and he let out a loud *"Bah-bah!"*

"What you got in the box, mate?" a man with a German Shepherd bellowed.

"It's a raven," I replied.

He was taken aback. "What, like a crow? Is it wild?"

It looked like we would have one of those conversations, and for once, I was not in the mood for talking. "Yeah, it's like a crow. Same family but a different species, and no, he's not wild; he's captive-bred," I replied bluntly.

The man thought about it. "Didn't know you could get one as a pet."

I was just about to launch into why Loki wasn't a pet until a softly-spoken lady entered the room.

"Loki?"

The vet was ready for us.

I picked up the box and happily left our conversation, but the man's voice trailed behind me: "That's a funny name; wasn't he in the Avengers?"

In hindsight, I probably came across as snappy and brash, perhaps even rude. I guess it's not the normal animal to have in a waiting room, and I should have been a bit more respectful, but all I could think about was getting in and getting out with a positive answer or solution.

The vet's room had that familiar clinical smell, hurling me back to fond memories of work experience. I prayed we would be on the winning team today. I crouched down and warned the vet just to take a step back: as soon as the box opened, he would explode out. As I opened the door, the black flash of corvid elegance ruptured into the room. I had a firm grip on his leash and let him acclimate to his surroundings. He strutted around for a few seconds, eyeing up all of the vet's shiny tools and equipment.

"Oh my god, he's stunning! I've never seen a raven before. Look at all those colors!"

Loki paid no attention to the pouring admiration from the vet. He stopped and yelled at me: a strong, definitive, *"Bah-bah!"*

I showed him my forearm, and he stepped up willingly.

The vet got closer and continued to admire him, Loki's chest firmly out, head crest fully deployed, ultimate show-off pose engaged! The vet continued to marvel at his presence, the pearlescent colors, and the sheer size of him. Normally, I would also be happy to engage. However, my heightened emotional state was struggling to subdue the seriousness of our visit.

"So...this is the toe," I said, subtly bringing the vet back into the room. She maneuvered so she could get a good look. She prodded and squeezed and prodded some more. My heart was now racing. Like a dentist sticking that obnoxious spike into a sensitive hole in your tooth, I expected a reaction—a violent one. Alas, our super proud corvid stood tall and proud without giving the vet a painful bite. She finished a physical exam and left the room.

I gave Loki a nice stroke on the head, using my fingernails to scratch his little scalp. The vet returned after a short while. When she went to speak, Loki clicked four times and blared out his trademark "Gwah!"

The vet chuckled, "That's a funny sound."

Loki did it again, and we all laughed, which provided me with a little bit of light relief. I couldn't help smiling at that call.

"He certainly likes to be the center of attention, doesn't he?"

The vet wasn't wrong. Even in times of despair, he cawed to his audience, relishing the adoration.

"So, it looks like it could be a tumor."

Bam! Straight out, no warning, like a car hitting a wall.

"We can try him on a course of antibiotics in the meantime. It looks like the solid mass that has formed is causing some irritation, which has led to Loki pecking his foot and exposing the tissue. If, after a week, the lump hasn't gone down, then we can take a biopsy of the lump. If it is a tumor, we would need to think about amputation of the toe, at least the foot, depending on the nature of the tumor. However, it might not be cancerous, in which case the antibiotics will clear it up."

"Okay, no worries,"—a lie we all tell ourselves. I was worried as hell. I stroked him down the back and returned him to his box, trying not to show any signs of emotion. My pride was determined to keep dry-eyed walking out of here.

We began the five-day course of Baytril. Every day, we carefully measured the correct dosage: this was incredibly important. Too little and the medicine would be inefficient; too much would kill him. We contaminated his food with the medicine and hoped for the best.

Loki has been an enemy, a challenge, and most importantly, a friend—one like no other. I would never have imagined the bond we would fabricate after that first night I saw him in my spare room all those years ago. I look back at the scars on my hands and arms not with anguish or discomfort but with pride. I wear the scars as a mark of commitment, a pledge I made that tested my patience as well as my pain threshold. This challenge was put in front of me, but I was under no duress to accept. When this intimidating, confused, and damaged soul came into my life, I could have passed. He wasn't my burden to accommodate, but the look in his eyes that first night changed everything.

My family has always had dogs, and like other serial pet adopters, there's always that one dog. You'll never have one like it again. Some people won't even get another one of the same breed. Loki, for me, is that one. There will never be a bird like him. There may be better, more well-behaved, or even be able to do more remarkable problem-solving puzzles, but they will never be Loki. His unique swagger brought smiles to so many strangers, and he gave so much without even realizing it. He pushed me to evolve my skills, to listen, and really see. I'd never been in a position where I would be working with a bird with severe mental conditions, and to be quite honest, I never in my wildest dreams imagined birds could possess such psychological capabilities. I've learned so much for which I am eternally grateful because Loki is more than a bird—he's more than a quirky attraction for people to come and see. To me, he is incredibly special, one of a kind, and a true landmark in my life that can never be compared to.

But all stories must end, and this account is no different. We administered the antibiotics religiously to the exact milliliter. The wound had cleaned up nicely and was healing, but the lump had not: it was prominent and stubborn, like me. It was time to realize that in the end, what will be will be. We, as custodians of these beautiful creatures, are faced with tough decisions: we need to do the best for those who cannot make welfare issues for themselves. It never gets easier, but the right decision must always be made.

We returned to the vet at the end of the five days and requested the lump to be examined. The vet took a biopsy and informed us the results would take around a week.

A week is an incredibly long time to be kept waiting on tenterhooks, but on the flip side, while we were together playing, it seemed to last forever. At the end of work, I headed over to see Loki every day. I took my camera to get some pictures of him during the golden hour, and he never looked so beautiful.

Loki came running over and sat on my lap. Curious as ever, he wanted to see my camera. I took a picture and showed him the image on the screen. He *"Gwah'd"* which I took as a mark of approval. I tilted my camera to see the dials on the top so I could change the setting, and Loki saw this as an invitation to jump onto my lens. I couldn't help but laugh—once again, he knew how to cheer me up, always the jester brimming with curiosity.

The next day would be five days: time to call in and face the music. Sarah-Jane made the call while I took refuge with Loki. He played his xylophone to me, and we kept ourselves occupied, enjoying each other's company.

In the corner of my peripheral vision, I could see Sarah-Jane making her way over to us. I pretended I couldn't see her, for I knew, like Hermes, she came bearing news: could I stomach what was coming? She greeted Loki, who was on my shoulder and gave him a bit of food. She told him he was a good boy, and Loki sauntered off to explore the play area.

She looked at me with warmth as she always did and grabbed my hand. The Oz effect was back in full swing: the sounds of nature were stolen from me. I looked over to Loki—he was happily wandering the arena, living his best life, the one he deserved. I turned to Sarah-Jane, and she told me the news.

Loki had been a massive part of our lives, a constant conversation starter. We marveled at him on a daily basis, and he astonished all the people who came to meet him, often bringing people to tears. His character was unique. Loki's presence would light up a room—his pearlescent colors, his size, the raw attitude, and the swagger he emanated all akin to his personality. There wasn't any raven like him, and fortunately, that wouldn't change.

Then I heard those two words: "He's clear."

I had built myself up so much all that week that I didn't quite understand the words that I was hearing—my stomach was coiled in a mess of nauseating stress knots.

"Loki is going to be okay."

It started to sink in, and guess who came scuttling over right on cue? He stood next to us and looked up, completely unaware of what this meant. Blissful ignorance allowed him to be his true, authentic self without the curse of worry. He wanted our attention, and we were apparently slacking! He pecked my boot and pulled on my laces, but on this occasion, I gave him a treat.

We managed to avoid any serious damage on this pothole, but the scare was real enough. The swelling eventually went down over the next few months, and the terror threat was reset.

Having these incredible animals in our lives brings profound comfort and joy. They awaken our humanity, drawing out our innate ability to connect deeply with other souls, binding us to the rhythm of the natural world. Yet their souls burn bright—and often far too quickly. It's a reminder, sharp and bittersweet, to cherish every moment we have with them.

And if we ever needed a reason to protect them, this is it.

TWENTY
ENDIRINN
THE END

"Live in five, four, three..."

Sunday, December 19, 2018.

The last two seconds were silent, yet were gesticulated emphatically by the floor manager and his mighty pen of commandment. The presenters launched into life, overly joyful and extremely enthusiastic. They were hiding their worry well.

Sarah-Jane and Loki were on set and being broadcast to the nation. Millions of people were tuning in while eating their breakfast. I was holding my breath and could feel my heart smashing against the inside of my chest. *So far, so good.*

Loki was silent as a button, his beady eye fixed on me the whole time. I locked my gaze, and with my imaginary telepathic skills, I spoke to him. *It's okay, Loki,* I said. *You're doing great. I'm here, mate!*

The presenters started to ask Christopher more questions about ravens, mostly about intelligence. Apparently, Loki felt he had the authority to chime in on the subject and had quite enough of being on the bench. He spoke up with vigor, his timing exquisite. I looked around at all the crew. They were all clinging to their clipboards, nervous team members anxiously chomping on pens, hoping he wouldn't continue and ruin the good start. Sarah-Jane gave Loki a treat. He seemed to almost say "thank you" with the most delicate little noise. Both presenters laughed and pointed this out before asking if he would do it again. Sarah-Jane plunged her hand into her pocket and gave him another morsel of food, and like before, Loki displayed his perfect manners and courtesy. He thanked her for the biscuit, bringing more genuine laughs from the presenters. He played his part perfectly, working with The Ravenmaster as if they had been appearing on TV together for years.

Perhaps we didn't get the script. Was all the worrying for nothing?

The flow of the segment was running incredibly smoothly. *Too* smoothly. Loki looked around the set as the audience at home was being treated to a prerecorded cutaway of him playing his xylophone. He seemed to be feeding off the positive energy from the presenters, his beak wide open, radiating the biggest corvid smile you could ever hope to see. He cocked his neck toward the monitor, clearly recognizing himself. Being self-aware is a true indicator of higher intelligence, something that sets humans apart from most of the animal kingdom. The cameras cut back to the studio. Loki chuckled like a human, seamlessly prompting The Ravenmaster to talk about their diverse vocalizations, which Loki happily provided testament to.

Loki behaved perfectly during the rest of the segment. No attempts to fly off, no attempts to bite Sarah-Jane, no surprise poos, and most of all, he spoke on cue. The presenters also seemed to relax and actively push more of the conversation toward Sarah-Jane and, more specifically, Loki. He was hogging the limelight and participating in the conversation when he felt he had something to contribute, which was often typical of him.

"Okay, we're off-air," the floor manager called.

I sighed with a tremendous sense of relief, exhaling a morning's worry in one joyous breath. Just like before, Sarah-Jane handed him back to me. She was shaking. He leaped into my arms, still wearing that big smile. It was as if he was saying: "Look, Dad, didn't I do well? Are you proud?" And I most certainly was. Never prouder. I scratched his beak and let him have half a cookie, both he and I oblivious to all the crew coming back for more photos. Sarah-Jane fended the questions while I gushed praise on our well-behaved star. He took residence upon my shoulder and plumped out his crest like a peacock. He now owned the place, and he knew it.

Suddenly, artist Paloma Faith flounced into the studio like a whirlwind, a personal photographer shadowing her closely. She made a beeline for us. "Oh my god, he is so beautiful!" she said. Much to my disappointment, she was referring to Loki—obviously. She asked if she could stroke him.

I was just about to advise her against it due to him having a nasty bite, but she had already started stroking his back by then. He was totally at ease, lording it up. She had the photographer snap a picture of her and Loki together before waltzing off to her next adventure.

Sarah-Jane and I returned to the green room. We hugged each other and shared a moment of blissful relief. Loki happily put himself back in his box, and we left the building. He had been a superstar.

A flurry of texts and tweets sent our phones into overdrive. Loki had won over the nation and was trending on Twitter and Instagram—he had well and truly stolen the show. He was a good boy. The best boy. I needn't have worried about conjuring spells in the middle of a sleepless night.

Loki's future is destined to be bright and colorful. There is no doubt in my mind he will continue to defy the odds, and his particular character will develop and grow, bringing smiles and laughter to those who are fortunate enough to meet him, be it in person or from afar.

It's a privilege for me to be involved with this incredible creature, and just when I think I know everything about him, he pulls a new trick out of his locker. I can't wait to discover new ways he will surprise me, and I hope you will stay with us on this journey.

Thank you all, from the bottom of my heart, for all of your support and kindness.

Gwah.

FURTHER READING

Heinrich, Bernd. *Mind of the Raven: Investigations and Adventures with Wolf Birds.* New York, Cliff Street Books, 1999.

Manarin, Sarah-Jane. *The Freedom of Falconry.* LR Price Publications Ltd., 2018.

Savage, Candace. *Bird Brains: The Intelligence of Crows, Ravens, Magpies, and Jays.* Vancouver, Greystone Books, 2018.

Shute, Joe. A Shadow Above: The Fall and Rise of the Raven. Bloomsbury Natural History, 2018.

Skaife, Christopher. *The Ravenmaster: My Life with the Ravens at the Tower of London.* Picador USA.

ACKNOWLEDGMENTS

Firstly, I'd like to thank Sarah-Jane. You have brought the magic of falconry to life; if it were not for you, I would never be able to connect with these amazing animals in the way that I can. The skills you have shared and the kindness you've shown, even in our darkest times, has allowed me to be here to write this account. I owe everything I know in this field to you, and I'm eternally grateful for this gift. Being able to be in the lives of these birds is a privilege.

Cassandra, Alma, and all the dedicated and talented team at Quill & Crow Publishing: you believed in me when hundreds of others didn't, and for that, I'm truly grateful. Your enthusiasm for bringing this story to the world has been heartwarming, and I'm proud to have worked with you.

Christine, your unwavering support and keen eye were instrumental in shaping this book into something ready to share. Your kindness and friendship have been a lifeline, and your determination often surpassed my own. Thank you for believing in this account and for pouring so much of yourself into its creation.

To the incredible team at Coda Falconry: Emily, your fierce dedication and tireless devotion to the birds are nothing short of inspiring. Watching you grow into the extraordinary falconer you are today has been a privilege. Luke, your easygoing nature and steadfast support over the years have meant the world to me. Your bond with Loki is a testament to your care and effort, and I'm grateful for all you've done. Emma, your friendship and persistence have been a source of strength. The trust you've earned from Loki in a short time is a beautiful thing. You are all family.

To all the volunteers at the center—you are the heartbeat of everything we do. Your enthusiasm, hard work, and willingness to forge bonds with each of the birds bring such vitality to our shared mission. Thank you for your invaluable contributions and for reminding me why this work matters.

And last but by no means least, you. From all corners of the world, I have been truly touched by all of your supportive messages. I read every single DM, comment, and message, and while it takes me time to respond, just know that I'm so grateful for all your support from whatever nook on this amazing planet we call home. We are sharing something very special—we have been enchanted by the same soul.

ABOUT THE AUTHOR

Elliot Manarin is a filmmaker, producer, photographer, and screenwriter based in Essex, England. He is also a trained falconer who has worked with raptors at the award-winning Coda Falconry since 2013. In 2021, he received a National Diploma in Zoology, and he is an expert on one special raven: Loki. This is his first book.

𝕏 ⭕

THANK YOU FOR READING

Thank you for reading *Raising Loki*. We deeply appreciate our readers, and are grateful for everyone who takes the time to leave us a review. If you're interested, please visit our website to find review links. Your reviews help small presses and indie authors thrive, and we appreciate your support.

Other Titles by Quill & Crow

Baba's Grimoire

The Bone Drenched Woods

The Ancient Ones Trilogy

www.ingramcontent.com/pod-product-compliance
Ingram Content Group UK Ltd.
Pitfield, Milton Keynes, MK11 3LW, UK
UKHW041319070325
4905UKWH00035B/391